EVERYDAY LINGUISTICS

This innovative introduction to linguistics connects language structure to everyday use, culture, and context, making the technicalities of language structure accessible, vivid, and engaging.

The first text to take a *socially realistic linguistics* approach, this exciting new textbook situates discussions about the building blocks of language like phonetics, syntax, and pragmatics within a social justice framework that recognizes that all language is shaped by sociocultural forces and reveals and reinforces ideologies. Uniquely, this text also introduces ecolinguistics, a new field that examines the relationship between language and its environment, again demonstrating how widely held views about language can have real-world consequences. Key features include:

- "Linguistics in your world" sections to connect concepts discussed with specific social issues
- "L1 acquisition in focus" sections to relate key concepts to first language acquisition
- "Explorations" sections at the end of each chapter to encourage students to test their knowledge, discuss in groups, and apply what they have learned to their own experiences
- End-of-chapter summaries and key term lists to conclude the main lessons and highlights of each chapter
- Recommendations for further reading

Everyday Linguistics: An Introduction to the Study of Language is an ideal starting point for students that are new to the study of language and those not majoring in language study.

Joanne Cavallaro is a professor emerita of English at St. Catherine University, Minnesota, U.S.A., where she has taught linguistics for 30 years.

Everyday Linguistics

An Introduction to the Study of Language

Joanne Cavallaro

Routledge
Taylor & Francis Group

NEW YORK AND LONDON

Designed cover image: © Getty Images | Jasmina007

First published 2024
by Routledge
605 Third Avenue, New York, NY 10158

and by Routledge
4 Park Square, Milton Park, Abingdon, Oxon, OX14 4RN

Routledge is an imprint of the Taylor & Francis Group, an informa business

© 2024 Joanne Cavallaro

ISBN: 978-0-367-21959-8 (hbk)
ISBN: 978-0-367-21963-5 (pbk)
ISBN: 978-0-429-26905-9 (ebk)

DOI: 10.4324/9780429269059

Typeset in Times New Roman
by Apex CoVantage, LLP

Contents

Acknowledgments

I'd like to thank the many teachers and students I have had the pleasure of working with. I am especially indebted to John Gumperz, my undergraduate advisor at Berkeley, who first started me on this path. And I'm indebted to all of the students I have taught over the last 30 years. Through their insistence on understanding what they were reading, they taught me to explain concepts in terms they could understand and relate to. Several students helped me think about this book in more detail, and I'd like to thank them specifically: Elizabeth Gadbois, Carly Fischback, and Sydney Robbins.

My editor, Amy Laurens, helped me through the publication process; I am grateful for her guidance, encouragement, and willingness to answer my endless questions.

I'd also like to thank my colleagues who read and responded to multiple drafts. My writing group, the Feministas—Lynne, Jane, Cindy, Ceil—deserve special thanks for their encouragement over numerous cups of coffee, glasses of wine, and various types of food. Cecilia Konchar Farr was an unflagging cheerleader, keeping me going through all the rough spots with her unwavering encouragement, even when I was not sure I could ever do this.

Special and deep-felt thanks to my partner, Toma Mulligan, without whose help, encouragement, support, and love this book would never have been finished. Merci, mon amour.

CHAPTER 1

Introduction

....

First glance

Diverse language experiences

Why study linguistics?

How we'll study linguistics

Socially realistic linguistics

Prescriptive and descriptive perspectives

Navigating through this book

DIVERSE LANGUAGE EXPERIENCES

Language both unites and divides us as humans. We are united by its importance to us as individuals, as members of communities, and as a species. Unless there is some unusual circumstance that prevents it, all human children learn a language. In fact, infants seem so hardwired to do so, it's hard to prevent it. Language use is part of everyday life for nearly all of us. It is difficult to imagine getting through a day without using language, if only by speaking to oneself. For us as members of human societies and cultures, language connects us and helps make us who we are.

The lived language experience is different for each of us. Some of us grew up and live in fairly homogeneous communities with little linguistic variation. Some grew up and live in diverse, even super diverse, communities, being exposed to multiple languages and multiple varieties of any one language. Some of us may be bilingual or multilingual ourselves; we may speak what is usually called proper English, or a variety of English not considered "proper," or one or more languages in addition to English.

Some people decry this linguistic diversity, claiming we'd be better off if we all spoke the same. Perhaps, but I don't think so. Diversity of experience and perspective is important in

DOI: 10.4324/9780429269059-1

any attempt to understand our world; if we all thought the same, we'd all likely make the same mistakes. Diversity in language is an equally crucial resource for all of us, one that *can* divide us but need not, a point we will come back to throughout this book.

This diversity in language experiences is also an important resource that I hope you will bring to your study of linguistics. Sharing your own experiences and learning about those of others can bring with it new perspectives, allowing us to learn from one another. I have an expertise in linguistics that I hope to share with you; you each have expertise in your own lived language experience that I hope you can share with one another; for no matter what it is, your experience is a valid example of how language works.

And how language works is exactly the focus of the field of linguistics and of this book.

WHY STUDY LINGUISTICS—AND WHAT IS IT ANYWAY?

When I tell strangers that I teach linguistics, they often look at me with a rather blank stare and ask—*What exactly is linguistics, anyway*? Even though language is so important to us in most of what we do, few of us have studied it in any meaningful way. Linguistics, the scientific study of language, is the field that studies language in all of its aspects: social, cognitive, cultural, ecological. Linguists examine the following, among other, aspects of language:

- How language is put together and how it is used
- How human language differs from animal communication
- What all languages have in common and how they differ
- How different varieties of the same language vary and how that variation carries social meaning
- How language originated and how languages have spread and changed over time
- How language is a cognitive phenomenon (how it functions in the brain) and a social/cultural one (how it functions in society).

These questions are standard ones addressed in the study of language. Here we will address not only those questions but also some additional ones, questions having to do with language and social justice, such as the following:

- How are linguistic structure and use connected to contemporary social issues?
- What are the real-world consequences resulting from common myths about language?
- How do attitudes toward grammatical correctness and linguistic variation contribute to social inequalities?
- How are gender, race, age, ethnicity, social status, power, privilege, and marginalization all integral to an understanding of language?
- How do beliefs about language serve to privilege some groups and disadvantage others?
- How is our language use related to how we treat the environment?

As you may guess from this list, linguistics is, in essence, interdisciplinary and related to many other fields. Linguistic insights are used in sociology, psychology, computer science, artificial intelligence, communication studies, history, paleontology, and criminology to name a few fields.

Insights from those fields help linguists understand language. Each of those disciplines is connected to one or more subfields of linguistics, of which there are many: psycholinguistics, historical linguistics, sociolinguistics, pragmatics, first language acquisition, second language acquisition, discourse analysis, phonology, syntax, morphology, semantics, conversational analysis, forensic linguistics, critical discourse analysis, ecolinguistics, and others. You'll learn more about most of these as you make your way through this book, so don't worry if you're not sure what they are now.

HOW WE'LL STUDY LANGUAGE

Since humans and their societies are so complex, one would expect the main tool of human communication to be similarly complex. And, indeed, language is amazingly complex, adaptable, variable, and productive. As we approach its study, we'll be doing various kinds of linguistic analysis, ranging from analyzing small details of pronunciation to examining less tangible concepts such as social identity and power. In each case, we'll be looking for patterns that can help us understand how language works. Each area of linguistics may require different types of analysis, but in each case, we'll be asking—how do we account for the linguistic phenomena we see around us?

I have titled this book *Everyday Linguistics* because I believe it is important to connect what you are learning to everyday life, both your own and that of others. The seemingly esoteric linguistic concepts presented here are related to what we do every day. They can help us understand not only everyday interactions but also the larger social contexts within which those interactions occur and the inequalities that are often part of those contexts. This book, then, asks you to notice language use around you—your friends, neighborhood, school, family, media—and to apply the linguistic concepts you learn to what you see.

My perspective here insists that the study of language needs to integrate what linguists often divide into subdivisions. That is, structural analysis should be connected to sociocultural analysis and the whole should be connected to social justice. Such connections can help us unmask social and linguistic prejudice and oppression. In our study here, we will connect our understanding of structure to attitudes and myths about language that support such prejudices. In doing so, we will explore the ethical dimension of linguistic study.

A SOCIALLY REALISTIC LINGUISTICS

What does it mean to explore the ethical dimension of linguistic study? First, it means as linguists we need to examine language not only as a system of rules, although that is an important aspect of any study of language. It means we also need to see language as a tool of social interaction and badge of social identity. And we need to take note of the fact that, as Winford (2003) notes, languages

> are shaped by sociocultural forces, and our perception of them is conditioned by social practice, social relationships, and attendant ideologies. Linguistic prejudice, as we all know, is simply race or class prejudice in a subtle guise. A socially realistic linguistics simply recognizes that fact.

> (p. 35)

This book presents a socially realistic linguistics, one that recognizes the intricate and complex ways that attitudes toward language structure, use, and variation are ethical as well as linguistic issues.

As a socially realistic linguist, it is important that I share some of my own language experiences to let you know who I am and where I come from, not as an expert, someone who has been teaching about language for 30 years, but as a person who has been both fascinated by language and perplexed by people's attitudes toward it since long before she became a professor. The following stories give you some idea of what propelled me into the study of linguistics, a fascination not only with the structure, the rules, and regularities but also with linguistic differences and a growing awareness of how much variation there is in what we normally call one language. So here are a few memories of that fascination, a brief language autobiography.

When I was a child, every summer I would visit my grandparents, neither of whom spoke much English although they had lived in the United States for nearly 40 years. They had emigrated from Sicily as adults, and when I visited them, they lived in an Italian neighborhood in Rochester, New York. I would often accompany my grandmother as she visited the neighborhood stores. All the shop keepers spoke to her in Italian; then, they would turn to me and speak English. Such easy control of both languages amazed me. And it was not only the adults who were bilingual. All the neighborhood children I played with spoke both English and Italian fluently, an ability that they took for granted and that I envied.

When I was slightly older, my family moved to Puerto Rico, and I found myself in school with children who also took bilingualism for granted. Classes were taught in English, but out in the playground, everything took place in Spanish, a language I knew nothing of when I arrived. With no instruction, I began picking up words and phrases. My efforts to do more were stymied, however, by the fact that everyone wanted to talk to me in English. Since English was a key to success in school, practice with me (a native speaker, though I did not know that term then) was something they all wanted. I remember feeling slightly uneasy in the classroom because I was seen as a star, not because I was necessarily the smartest but because I knew English. Today I would say that my knowledge of English privileged me unfairly; then I merely felt uneasy about something I could not put into words.

Years later, after graduating from college, I found myself in a small town in Northern Wales, trying to talk to a few locals. There was one very attractive young man who obviously wanted to talk to me. We had one big problem, however. We could not understand each other without the help of my companion, who ended up translating for us. She would repeat what I said to him; he would respond, looking at me inquiringly, whereupon she would repeat his words for me. He could not understand me; I could not understand him; she could understand us both and we could both understand her. You might assume that my companion spoke Welsh and English, but she didn't. She spoke only English. In fact, all three of us were speaking *only* English, just different types of English, what linguists call different dialects or varieties.

I had been living in London for several months when that trip took place. During that time, I used to shop at Portobello Market to buy fresh fruits and vegetables. At one vegetable stall, which had some of the best produce in the market, the owner used to regularly refuse to understand me when I asked for tomatoes in my American accent. Not until I said, *a pound of tomahtoes, please,* using the British pronunciation, would he "hear" me. At first, I thought it cute, an effort to help me acculturate. After a few months, however, I began to resent it, feeling as if I were being forced to give up a piece of who I was. I remember thinking, *I'm American, and as much as I love living in London, I'm not a Brit and never will be, and I don't really want to sound like one.*

These early experiences helped create my interest in language and led me to the study of language as my life's work. Your experiences may be similar to, or very different from, mine. Regardless, for each of us, our early interactions with the language or languages used around us gave us some of our first knowledge about language and how it is used. This book is meant to enlarge that pool of knowledge.

PRESCRIPTIVE AND DESCRIPTIVE PERSPECTIVES ON LANGUAGE

Linguistics takes a descriptive perspective on language, so it is important to differentiate descriptive and prescriptive perspectives.

Prescriptive perspective

A prescriptive perspective on language is probably the one you were exposed to in school. It is full of rules about what you should and should not do: never end a sentence with a preposition; don't use double negatives; don't split infinitives; never start a sentence with *but*; avoid using *ain't*; use *I* with linking verbs (*It is I* rather than *It is me*). These and other prescriptive rules are usually applied to written language, though people often try to prescribe them for spoken language as well. The purpose of prescriptive rules is to tell you how you *should* speak or sign or write, like rules of etiquette or politeness that delineate how we should behave, speak, or dress when we are on our best behavior or in formal situations. They are, therefore, better seen as rules for appropriateness rather than rules for grammatical correctness. The reasons behind these rules are a matter of debate, but linguists agree that they are arbitrary. In other words, there is no linguistic or logical reason why we should consider *I didn't do anything* more correct than *I didn't do nothing*.

You may think that if these rules are not followed, then it's just bad grammar. And that, in some ways, is the point of prescriptive rules. They set up expectations about what good behavior is supposed to be, always according to some group, of course. As we will see throughout this book, such linguistic expectations vary across groups, are based on false linguistic premises, and serve to unfairly privilege some groups and marginalize others.

Descriptive perspective

The perspective we will take here is not prescriptive but descriptive. That is, our focus will be on how language is actually used, and our purpose is to describe how people actually speak or sign. Using this descriptive approach, we will look for the regularities or rules that constitute how we produce and understand language. More on this in Chapter 2.

A prescriptive approach would ask of a particular utterance: Is it correct or incorrect? A descriptive one would ask: Is it a possible utterance in English (or any other language)? If so, it is grammatically correct. The socially realistic perspective we use here would go on to ask who gets to say whether or not it's correct.

NAVIGATING YOUR WAY THROUGH THIS BOOK

This book is divided into four sections, each covering an aspect of language, introducing basic theory, and giving you a chance to apply that theory to the language you hear or see around you.

- Chapter 2 introduces some basic concepts in the field of linguistics, discussing key aspects of the nature of language. It lays the foundation for further discussion of the intersection of language and social issues, asking why, for example, some variation in language use is seen just as variation while other variation is seen as wrong.
- Chapters 3–7 begin our exploration of linguistic structure: how languages are put together: the units that make them up and how those units are combined to form meaningful utterances. We'll look at the lexical system (words, their origins, and structure), the sound system (sounds, their variants, and how sounds are structured within words), the syntax system (how sentences are structured), and a first foray into meaning (semantics). Along the way, we'll connect aspects of that system to social issues.
- Chapters 8–12 examine language use in its social context. After an examination of language use in everyday interaction, our focus will shift to variation, a key concept in linguistics, one that highlights the obvious fact that not all speakers of any one language speak or sign the same. We will investigate linguistic variation in North American English across region, class, gender, and ethnicity, including the social meanings of such variation. We'll examine real-world consequences of common beliefs and attitudes about language, connecting linguistic theory to our lives, the lives of others, and social issues that affect us all.
- Chapters 13 and 14 move us out in time and space, as they examine the origins and spread of language, language contact, endangered languages, and the ways that language and the environment are interrelated.

I've included several features designed to help you make your way through the book. The examples I've used, mostly from North American English, are ones that I hope will make sense to beginners in linguistics, which I assume you all are. My hope is that you'll be able to make connections as you read through the theory and the examples and notice if any of the concepts discussed connect to or illuminate any of your experiences. I've also tried to use a personal voice throughout, though I do have to use some technical terminology and abstract concepts to explain things. I share my own experiences at times and hope you will have a chance to share yours as well.

So that you know what to expect, here's a list of what each chapter includes.

- A chapter preview, "First glance," at the beginning, and a summary and a list of key terms at the end of every chapter
- Bolding of key terms when introduced
- Interspersed throughout each chapter, "Linguistics in your world" sections that relate concepts from each chapter to contemporary social issues
- Exploration activities at the end of each chapter that give you an opportunity to review and practice what you've learned or to apply new concepts to the language use you see

around you. These include activities that ask you to observe language you hear or see, not as a member of the grammar police nor as a possible victim of such police but as an interested observer.

I hope you enjoy reading this book as much as I have enjoyed writing it.

EXPLORATIONS

Exploration 1: Language autobiography

What is your language story? Perhaps you grew up in a place where those around you all spoke the same language in much the same way. Or you may have had experience with a great deal of language diversity. In either case, you have a rich tapestry of language experiences to draw upon. The fact that your experiences are not the same as your classmates will only enrich any discussion.

The questions below can help you recall and elaborate upon your experiences and attitudes, both now and as you were growing up.

1. What language(s) did you speak at home while growing up?
2. What language(s) were spoken in your community?
3. How about now—what language(s) do you speak or sign? If more than one, can you identify which one(s) you use in which circumstances?
4. What language(s) do people around you use – in your family, your community, your school, your workplace? Are home and school languages different for you, for example?
5. When did you first realize that not everyone speaks the same as you and your family? How did you come to this realization?
6. Have you lived in or visited different places where people spoke differently from you, a different version of English or a different language? What were your reactions to these differences?
7. Have you noticed any times when someone's way of speaking left a good or a bad impression on you, even before you really knew them? What left that impression?
8. Have you ever experienced what you perceived as prejudice or discrimination because of the language or the dialect you spoke? When?

There are no right or wrong answers here. Your story is always your story and you are the one who should tell it.

Class discussion: Bring your notes into class and compare them with those of your classmates. What differences do you see? What similarities?

Writing assignment: Write a two-page reflection on your language history and current situation, touching on the questions above as relevant.

REFERENCE

Winford, D. (2003). Ideologies of language and socially realistic linguistics. In S. Makoni, G. Smitherman, A. Ball, & A. Spears (Eds.), *Black linguistics: Language, society and politics in Africa and the Americas* (pp. 21–39). Routledge.

CHAPTER 2

A language is a language, right?

....

First glance

What is language?

Dialects, varieties, and languages

Design features of language

Do animals have language?

Speaking, signing, writing

Characteristics of language:

- All languages change over time
- All children acquire language in similar ways
- All languages are rule governed
- Variation is an intrinsic aspect of all languages

INTRODUCTION

Let me start our discussion with a seemingly simple but actually quite complex question. In British English the word *schedule* is pronounced *shed-yule*, not *sked-yule* as it is in most parts of North America. Speakers of both North American English and British English often notice this but don't make a big deal about it. They talk their way; we talk ours. Both are okay. In African American English, to use a different example, the word *ask* is not pronounced *ask*, as it is in most parts of North America, but *axe*. Many people notice this too, but unlike their reactions to *schedule*, they do make a big deal of *axe*. The question I want to ask is, Why do we make a big deal about a minor pronunciation difference between African American English and Standard English yet accept a similarly minor pronunciation difference between British English and American English?

The answer to that question concerns much more than those two words. It concerns what we consider a language, of course, but also issues of privilege, power, difference, and ways

DOI: 10.4324/9780429269059-2

of thinking about and reacting to variation in language. To answer our question, we'll need to examine some basic concepts about language and perhaps adjust our ideas about what language is. We'll come back to our question about *schedule* and *ask* after this discussion.

WHAT IS LANGUAGE?

We can start by noting the distinction between language and a language. When we talk about a language, we are talking about a specific communication system used by a particular group or groups of people. English and Italian, Burmese and Tibetan, Swahili and Xhosa, Quechan and Navajo, American Sign Language and Chinese Sign Language are all easily recognized as separate languages. Even here, however, in trying to create a list of languages, problems arise. How do we know if two different communication systems are two different languages or just variations of the same language? Is Sicilian, for example, a different language from Italian or a dialect of Italian?

One way of distinguishing is to ask if they are **mutually intelligible**, that is, users of one can understand, and be understood by, users of the other. If they cannot understand one another, then their speech is not mutually intelligible, and we might assume they are speaking or signing different languages.

Mutual intelligibility doesn't always work to distinguish languages, however. Speakers of what is considered the same language can have difficulties understanding one another, as my story in Chapter 1 of trying to speak to people in Wales illustrates; we were speaking mutually unintelligible varieties of English. Similarly, speakers of different dialects of what we usually call Chinese are totally unintelligible to one another, yet we call it all Chinese. On the other hand, educated speakers of Danish, Norwegian, and Swedish can usually understand one another, yet we call them different languages. In fact, until Norway separated from Denmark and became an independent nation, what we today call Norwegian and Danish were seen as the same language, with Norwegian considered a dialect of Danish. Other languages too used to be considered dialects of the same language. Serbian and Croatian used to be seen as different dialects of one language, called Serbo-Croatian. After the break-up of Yugoslavia (a nation that contained Serbia and Croatia) and the Serbs and Croats established their own separate nations, both groups began calling their "dialects" separate languages, and the rest of the world followed suit. The languages themselves did not change much; what we call them changed because the social and political realities of their speakers changed.

Those political and social factors play an important role in what gets recognized as a language and what gets called a dialect or variety. (More on dialects and varieties later.) There is a saying among linguists, in fact, that a language is just a dialect with an army and a navy, in other words, a nation. We often conflate languages and nationalities: the French speak French, the Japanese speak Japanese, the Russians speak Russian. We tend to think that one nation means one language. It's a bit more complicated than that in real life, however. Many French people who live in Breton speak Breton, not French, as their native language. And many Sicilians believe that what they speak is not a dialect of Italian, but a separate language altogether. Even nations where most people speak the same language consist of populations that speak different languages. If we move beyond the confines of Europe, it gets even more complicated. India, though one country, has speakers of hundreds of different languages as citizens. In fact, most countries in the world are multilingual; that is, their citizens speak many different dialects and languages.

Dialects, varieties, and languages

I've used the terms standard language, dialect, and variety several times already without defining them, so let me do so here. The **standard language** (or the **standard**) is the variety used in schools, the government, and the media, especially the print media. It may be the one spoken by most people in a country, but that is not always the case. It is what most people think of as the language, devoid of dialect features and with no discernable accent and what most people think of as correct and proper language. That perspective misrepresents what we know about language, as we will see later. We'll return to standards and how they develop in Chapter 13.

A **dialect** is defined as a variety of a language shared by a group of speakers that is distinguished from other varieties of that language by differences in vocabulary, pronunciation, grammar, and more intangible aspects like politeness.

Now many of us are used to thinking of dialects as something other people speak. For English speakers, we talk about British, Irish, American, and Australian English, among others. Each of these is itself made up of dialects. In the United States, we distinguish among the New York, Boston, Appalachian, and various Southern dialects. In the United Kingdom, they distinguish among many regional dialects. In England, we find West Country dialects, Midlands dialects, and Southern and Northern dialects. In Wales, there are various forms of Welsh English (not the same as Welsh itself); in Scotland, there is Scottish English, and in Northern Ireland, there is Ulster English. In other parts of the world, we find Singapore English and Nigerian English, to name a few. These and other varieties around the world can differ greatly, but they are all English.

So how can we distinguish a dialect from a language? From a purely linguistic perspective, we might say that trying to distinguish a language from a dialect is a waste of time. In fact, there are only dialects, some of which resemble one another enough to get clumped into a single language, if, and only if, the cultural and political conditions favor such clumping as well. English, like all languages, only exists as a constellation of various dialects such as those mentioned earlier.

We all speak a dialect, even if we speak what is considered the standard language. We don't usually think of Standard English as a dialect, but it is. It is merely one variety of English among many, as we will see.

Dialect is a term that for many people denotes something less than a real language, something spoken by uneducated or rural people. We know that's not true, but the term dialect is still used that way by the media and many others. For that reason, linguists often use the term **variety**. The two terms mean the same thing; the latter just comes with less baggage and fewer judgments. I'll use both here.

DESIGN FEATURES OF HUMAN LANGUAGE

When we talk about language as a human phenomenon, we are acknowledging that there are some underlying similarities among them all. Linguists examined these similarities and have determined there are several characteristics that all languages and all varieties of all languages share, what are called **design features**. Linguists continue to debate how many design features there are, but most agree on the following.

Semanticity

Perhaps the most basic characteristic is **semanticity**: we use language to convey meaning. We manipulate sounds or signs, words, and the form and order of those words, according to a system of rules to create meaning. That is, we manipulate the three major components that comprise all languages: a system of sounds or gestures, a lexicon or vocabulary, and a grammatical system.

Arbitrariness

In all languages, the relationship between a word and the object or concept that word refers to is **arbitrary**. In other words, there is no inherent or logical relationship between words and their meanings. This lack of any inherent relationship is referred to as **arbitrariness**, a design feature shared by all languages.

For example, take the English word for the object upon which we put our dinner: *table*. As English speakers, we have an arbitrary set of sounds that make up the meaning of our word *table*. Spanish speakers use a different set of arbitrary sounds for the same object, *mesa*, and Italian speakers use still another arbitrary set of sounds, *tavolo*. And users of sign languages do not have a spoken word at all, but rather a sign that indicates what we mean by *table*. None of these words is any more inherently connected to the meaning of *table* or more able to embody the essence of tableness; they are all equally arbitrary.

Arbitrariness is sometimes contrasted with **onomatopoeia**, the characteristic of a word sounding like what it means. Words like *buzz*, *meow*, or *oink* are onomatopoetic. In some ways, these words are non-arbitrary as there is a relationship between sound and meaning. Even with sounds such as these, however, there is some arbitrariness present, for not all languages use the same linguistic sounds to indicate the same natural sounds. In English, for example, roosters crowing at the break of dawn say *cock-a-doodle-doo*. In Russian the same rooster would say *kikiririki*.

It's not just words that are arbitrary; other parts of language are as well, including grammar. For example, English speakers use articles to distinguish a specific or known object (*the book*) from an unknown object or general idea (*a book*). In many other languages, such as Russian, there are no articles at all, no equivalent to the word *the*. Our use of articles is an arbitrary convention; Russian has other arbitrary conventions. English speakers also generally place adjectives before nouns; Spanish speakers put them after nouns. Both systems are arbitrary.

As another example of the arbitrariness of grammar, let's look at plurals. How a language marks a word as plural, or even if it does so at all, is arbitrary. In English, we mark nouns by adding an {s} at the end to indicate they are plural. Some languages do not mark nouns at all to indicate plurality; the context or a number word indicates plurality without any other marking, the equivalent of *three book*. Some languages mark nouns as either singular or plural; some mark them as singular, dual, or plural. All are equally arbitrary and equally logical.

Linguistics in your world: But that's wrong, isn't it?

How about grammar rules? Aren't they based on logic and therefore non-arbitrary? Grammar, despite what you might have been told, is not based on logic. In fact, grammar rules are arbitrary too. Take double negatives. You've probably been told that double negatives are incorrect because they are illogical. Not so. In some languages, making an assertion negative requires at least two negative elements. To say *I never saw her* in French, for example, one needs both a *ne* and a *jamais* (both negativizers): *Je ne l'ai jamais vue*, literally *I did not see her never*. The French use of what we might call double negatives is not illogical; it's just the way they say it. The same goes for some varieties of English that use two negative elements. We will discuss double negatives in more detail later; for now, it is important to realize that both ways of making a sentence negative are arbitrary; neither is more logical.

What is grammar?

A useful question here might be, What is grammar? The term grammar has many meanings. We talk about good grammar and bad grammar; we've all probably sat through grammar lessons in school; we may have had our grammar corrected by teachers or even by friends. When we talk about correct or incorrect grammar, we're using the prescriptive perspective described in Chapter 1, a perspective that assumes there is one and only one correct way to sign, say, or write something.

You'll remember from Chapter 1 that linguistics uses not a prescriptive but a descriptive approach. As a result, a radically different definition of grammar prevails. In linguistics, **grammar** refers to a system of rules that governs how we put sounds together to form words, put words together to form phrases, and put phrases together to form sentences. Sign language users put together what are called primes rather than sounds to form words using their grammar to do so. It is our knowledge of this system, our grammatical competence mentioned in Chapter 1, that allows us to speak or sign. Linguistics as a field seeks to describe this system of rules and its phonological, morphological, and syntactic components.

Cultural transmission and innateness

The ability to learn a language is **innate** in humans; we're born with this ability. Which language we learn, however, depends on which language we are exposed to as children. Children learn what they hear or see around them; the design feature known as **cultural transmission**. Which language a child learns depends not on what language her ancestors spoke, but on what language she hears around her as she is acquiring language. If a child of Norwegian parents is raised hearing only Chinese, she will learn Chinese as her native language. Unless she is also exposed to it as a child, Norwegian will be just as hard for her to learn as it is for any other speaker of Chinese. We'll discuss how children learn language in more detail later.

Displacement

All languages allow their speakers to refer to the past and the future; to refer to people, things, or events that are not present; and to refer to things that do not exist. That is, all human languages have a design feature known as **displacement**. Languages display this characteristic whenever their speakers communicate about events from the past, predictions about the future, or imaginary objects. We are, in our language use, not confined to the here and now.

We can talk about holodecks and intergalactic travel, about unicorns and sea serpents, or about what we had for breakfast yesterday and what we hope to have tomorrow.

Discreteness and duality

Discreteness refers to the quality of being composed of discrete units. When we learn a language, we learn to perceive it as made up of discrete units. Take language sounds, for example. When we think about the [o] sound and the [u] sound in English, we tend to think of them as discrete, separate sounds. And when we hear them, we generally hear either one or the other, not something in-between. If we looked at the acoustic realities of these sounds, however, we'd find that there is a continuum of sound from [o] to [u] and no one clear spot in which the [o] becomes the [u] or vice versa. Our minds, because we have learned that these are separate sounds in our language, do not hear the continuum but rather two separate discrete entities.

This concept is perhaps easier to grasp with words. Think about the phrase, *an orange*, for example. We would expect to hear it pronounced with a pause between *an* and *orange*. If we listen carefully, however, we notice that it sounds more like *a norange*. Because we know the words *an* and *orange* as discrete units in English, however, we hear *an orange*.

Related to the design feature of discreteness is the design feature **duality**. All languages are structured such that discrete smaller units can be combined into larger units, so for spoken languages, sounds combine to form words, words combine to form phrases, and phrases combine to form sentences. In sign languages, primes combine to form words, words combine to form phrases, and phrases combine to form sentences. Discrete words and phrases can be recombined in different ways to form different meanings.

Duality and discreteness form the basis for what linguists call grammar—that is, the ability mentioned earlier to combine discrete units into larger units to create meaning. The smallest of these units tends to be meaningless. Take the [t] sound, for example. By itself, it has no meaning. But if we combine it with another meaningless sound [o], we create an utterance with meaning, the word *toe*. It's actually quite an amazing feat all languages do: they take these small discrete meaningless units and, by combining them with other units, create meaning.

Productivity

Discreteness and duality are key to productivity as well. The design feature of **productivity** refers to the ability of speakers of any language to produce an infinite number of sentences and to produce novel sentences, sentences they have never uttered nor heard before, an ability enabled by the ability to combine the same discrete units in different ways to create different meanings. This ability allows for the creativity all language users are capable of. As an example of a novel sentence, take the following: *Get that silly pink hippo off my tutu at once.* Chances are you've never heard that sentence before. Yet you have no problem understanding it. In similar fashion, you can produce sentences you've never heard or produced before. There are, in fact, an infinite number of sentences or utterances possible in any language. Although the number of words is obviously limited (very large, but not limitless) and the number of rules for combining them is similarly limited, in theory the number of sentences or utterances we can produce is infinite.

DO ANIMALS HAVE LANGUAGE?

Productivity is, perhaps, the property that most clearly sets human language apart from animal communication, for no animal forms of communication allow their users to produce an infinite number of utterances. There are some forms of animal communication, however, that share some characteristics of human language. Bird song, for example, at least for some species, seems to be culturally transmitted, as human languages are. Some birds won't learn to sing at all if not exposed to the song of their species, while other birds will learn the song of whatever species they are exposed to, much like human infants will learn whatever language they are exposed to.

Although some animal modes of communication share certain characteristics with human language, none shares all of them, so they are not language as we have defined it. The European honeybee, for example, does an intricate tail-wagging dance to communicate to its mates the location of a good source of nectar. It can communicate direction, distance, and the richness of a source that is up to 7 miles away. It does so by wagging its tail in both a circular and a straight-line manner, using the angle of its line to indicate direction and the excitability of its wiggling to indicate the richness of the food source. Certainly, this is a complicated communication system that serves the honeybees well. It is not, however, human language.

If I say that non-human animals do not have language, I am not implying that they are somehow less than we are. Like humans, many other animal species have developed complex systems of communication that serve their purposes well. Those forms of communication are not part of our makeup, either genetic or social. They are not the forms of communication that have evolved as humans have evolved. We can study animal modes of communication and write learned treatises on them, but as for being able to wiggle our rear ends to indicate how far and in what direction the flowers with the best nectar lie, we as humans can probably never manage that. The various skills and types of intelligence needed in non-human animal worlds are different from those needed in our human world. As such, they have led to the development of their systems of communication, which are different from human language.

Many people, linguists included, have tried to teach human language to various non-human animals, usually chimpanzees. The results have been mixed, and linguists disagree about whether it is possible. One problem in the early attempts was that chimps' vocal apparatuses are not able to produce the kinds of sounds that humans use for language. The solution was to try to teach them a sign language, often American Sign Language (ASL). The most successful attempt seems to have been Washoe, a chimpanzee raised in the 1960s by Allen and Beatrix Gardner, who raised her like a human child as much as possible, using ASL to communicate with her. Washoe learned to use around 200 signs and seemed to understand many more. Even more telling, the Gardners claimed that she could produce new combinations of signs, ones not seen by her before, a key characteristic of language use.

A decade later, Herb Terrace tried to teach another chimp, Nim Chinsky, language signs but eventually concluded that the signs Nim produced were merely repetitions of signs used by his trainers and that Nim had not really acquired language. In the 1990s, Sue Savage-Rumbaugh and Dwayne Rumbaugh claimed some success with a bonobo chimpanzee named Kanzi that they had socialized much like a human child. They showed that he could understand a complex sentence such as *Get the ball which is outside*. That sentence required him to understand the relative clause (*which is outside*) and its relation to the ball, while ignoring the ball that was inside, which he did. The debate about whether chimps, or any non-human animal, can acquire human language continues.

OTHER CHARACTERISTICS OF HUMAN LANGUAGE

In addition to the design features discussed thus far, there are a few other characteristics of language:

- Spoken, signed and written language are different modes of communication.
- All languages change over time.
- Children everywhere learn their first language in very similar ways.
- All languages are highly structured and rule governed.
- Variation is a natural part of all languages.

We'll touch on each of these here and discuss them in more detail in later chapters.

Linguistic modes of communication

When we examine language, especially in an educational setting, many people first think of the written language. However, language exists independent of any writing system. Writing is only one mode used in language; speaking and signing are the other two. Historically for all languages, the written form derived from the spoken form. Both as a species and as individuals, we spoke before we wrote. Indeed, many languages throughout the world today do not have a written form. People in developed, highly literate societies often consider oral societies as somehow more primitive than literate ones. Not so! There are, in fact, no primitive languages. Like all languages, both oral and signed languages meet the needs of their users. Indeed, as Burgess (1993) notes, "We forget that language is primarily sounds [or signs], and that sounds existed long before visual signs were invented. The illiterates of the . . . world are not dumb" (p. 173).

Speaking is the most common mode of linguistic communication. Spoken language is different from written language in important ways. It is learned as a child, before going to school. We can speak to others without seeing them, in the dark, for instance, and since it does not require the use of hands, we can use our hands for other things as we speak. Because the human voice can easily vary its pitch, speed, and rhythm, speaking can indicate emotions as well as content. Speaking usually occurs in a shared social and temporal context, one in which confusion and ambiguity can be resolved directly by those involved. More so than writing, spoken language is inherently and inevitably variable. It varies at all levels of language: pronunciation, vocabulary, grammar, and more. This variation allows it to signal more information than is apparent on the surface, such as social roles and identities, for example. It is not just poets who mean much more than they say; we all do it every day. We'll come back to this idea of variation later in this chapter.

Writing, unlike speaking, is a skill usually learned in school, after children have already acquired the basics of their language. It is derivative of speech: while a spoken word directly represents objects in the world, writing represents the spoken word, so it is an indirect representation of those objects. If I say *dog*, you probably think of the animal. If you read *d-o-g*, you think of the word *dog*, which then leads you to think of the animal. Because of the different functions it serves, writing tends to contain less variation than spoken language. It functions to impart information across time and space, to record things we cannot remember, to express our creativity, and more. Unlike speaking or signing, writing is designed to work outside of the context in which it is produced. I'm writing this now at a coffee shop in St. Paul, Minnesota; you are reading it at some other time and in some other place. Writing needs to have a certain level of consistency for that to happen.

Signing is the use of hand movements and facial gestures to communicate meaning. Sign languages are just as much language as spoken ones; they show all the design features discussed earlier. Instead of using a system of grammatical rules to combine sounds into words and then phrases and sentences, however, sign languages use a system of grammatical rules to combine hand shape and orientation, hand location, and hand movement to create words that then are combined into phrases and sentences to create meaning. A word in a sign language can differ from another word by the shape of the hand (fingers opened or closed; palm facing outward or inward) just as a spoken word can differ from another word by one sound (*cat—bat—mat*).

A discussion of the differences between written, spoken, and sign language could fill an entire book; here I've just touched on a few basics. As we discuss language throughout the rest of this book, remember that speaking or signing, not writing, is the primary mode of communication of language users.

All languages change over time

Language change is not only natural and normal; it is also inevitable. English, like all languages, has gone through substantial changes throughout its history. If we try to read *Beowulf*, for example, as it was originally written over a thousand years ago, we'd have a hard time comprehending it, even though it is written in English, what we now call Old English. Even reading Chaucer is difficult, and he wrote only 700 years ago. (We discuss the history of English in Chapter 13.)

What is it that changes over time to make it so hard to understand our language from centuries ago? Obviously, words do; old words disappear, new words appear. You can probably identify words that were once common but are no longer used: *davenport, floppy disk, rotary phone*, for example, or words that have entered the language in the last 30 years or so: *cell phone, Twitter*. The meanings of words change too, of course. The word *way* used to be strictly a noun; now it is often used as an adjective meaning *very*—as in *way uncool*. Pronunciations change too; *name*, for example, used to be pronounced *nah-muh* in Old English and gradually changed to how we pronounce it today. Pronunciation changes are not just things of the past; they go on all the time, even if we don't notice them. Currently, in the United States we are experiencing what is known as the *cot/caught merger*. Younger people tend not to make a distinction between the vowel sound in *caught* and the one in *cot*. Say them aloud and listen to how you pronounce them. I make a distinction; that is, I pronounce those two words quite differently. You may not. Which way is right? Both are!

Our ideas of what is grammatically correct change too, though less quickly than vocabulary. One change I've noticed recently can serve as an example. For me, the preposition used with *base* is *on*, not *off of* (*based on your opinion* not *based off of your opinion*). The latter sounds decidedly odd to my ears, and I'd be tempted to correct it in an essay. To my students, however, it sounds perfectly normal and correct. I've had to change my ears, if you will, and accept that *based off of* and *based on* are both grammatically correct; it's just an example of normal language change.

That change seemed to just happen. Sometimes, however, language changes as the result of social changes. All languages will change as the needs of their speakers change. In Germany, for example, the use of two common terms of address for women, *Frau* and *Fraulein*, has been changing. *Frau* was used with older or married women, *Fraulein* for young or unmarried ones. There was, of course, no such distinction made for men; *Herr* referred to both married and unmarried men. As the result of changes in women's roles since the 1970s, *Fraulein* is gradually falling out of use and being replaced by *Frau* for all women.

People often think that there is only one correct way to pronounce a word or only one correct way to say something. As we'll see in more detail later, that's not true. If we see new ways of pronouncing a word as wrong, then we'd need to say that how we now pronounce *name* is wrong too. It's not wrong, just different from the way it used to be pronounced—the result of natural language change. In the case of how *caught* and *cot* are pronounced, the change from making a distinction to not making one doesn't indicate a decline in the English language. Like all language change, it is not decay or corruption at work, just simple change.

All children learn their first language in similar ways

Most adults find learning a new language a daunting task, yet children everywhere accomplish this task with little or no overt instruction from adults. All children, if they are exposed to a language and if there are no physiological or mental disabilities that prevent it, will learn, or more precisely acquire, a language, mostly without conscious effort or awareness. Linguists make a distinction between learning a language, a conscious effort that usually requires practice and instruction, and acquiring a language, an unconscious process that does not require overt instruction. They call this process **first language acquisition** or **L1 acquisition** for short. We'll discuss some general principles of how children acquire their first language here; in subsequent chapters, we'll discuss how children acquire specific aspects of language.

Despite common misconceptions about language acquisition, children don't learn their first language by adults teaching them, nor do they learn it mainly through imitation. No tests, no homework, no drills, yet by the age of five, before they go to school, they have mastered a complex system of grammar, the ability to combine discrete units into larger units to create meaning. They have mastered the sound system (or primes for sign languages), a great deal of vocabulary, and a complex syntax system. To accomplish all that so quickly, they must have some predisposition for language learning. The exact nature of that predisposition is debated, but linguists generally agree we are hardwired to acquire language, no matter the language.

Many linguists point to what is called **Universal Grammar**, or **UG**, a set of core grammar principles that all languages adhere to, as an important part of that hard wiring. Many linguists posit that UG is part of our biological endowment, a sort of genetic blueprint for all languages. Since children already have this blueprint, they don't need to figure everything out, just how the universal principles apply in their language. Evidence for this view includes the universal nature of language acquisition, the uniformity of the acquisition process, and the ease and rapidity with which children acquire language.

Other linguists contend that we are not born with knowledge of these principles; rather, we are born with certain cognitive strategies that allow us to quickly deduce the underlying principles or system of language. They note that even with advances in brain scans, no one has yet found any evidence for any innate blueprints.

Both sides agree that children learn very quickly from what is called a poverty of data. That is, the language they hear (or see in the case of sign languages) around them is full of stops and starts, incomplete sentences, non-language noises, slips of the tongue or hand, and other features that make it hard to figure out the underlying rules. Yet children everywhere do it.

They appear to go through similar stages as they do so, whether their language is oral or signed. These stages and their timing are general patterns, so not all children move through them at exactly the same time. Nor do they move from one to the other in one day. It's a gradual process, but one that shows remarkable similarity in children learning languages as different as Chinese and Swahili. What follows is a summary of these stages:

- A prelinguistic stage where children learning a spoken language learn to distinguish speech sounds from other noises in the environment. They also learn to recognize the intonation patterns of their native language and can reproduce those patterns well before they produce any recognizable words.
- A babbling stage (4 to 8 months of age): At around 6 months, children learning a spoken language begin to master the sounds of their language and practice producing them, often repeating the same syllable over and over: *dadadada*. Early babbling seems to be similar across languages, with children producing much the same sounds. Interestingly, children even babble when they are alone. Children learning a sign language also babble, except with their hands instead of their mouths.
- A one-word stage (9 to 18 months): Here children start producing identifiable words, usually referring to familiar people, actions, or objects: *mama, doggie, up, milk*. They soon start producing around 50 or so common words, though the production is often not quite adult-like, sometimes to the point that only family members can understand them. During this stage, children's use of a single word can function much like a complete adult sentence; *milk*, for example, can mean *I want milk* or *There's the milk*.
- A two-word stage (18 to 24 months): At about 18 months, children begin using two-word combinations to mean what would be expressed in adult language with a complete sentence. These combinations are usually made up of nouns, verbs, and adjectives: *Mommy shoe* could mean, for example, *That's Mommy's shoe* or *Give me Mommy's shoe*. At this stage, children learning different languages seem to express similar things as they learn to express content more efficiently.
- A multiword stage (24 to 48 months and older): During this time, children begin using more and more words as they also begin to acquire more complex syntactic rules. This acquisition proceeds rapidly, with children learning to produce more complex sentences, including questions and negatives. At about 3 years of age, for example, they start using multiple clauses, first joining clauses coordinately with *and* then using subordination in utterances like *Don't see where Sally is*. These utterances show that they are beginning to understand and apply the rules of grammar, though these are not yet fully adult utterances.

By the age of five or so, children have mastered the basics of their language, adult-like phonology, morphology, and syntax, though there may still be many overgeneralizations. Obviously, they continue to learn more as they age. The growth in vocabulary is especially noticeable after five. It is estimated that on average, 6-year-old children know about 8,000 words. By the time they have reached the age of eight, that number will have expanded to around 17,000. And of course, they will continue to learn more complex syntactic structures as they mature.

Children, then, become competent users of their native language or languages in a few short years. What does it mean to say they are competent? In linguistics, that word has a specific meaning slightly different from the one used in everyday speech. **Linguistic competence** refers to the unconscious knowledge all speakers of a language have, knowledge that allows them to produce and understand their language. By definition, all native speakers/ signers of a language are equally competent.

If we start to judge some people as better users of language, we are then referring to **linguistic performance**, not competence. Linguistic performance refers to what is produced using one's linguistic competence, what we say, sign, or write. Obviously, some of us are better orators than others, some of us are better writers than others. That judgment is about our performance, not our competence.

All languages are structured and rule governed

As we saw earlier, all languages are made up of discrete units and rules for putting those units together into meaningful and well-formed utterances; that is, all languages are structured and rule governed. In linguistics, the term **structure** refers to all levels of language: sounds, words, phrases, and sentences. When we examine the units of sound in a language, for example, and how those units are put together to form words, we're examining the structure of language. We can examine the structure not just of sounds, but of words (yes, words have a structure too), phrases, sentences, and units of language beyond the sentence, what is called discourse. The next few chapters examine that structure; here I'd like to discuss the term **rule governed** as it is a key concept in linguistics.

When we talk about rules in this context, we do not mean the ones you may have learned in school, such as rules for spelling and writing. Nor do we mean those prescriptive rules mentioned in Chapter 1 that tell us how we should talk or write. Instead, we are talking about the unconscious rules we use to produce and understand language as we speak or sign it every day. What linguists do is try to describe those rules.

Some examples might help here. In school, you were probably taught that to make a noun plural in English, we add an *s*, with a few exceptions such as *children*. This is true to some extent. But if we listen carefully to how we talk rather than how we write, we discover that the rule is a bit more complex than that. Try making *cat* plural: *cats*. What sound do you hear at the end of the word? That sound seems to clearly be an [s] sound. So far, the school rule works. Now try making *dog* plural: *dogs*. What sound do you hear at the end of that word? Although we spell that sound with the letter *s*, we don't pronounce it that way. In fact, we make *dog* plural by adding not the [s] sound, but the [z] sound. (Those brackets are a convention in linguistics to indicate we are talking about sounds, not letters.) What rule is operative here? Certainly not the one we learned in school.

There is a rule here, and we know this because children as young as two, who most likely have not yet been to school, also use [s] with *cat* and [z] with *dog*. In fact, young children will add [s] to some words they have never heard before and [z] to other novel words. They are using a rule when they do so, for their answers are all the same; [s] is added to one set of words, and [z] to a different set; those sets are the same for all children. (We will investigate the exact nature of this rule in Chapter 5.)

As another example, take the following words and put them in an order that sounds like English to you: *French, four, girls, young, the*. Chances are you put them in the following order: *the four young French girls* rather than *the French young four girls* or *young four the girls French*. Why? You might say, "*It just sounds better*." But that raises the question: Why does it sound better? Surely, it's not by accident or just a matter of personal taste. If it were, some would prefer *the French young four girls,* and others would prefer *the four young French girls*. But all English speakers will come up with the latter not the former. If we all do the same thing, then there must be some underlying rule or pattern that we follow. You may not know that rule consciously, but you do know it. And as speakers of English, you use it.

Here's one more example: Say the word *fin* aloud. Listen carefully to the [n] sound. Now say the word *finger*. Again, listen carefully to the [n] sound. What happened? Is it the same [n] sound? Probably not. Why not? You might guess here that the fact that the [g] sound follows the [n] sound influences how we pronounce it. And you'd be right. But what is it about the [g] sound that has this influence? In other words, why did we all adapt the [n] sound in the same way when it preceded the [g] sound? You might say, "*That's just how the word is pronounced*." True enough. But if given a made-up word, say *langel*, one they do not already know how to pronounce, English speakers will again adapt the [n] sound to be like the one in *finger*, not like the one in *fin*.

The rules that we follow to make that adaptation are among the type of rules we are referring to when we say that all language is rule governed. And the rules we follow when choosing [s] or [z] with plurals and when ordering adjectives before nouns are similarly examples of the rule-governed nature of language.

Two important points to remember here: 1) these mostly unconscious rules are the ones we draw upon whenever we speak or sign or write, and 2) all language is rule governed, even if it does not sound correct or proper to you. If all language is rule governed, then whenever we speak or sign or write any language, we are always following the rules of our language. There is no other way to do it. We'll come back to these points later in this chapter.

Variation is a natural part of all languages

Variation, like structure and change, is intrinsic to language, both variation among languages and variation within any one language. Most of us are used to accepting variation among different languages. It is estimated that there are around 7,000 languages in the world, all of which do things differently. Perhaps we're not so used to accepting variation within one language. All languages spoken by a substantial number of people, however, are made up of different varieties. These varieties are connected to our social identities—regional, class, ethnic, gender, and racial identities. That is, people from a particular region tend to speak a similar if not identical variety of a language if they also share a similar class, ethnic, racial, or gender identity. It is this patterned variation that allows our language use to serve as a badge of social identity, an important function of language. We show others who we are by how we talk.

This function of variation seems to be important in some other species' communication too. Recent studies of bird songs have found that swamp sparrows, for example, have what we can call dialects. That is, birds in different locations have slightly different songs. What's interesting here is that the birds seem to use these differences to identify other swamp sparrows that belong to their own or to a different group. Thus, this variation serves a social purpose similar to variation in human language; it marks speakers' (or in the bird example, singers') social identity and allows them to identify the social identity of others.

For the swamp sparrows, we probably would not ask which variation of the species' song is correct, but for human languages, we often do ask that question. Can two different varieties of a language both be correct? If variation is an intrinsic part of human languages, then the answer must be yes. Earlier we saw that some English speakers pronounce *caught* and *cot* with the same vowel sound, while others use different vowel sounds. And we noted that both are correct. Just as there is no one correct way to pronounce a word, so there is no one correct way to speak any language. There are many correct ways of pronouncing a word and many grammatically correct ways of speaking.

There are different ways because there are different language varieties. What is key here is that each variety is correct in its own terms; such variation is natural, normal, and inevitable. Variation—different ways of pronouncing a word or constructing a sentence—is thus not something to be condemned; indeed, all languages, and all varieties of all languages, are equally correct, rule governed, and valid forms of communication.

Variation in accent—differences in how different groups pronounce words—tends to be acceptable. Variation in grammar, however, is often seen as bad grammar. If all language is rule governed, however, then there is no such thing as bad grammar. That statement may be a bit hard to swallow at first, so let me explain. As we've seen, linguists have established that all language use is rule governed; it is impossible to speak or sign without using the constitutive rules of the variety you are speaking or signing. Does all this mean that there is no such thing as a grammatical mistake? The answer is—yes and no. People do make mistakes when they speak: slips of the tongue (*fed rish* for *red fish*); mispronunciations of words they come across for the first time (how would you pronounce *desuetude*, for example?); or getting lost in a long sentence and forgetting where it started. These can be caused by tiredness or inattention or other non-linguistic factors.

What most people call mistakes, however, are not slips of the tongue or mispronunciations of novel words. Utterances such as *ain't*; *he be tired*; *they don't need nothing*; *you shouldn't oughta had done that*; or *I seen it*, for example, are often cited as grammatical errors. Those utterances are not grammatical errors; they are rule-governed constructions common in certain varieties of English but not common in Standard English.

It ain't necessarily so

Ain't can serve as an illustrative example here. Most of us have probably been told that there's no such word as *ain't*. All of us have also probably heard people use that word and understood it. In fact, it's been in use for hundreds of years. If that's not a word, what is?

Ain't began its life in the early 1600s, a time when many contractions entered the English language: *isn't, aren't, can't, won't*, etc. It seems to have originally served as a contraction of *am not* and was written as *amn't*. In English, two nasal sounds ([m] and [n] are both nasals) next to one another are often disfavored; that is, they can sound a bit odd and be a bit hard to pronounce. As a result of this phonological aspect of the word, it came to be written (and we assume pronounced) as *an't*, then as *ain't*.

Surprising to many people today, throughout that time, *ain't* was considered a perfectly acceptable word. It's not clear exactly why it became unacceptable in Standard English. One theory is that it fell out of favor in the mid to late 19th century, beginning in the United States when it became associated with new immigrants. Because these new immigrants were seen as less desirable by the dominant group, that word also came to be seen as less desirable and then as ungrammatical.

Let's look at what happens because we no longer use *ain't*. There is a construction in English known as a tag question. It functions a bit like the *n'est-ce pas* in French: It comes at the end of a sentence and adds a little question to it. For example, we can say, "She's invited to the party." To add a tag question to that sentence, we'd add, *isn't she*? Thus, you get the following:

- She's invited to the party, isn't she?
- They're invited to the party, aren't they?
- We're invited to the party, aren't we?
- You're invited to the party, aren't you?
- He's invited to the party, isn't he?

Now, what happens when you want to add a tag question to the sentence "*I'm invited to the party*"? Most people end up saying, "*I'm invited to the party, aren't I?*" Doesn't that strike your ears as rather odd—*aren't I*? If we had a contraction for *am not* analogous to *isn't* and *aren't* (which the much-maligned *ain't* is), we could use a form that makes more sense as part of the English verb system. Instead, we are stuck with *aren't I*—or *am I not*—a construction that definitely changes the tone of the entire sentence.

I am not saying by all this that you should go out and use *ain't* in your next essay or job interview. You know as well as I do that there are consequences to doing so. I am saying that we should realize that there is nothing inherently wrong with *ain't* and similar stigmatized forms except for the fact that they are stigmatized. And it is their stigmatization that is the problem, not forms like *ain't* per se.

Other so-called grammatical errors

If we examine some other examples of stigmatized so-called grammatical mistakes such as those mentioned earlier (*he be tired*; *they don't need nothing*; *you shouldn't oughta had done that*; *I seen it*), we would see that most of what people call bad grammar are not mistakes at all. Instead, they are the normal, rule-governed usages of a particular group or groups of speakers, in other words, of a particular variety of English.

To return to an example mentioned earlier, double negatives are often cited as obvious grammatical mistakes. Two negatives, we are told, make a positive. Well, in math that is true, but only in certain circumstances. When multiplying negative numbers, that's true; you do get a positive. It is not true, however, when adding two negative numbers; there you get a larger negative. It's not true in language, either. Many languages use two negative units to indicate negation, as we saw with French. And English used to do so as well. Even in Modern English, if we hear, *I didn't see nothing*, we most likely do not think the speaker is admitting to seeing something. We know that sentence is not a positive, no matter what the grammar police might say.

Why are *ain't, he be tired; they don't need nothing; you shouldn't oughta had done that;* and *I seen it* considered bad grammar? The answer is that they have come to be seen as errors not because of anything inherently wrong in them but because of the speakers these varieties are associated with. Basically, it can be boiled down to this: if a group of people is considered less desirable by the dominant group, then their language variety will be seen as wrong. The varieties of groups who face social discrimination also face linguistic discrimination. That helps explain the question I started this chapter with: why is it considered okay to pronounce *schedule* the way many British do, but not okay to pronounce *ask* the way many African Americans do?

Does all this mean that if someone says, *I seen it*, and someone else says, *I saw it*, they are both correct? Yes, that's exactly what it means. We need to recognize that all speakers follow the rules of their variety of English; it's just that different varieties have different rules.

But isn't there one dialect of English (or any language) that is most correct, one that is the best? As uncomfortable as it may be to believe, the answer is *no*. Most people think that there is one correct way of speaking English, variously termed Proper English or Standard English or Broadcast English—the English generally described in grammar handbooks and taught in school. This English is usually seen as the only correct form of the language; variations of it are termed dialects and viewed as aberrations of the standard. The truth is, however, that if this variety of English exists (and most sociolinguists would insist it does not), it is still only one dialect among many, all of which are equally correct.

To reiterate: All dialects—*all of them*—are rule governed. Thus, if a person says *I seen it* on a regular basis as part of her normal speech, she is not speaking bad English. It is not that she does not know the rules of English; it is merely that the rules of her dialect are different than the rules of the dialect of someone who says *I saw it*.

Not only are all varieties equal linguistically, but from a linguistic perspective, there are only dialects. Each of us speaks a particular dialect of our language. Some of us may speak two; we may have grown up bi-dialectical. And since dialects include **accent** (in linguistics, accent refers specifically to pronunciation), all of us necessarily speak with an accent. We may not hear it ourselves, but if we travel far enough away from our region of origin, we usually notice that we don't sound exactly like others in this new area, even if we speak the same language. We may hear them as having an accent; they, in turn, hear our speech as accented. The truth is both are right, for no one speaks without what others would consider an accent. Sometimes this is to a speaker's advantage; in the United States, for example, British accents are often considered sophisticated. Sometimes, though, it is not so advantageous; Southern U.S. accents in the United States are often seen as ignorant and backward by those living in other regions of the country. Neither judgment is true, but these are strong stereotypes that can be hard to dispel.

Judgments about language varieties and accents are more than merely judgments about correct or incorrect grammar or pronunciation. They are, in essence, judgments about the people who speak those dialects. Linguistic stigmatization, then, has to do with who speaks the varieties in question and what associations the dominant culture has about that group and their language. It is not the case that a certain variety is grammatically incorrect and then society looks down on those who speak it. The real situation is that when a certain group is looked down on, their language becomes stigmatized, and then the stigma about their language is used to further stigmatize and oppress that group. It starts with the speakers, not the speech.

The flip side is also true. If a group has power and prestige, if they are somehow dominant, their speech comes to be seen as correct and proper, as standard. Their use of that speech is then seen as further evidence that they deserve the power and prestige they enjoy. Again, such perceptions are not true, though they do form a powerful myth.

Speaking Standard English brings with it certain privileges, not the least of which is the fact that the educational system is conducted in, and asks participants to use, that variety. Think about standardized tests common in the United States that many students take to get into university. Using *I seen* on such tests, even if such usage is a normal part of your variety, merits punishment in terms of points; using *I saw* merits rewards. Standard English is the preferred dialect not only in the educational system, but in business, government, law, and the media as well. As such, it is accorded a special status that other dialects are not. Most educators and politicians and many others continue to believe that those who speak what are sometimes called nonstandard dialects are speaking a *substandard* form of the language. Despite the fact that linguists have established beyond any reasonable doubt that no dialects are substandard and that all dialects are equally rule governed and equally valid, useful, and well-structured systems, society continues to privilege some dialects and thus some speakers over others.

We will discuss linguistic prejudice in more detail later in several chapters. For now, when we are tempted to disparage other people's ways of speaking, we should perhaps take Einer Haugen's (1973) admonition to heart: "Any scorn for the language of others is scorn for those who use it, and as such is a form of social discrimination" (p. 52).

CHAPTER SUMMARY

- Mutual intelligibility is not necessarily a reliable way to distinguish languages because political and social factors often play a more important role than do linguistic factors.
- All languages, oral, signed, or written, share certain design features: semanticity, arbitrariness, cultural transmission, displacement, duality, discreteness, and productivity. No animal communication system is thought to contain all of these features.
- In linguistics, grammar refers to a system of rules that governs how we speak or sign, that is, how we put sounds or signs together to form words, put words together to form phrases, and put phrases together to form sentences.
- All children, if exposed to language, will acquire it without conscious instruction or effort, going through similar stages as they do so.
- All languages, and all varieties of all languages, are able to express meanings needed by those who speak them.
- Spoken and written language differ in important ways. Those who speak a language without a written form do not speak a primitive language.
- All languages are structured, rule governed, constantly changing systems that are made up of dialects or varieties, which are equally rule governed, structured, constantly changing systems.

- Language change is natural, normal, and inevitable.
- Since all languages are made up of varieties, we all speak one of these varieties.
- All varieties of all languages are correct, even if society privileges certain ones over others.
- Prejudice against linguistic varieties are prejudices against those who speak those varieties.

KEY TERMS

mutual intelligibility
standard language
dialect
variety
design features
    semanticity
    arbitrariness
    cultural transmission
    innateness
    displacement

discreteness
duality
productivity
onomatopoeia
variation
rule governed
L1 acquisition
Universal Grammar
linguistic competence
linguistic performance

EXPLORATIONS

Exploration 1: Discussion prompt

I've provided some examples of animal communication. Determine if the communication systems described here share any of the design features of human languages. If there is not enough information to decide, determine what more information you would need. Share your conclusions with your small group.

- Vervet monkeys have an interesting set of alarm calls they use to warn of danger: one call means the danger is from a snake, a different one from a leopard, and a still different one from an eagle. These calls always refer to the here and now, and as far as we can tell, monkeys don't take parts of one call and add it to another or manipulate it in any way.
- Prairie dogs also have a complex system for communicating about predators, using alarm calls that can let others know not only the type of predator but also its size and shape. These calls seem to communicate even when the predator is not present. Current research evidence indicates that they can create new calls for new types of predators and that they can put together different vocalizations to create what we might call words that are then combined to create structures analogous to sentences.
- Dogs can communicate their emotions to other dogs by the way they position their lips, ears, and tails. They can communicate threat, fear, defensiveness, submission, confidence, depression, and lack of tension. They can solicit play from other dogs through their body language; they can express curiosity by cocking their head, holding their ears forward, and showing alertness by skin creases around the eyes; they can communicate threat and

antagonism by vocalizing, growls, or snarls, for example. The meanings of these positions and vocalizations are generally consistent across canines, no matter the breed.

- My cat communicates with me in what seems to me a direct manner. Although this is not a communication system per se, we can examine it for design features. When he is hungry, he scratches at the cupboard where I keep his food. Let's assume he means to tell me to feed him now, not in 2 hours. He does the same thing each time, never varying it nor using parts of the scratch in other ways.

Exploration 2: Arbitrariness

Our number system (1, 2, 3, etc.), like our language, is mostly arbitrary. We use symbols to mean quantities that have no inherent connection to the symbols themselves. It is not totally arbitrary, however. Which of our numbers is not arbitrary?

Contrast our number system with the Roman system (I, II, III, IV, V, etc.). Is this system arbitrary? Are there parts that are arbitrary and parts that are not?

Share your conclusions with your small group.

Exploration 3: Onomatopoeia—oink, oink

Different languages use different words to represent animal noises. Find as many words for animal noises in different languages as you can. Share them with your small group without telling them the English translation. See if they can guess what the analogous word would be in English.

Exploration 4: Language myths

In this chapter, we discussed several characteristics about language that may have contradicted what you have been taught previously. You may have been taught, for example, that some language used by some people is bad grammar or that those who are illiterate are dumb. Choose one of the characteristics that contradicted what you had been previously taught and decide how you would rebut that teaching now, given what you have learned here.

Small group discussion: In small groups, discuss what you would say.

Writing assignment: Write a one-page rebuttal of your previous ideas.

Exploration 5: Linguistic pet peeves

For all of us, there are probably certain ways of speaking (accents, certain pronunciations or words, or phrasings) that drive us crazy. (One that drives me nuts is saying *expresso* for *espresso*, I think because I'm a bit of a food snob!) Identify those that drive you nuts; see if you can determine why those particular ones bother you. What might you say to yourself after reading this chapter? Discuss these in your small group.

Exploration 6: Accents

As noted in the chapter, we all speak or sign with an accent, even if we don't usually notice it ourselves. Have you even been made aware of your accent? What happened? Have you noticed other people's accents? What was most noticeable for you? What was your reaction? Discuss these in your small group.

FURTHER READING

Napoli, D. (2003). *Language matters: A guide to everyday thinking about language.* Oxford University Press.

The Human language series—a series of videos from PBS that engagingly discuss various topics about language. http://thehumanlanguage.com/. You can watch these on YouTube.

The website of the Linguistic Society of America, The Domain of Linguistics, has short introductory units on various topics: www.lasdc.org/info/lings-fields.cfm.

REFERENCES

Burgess, A. (1993). *A mouthful of air: Language and languages, especially English.* William Morrow & Co.

Haugen, E. (1973). The curse of Babel. *Daedalus, 102*(3), 47–57.

CHAPTER 3

Morphology

Word histories and structure

....

First glance

How do we put words together?

Word formation processes:
- When is borrowing theft?

Word structure: Morphemes
- Derivational and inflectional morphemes

- Grammatical meaning

Morphology in other languages

Hierarchical structure of words

Acquiring words

INTRODUCTION

Most people probably think of words as the basic, most important part of a language. When we learn a foreign language in school, aren't we asked to memorize all those words at the end of each chapter? If we do memorize them, we're often not much further along in learning to speak the language, though, because every language consists not only of a lexicon—a vocabulary—but also a phonological system, a morphological system, a syntactic system, and a grammar for putting them all together. Each system has a structure that we'll examine in the following chapters. Here we'll start with those words by examining **morphology**, the study of words and their structure.

What is it we know when we know a word? We know its meaning or meanings, its pronunciation or sign, how it's used in a sentence, and how to use it appropriately. We know that, even within the same language, the word for something in one area may be totally different in another area. A submarine sandwich (or sub) in Minnesota, for example, is a hoagie in Philadelphia and a hero in San Francisco. We know that words vary across time as well as space; that is, they

DOI: 10.4324/9780429269059-3

come and go. How many of you still speak of an *ice box*, a *davenport*, or *consumption* (*refrigerator*, *sofa*, and *tuberculosis*, respectively) or use slang terms like *groovy* or *phat* or *rad*?

We know, even if we're not aware of it consciously, that words are made up of separate parts that have meaning. *Doors*, for example, is made up of two parts, *door* and an {s} that means it is plural. We also know that each word is a particular part of speech (a noun or a verb, for example), what linguists call **lexical categories**.

We begin our discussion of words first by examining those lexical categories. We then move on to how new words enter a language and how the parts of words are put together.

LEXICAL CATEGORIES

Most of us were taught about lexical categories in school, though they were most likely called parts of speech then. All of us knew these categories even before we went to school, as they are part of our internal grammar—the system of rules we use every day to speak or sign. That knowledge is mostly unconscious, however, and it is sometimes hard to bring into conscious awareness. Here we'll examine lexical categories to help you make that knowledge conscious so you can use that knowledge in the morphological and syntactic analysis we'll be doing later.

We can classify words in general into two broad categories: **open classes** and **closed classes**. **Open classes** consist of the lexical categories of **nouns**, **verbs**, **adjectives**, and **adverbs**. They are called open because, unlike closed classes, they regularly admit new members (new words). As a result, they are a much larger class; in fact, most of the words in a lexicon belong to the open classes. They provide lexical content in sentences. **Closed classes**, as their name implies, tend not to admit new members, and in English they have remained fairly constant for centuries. Determiners, pronouns, auxiliaries, prepositions, and conjunctions are closed classes; their function is to signal grammatical relationships within sentences. They are much smaller classes, numbering only in the hundreds.

We'll start with how to distinguish nouns, verbs, adverbs, and adjectives, using meaning, form, and function to do so.

Nouns

In school, we're taught that a noun refers to a person, place, or thing. That's a meaning definition, which is sometimes useful and sometimes not. A definition that relies on form is more helpful, for each open lexical category has a set of inflectional endings that distinguishes it from other open lexical categories. For nouns, we know that they can be made plural and/or possessive by using those endings: *chair* can become plural *chairs* by adding that {s} ending; *sister* can become possessive *sister's* (*my sister's book*) by adding that apostrophe {s} ending. That's one good way to tell that a word is a noun: it can be made plural or possessive. Granted it gets a bit complicated because both of those endings are {s}, but even if we're not sure whether to use an apostrophe when we write, we know the difference between plural *sisters* (My *sisters* all live in California.) and possessive *sister's* (My *sister's* book is on the table.).

Nouns are usually, though not always, preceded by a **determiner**, a small words that signals a noun: *the*, *a/an*; *that*, *this*, *these*, *those*; *my*, *your*, *his*, etc. We can say *the vase*, for example, but not *the pretty*. We can, of course, say *the pretty vase*; nouns are often preceded by adjectives as well as determiners.

Verbs

Verbs, unlike nouns, refer to actions or states of being, at least according to my fifth grade teacher. Again, that's a meaning definition and only sometimes useful. A more useful way to distinguish verbs is to use a function definition and note that verbs are words that can show tense: present or past. And most of them can take a specific set of inflectional endings, such as {s}, {ed}, or {ing}: *walk, walks, walked, walking*. There are many irregular verbs that do not take these endings; instead, they indicate past tense, for example, without adding {ed} (*drive/drove*; *eat/ate*; *stand/stood*) or use {en} in their past participle form (*eat/eaten*). These are exceptions to the inflectional endings but not to the general rule that verbs show tense, one of their functions.

Adjectives

Adjectives are often defined by their function: they modify nouns. We can use that idea by trying out what words might fit in the following slot: *The _____ cat sat on the mat.* The words that fit in that slot are pretty sure to be adjectives: *tired, hungry, fluffy, angry, indignant*. We can also define adjectives by the endings that can attach to them: {er} and {est}: *pretty–prettier–prettiest*; *large–larger–largest*. Not all adjectives indicate comparative and superlative this way; if they consist of more than one syllable and don't end in -*y*, we use *more* and *most* instead of {er} and {est}: *more fragile, most fragile*; *more intelligent, most intelligent*. Adjectives can also be directly preceded by *very* or *too*; nouns and verbs cannot: *very smart, too hot, very spicy, too long* but not *too book* or *very sit*.

Adverbs

Adverbs are in many ways the trickiest lexical category to figure out. They often, but not always, end in -ly: *quickly, suddenly, happily*. To complicate things, not all words that end in -ly are adverbs; *lovely, chilly, lonely,* for example, are adjectives. One good way to identify adverbs is through their meaning; they tell us *when, where, why, how,* and *how often*. We can also identify them through their function: they are modifiers. In fact, they modify several parts of a sentence: verbs, adjectives or other adverbs, and even entire sentences. In *Unfortunately, it's raining really hard*, there are three adverbs: *unfortunately*, modifying the entire sentence; *hard*, modifying the verb *rain*; and *really*, modifying the adverb *hard*. One other characteristic of adverbs can help distinguish them from adjectives; many adverbs, especially those that modify sentences or verbs, can move around in the sentence. In the previous example, we can move *unfortunately* from the beginning to the end of the sentence.

To sum up, we've seen that nouns are words that can be made plural or possessive and are usually preceded by a determiner and sometimes an adjective; verbs are words that indicate tense and can take {s}, {ed}, and {ing} as endings; and adjectives and adverbs are both modifiers, modifying different parts of the sentence. Adjectives can be made comparative ({er} or *more*) and superlative ({est} or *most*). Adverbs are often movable in the sentence and tell us when, where, why, how, and how often.

WORDS AND THEIR HISTORIES

If we look at the history of words, we are approaching them from a **diachronic** perspective, one that examines how language changes over time. One of the places where language change is most evident is in the **lexicon** (the words in a language), and the study of the origin and history of words, known as **etymology**, has long been a part of linguistics. Words are constantly added to and disappear from languages. Some words change their meaning so much so that their current meaning seems completely unrelated to their earlier one and they seem like new words. (Does the word *tweet* conjure up a bird's sound or a post on Twitter?) New words enter the language all the time; most, however, never catch on. It is not always the cleverness of the new word that determines its fate. That determination usually has more to do with social factors: the word meets a need in society. When any new word catches on, we say that it has become **lexicalized**.

Word formation processes

The processes by which new words enter a language's lexicon are collectively known as **word formation processes**. Some languages make use of some processes more than others, but the processes discussed here are common in languages around the world.

Eponyms are words created from names of people or places. The Earl of Sandwich, for example, gave us the word *sandwich*. *Denim* comes from the French phrase *de Nimes*, in English *from Nimes*, a city in France that produced heavy-duty material. *Diesel* was the name of the man who invented the diesel engine, and *cardigan* comes from the Isle of Cardigan, whose inhabitants often wore what we now call cardigans.

Coining, also known as neologism, is simply inventing new words. It is not very common in English, though it is often used by clever marketing departments: *Teflon*, *aspirin*, *zipper*, and *xerox* are all coined names of products. Sometimes these nouns shift to become verbs; we can now xerox papers, not just use a Xerox machine. Recently, technology has led to an explosion of new terms: *quark* and *google* being two examples. Many new words are coined using other word formation processes, as described further.

Borrowing, a common process in English, occurs when one language borrows a word from another. English has borrowed from dozens of languages around the world. *Alcohol*, *boss*, *influenza*, *tycoon*, *yogurt*, and *klutz* were borrowed from Arabic, Dutch, Italian, Japanese, Turkish, and Yiddish, respectively. Some words take a circuitous route into English: *algebra*, for example, is an Arabic word that came into English via Spanish. English has borrowed so many terms that, according to some experts, over half of the 20,000 most commonly used words are borrowed.

Borrowing or theft?

Some of these word formation processes are neutral, not socially contested. Sometimes, however, seemingly innocuous word formation processes are fraught with social complexities. This is especially true with what are called borrowed words, a neutral term that can hide a far from benign past. What makes borrowing so socially and ethically fraught? For one thing, many terms in English were "borrowed" from peoples who were colonized by English speakers. To those colonized peoples, such borrowing may well feel more like theft. Certain borrowing is now recognized as a sort of theft, what we call **linguistic appropriation**. A form of cultural appropriation, linguistic appropriation occurs when a dominant language group adopts linguistic resources (words, in this case) from a minoritized or subordinate group while also denigrating that group and its language.

We find examples of this across the United States. The use of Native American terms as place names is common in housing subdivisions, cities, and some states, and it almost always occurs without any acknowledgment that these lands once belonged to Native Americans. Words from Spanish and from African American English (AAE) are common in the everyday language of many people. In and of itself, such borrowing is not a problem. The problem is that it coexists with both overt and subtle attacks on those languages and varieties and the people who speak them. Thus, the widespread use of Spanish words (*manana, cojones, hasta la vista*) coexists with efforts to pass laws prohibiting Spanish in public spaces. A similar situation exists with borrowed African American terms. Such words often convey a sense of being cool, itself a word borrowed from AAE, and are used simultaneously with attacks on AAE as lazy, vulgar, ungrammatical speech, which we know it is not.

Flattening, a common phenomenon in linguistic appropriation, refers to eviscerating the meaning of a term. *Cool*, for example, when first used in African American speech, referred to the ability to survive, even when threatened by lynch mobs and police brutality. It has now been flattened in White speech to a general term of approval (*Cool shoes!*) or to refer to a sense of self that is stylish and confident. In Spanish, perfectly normal terms such as *el presidente* or *generalissimo* are often used mockingly in English to portray Spanish-speaking leaders as foolish. Similarly, *macho* in Spanish simply means manly, not overly manly or patriarchal. In English it is often used as a synonym for chauvinist males who try to prove their manliness through a degrading attitude toward women.

Modifying existing words

Most new words are not brought into the lexicon by borrowing or being created through coining; instead, they are formed by modifying existing words, as in the processes explained in this section.

Acronyms are shortenings in which the initial letters of each word in a phrase are combined into a new word that is then pronounced normally, like any other word, not as a collection of its initial letters. For example, WASP (White Anglo-Saxon Protestant) is pronounced the same as the flying insect that stings, not as a collection of its letters W-A-S-P. Laser (light amplification by simulated emission of radiation), RAM (random access memory), and ROM (read-only memory) are other common acronyms.

Abbreviations differ from acronyms in that each individual letter is pronounced. NATO is pronounced as a word, so it is an acronym. The UN is an abbreviation, as each letter is pronounced separately. Similarly, HIV is an abbreviation; AIDS is an acronym. ATM is an abbreviation; PIN is an acronym.

Compounding, whereby two words are combined to form a new word, is extremely common in Germanic languages such as German, English, or Dutch. We see it in our everyday language: *bluebird, underfed, outlaw, coatroom, strawberry, rowboat, overeat, afterbirth,* *snowstorm, breakfast,* and *weekend* are just a few examples. Terms for new technology are often created through compounding: *screensaver, flash drive, cyberspace, swapspace,* to name but a few. *Pandemonium* is a good example of creative compounding from which a new word emerged. It was created by John Milton by combining the prefix *pan,* meaning all or everywhere, with the root *demon.*

Blending is similar to compounding but here it is parts of words, not entire words, that are joined. *Gasohol* (gasoline and alcohol), *infomercial* (information and commercial), and *brunch* (breakfast and lunch) are all examples of blends, as is *mansplaining,* a fairly new word to describe the lecturing discourse style of some men. Blending appears to be a less commonly used process than compounding in most languages.

Clipping is a process that produces new words by shortening old words or phrases. Clipped words are formed by shortening an existing multi-syllabic word, the new word retaining the same meaning as the original. *Bus, flu, condo, narc,* and *bra* are all examples of clipping (from *omnibus, influenza, narcotics agent,* and *brassiere,* respectively). Similarly, *dis, bike,* and *installs* were formed by clipping *disrespect, bicycle,* and *installations.*

Backformation is another process whereby a new word enters the language through shortening, in this case by dropping off an ending. The verb *edit* was backformed from *editor,* that is, the *-or* ending was dropped from the original noun, *editor,* to form a verb describing what an editor does. *Compute* was backformed from *computer, opt* from *option, televise* from *television,* and *donate* from *donation.* Backformation differs from clipping in that a word with a new meaning and new lexical category is created, whereas in clipping, the word is shortened but the meaning and the lexical category stay the same.

Reduplication, although not common in English, is common in many languages of the world. Reduplication forms new words by doubling an entire word or a part of it. In Italian, *piano* means softly; *piano piano* means very softly. Some languages use reduplication to make nouns plural: in Malay, for example, *rumah* is house, *rumah-rumah* is houses; in Indonesian, *ibu* is mother, *ibuibu* is mothers. In English we can see reduplication in such words as *bye-bye, boo-boo,* or *night night.* We also see rhyming reduplication: *hanky panky, itsy bitsy, eeny meeny,* or *flim flam.*

Derivation, adding **affixes** to existing words to derive new ones, is among the most productive processes by which new words are created in English. Affixes in English are either **suffixes** (added to the ends of words) or **prefixes** (added to the beginning). **Productive** refers to the relative freedom with which affixes can attach to existing words to derive new ones. Derivational affixes are used to change the lexical category of a word or give it a new meaning: *girl* becomes *girlish, affection* becomes *affectionate, happy* becomes *unhappy, annual* becomes *bi-annual, health* becomes *healthy, conform* becomes *conformist,* or *theory* becomes *theorize.* Suffixes often change a lexical category. Nouns become adjectives through the addition of suffixes like *-ish, -ful* (*girl–girlish; health–healthful*) or become verbs through the addition of other suffixes like *-ize* (*theory–theorize*). Verbs can become nouns with such suffixes as *-ist* (*conform–conformist*). Some suffixes derive new words without changing the lexical category: *music* can become *musician, vicar* can become *vicarage,* and *dump* can become *dumpster,* all of which are nouns.

While derivational suffixes often change the lexical category of a word, prefixes often derive new words that can have opposite or very different meanings: *likely/unlikely; partner/ ex-partner; print/reprint; standard/substandard.* Prefixes are very productive in English.

TABLE 3.1 Derivational affixes in English

Affixes that change lexical category

Noun to adjective	Noun to verb	
passion + *ate*	priority + *ize*	
joy + *ous*	vaccine + *ate*	
mirth + *ful*	*im* + power	
Roman + *esque*	length + *en*	
girl + *ish*		
Shakespeare + *an*		
athlete + *ic*		
Adjective to noun	**Adjective to verb**	**Adjective to adverb**
happy + *ness*	valid + *ate*	quick + *ly*
pure + *ity*	legal + *ize*	
free + *dom*	pure + *ify*	
	en + large	
Verb to noun	**Verb to adjective**	
teach + *er*	*manipulate + ive*	
migrate + *ion*	*accept + able*	
contain + *ment*		
attend + *ance*		
rebut + *al*		
alarm + *ist*		
validate + *ation*		

Affixes that change meaning

Affixes attaching to nouns	Affixes attaching to verbs	Affixes attaching to adjectives
mono + theist	*re* + print	*un* + attractive
ex + partner	*dis* + cover	*a* + theoretical
auto + biography	*un* + pack	*in* + operative
music + *ian*	*auto* + correct	*dis* + enchanted
	de + regulate	*sub* + standard
	brown + *ish*	

Table 3.1 lists some common derivational affixes in English. Note that each affix attaches to a particular lexical category, some changing that lexical category (a noun to an adjective, for example) and others changing the meaning in some substantial way, with the new word remaining the same lexical category as the original word.

Many of the most productive derivational morphemes common in English come from Latin or Greek: prefixes such as {neo} *neo-liberal*; {pan} *pansexual*; {mega} *megastore*; {e} *e-commerce, e-trade, e-file, email, eBay*; or {tele} *telecommute, telemarketing, telemedicine*.

With some word formation processes, it is not so much that new words are created, but rather that old words take on new meanings or new grammatical functions while retaining the same form.

In **functional shift**, also known as **conversion**, the meaning of a word shifts to add a different lexical category (a new grammatical function) to its meaning. For example, until the beginning of the 20th century, *test* was used exclusively as a noun: *The test is tomorrow.* Over time, it shifted in function so that now we can also use it as a verb: *They tested us on our knowledge of anatomy.* A similar shift happened to *impact.* It was originally a noun, with the verb sense of the word being expressed through the phrase *to have an impact on.* Now it is common to hear people say *That impacted me a lot,* so the word has shifted functionally to become a verb as well as a noun. Recently, the adjective *bad* has taken on the additional function of a noun, so we can apologize by saying *Sorry, my bad.*

Semantic shift is a slightly different way for words to shift meaning. In this case, over time a word will shift its meaning so that the old meaning is lost and only the new one remains. Words can broaden their meanings, narrow them, or change them altogether. *Lust,* for example, used to mean *pleasure, lewd* used to mean *wicked,* and *nice* used to mean *ignorant.* Our word *junk* has broadened in meaning over time; in Middle English *jonk* meant an old cable or rope used on ships. It shifted semantically through the term *junk shop,* a store where old materials from ships were sold, and came to mean any old and useless material. The meaning of *ketchup,* on the other hand, has narrowed. It came from the Malay term for fish sauce, *kechap,* which was brought to Europe by sailors. In the 17th and 18th centuries, it meant any sauce made with vinegar; only later did it narrow its meaning to a specific type of condiment made from tomatoes.

Glamour words?

When we examine the etymology of words, some interesting things come up. Take the words *glamour* and *grammar,* for example. We might think these two words are mutually exclusive— grammarians are not often thought of as glamourous. It turns out, however, that *glamour* and *grammar* are related words. *Glamour* was a variant form of *grammar* in Scottish. So how did we get from *grammar* to *glamour*? *Grammar* referred to scholarship or learning, which was then often associated with occult practices. *Glamour* contained this sense of occult learning or magic and came to mean a magic spell, something that could bewitch a person. In the mid-19th century, it came into the English language with a related meaning: a charm that could enchant through illusion or deceit. Only later did *glamour* come to its current meaning related to charm or physical allure.

If you're a Harry Potter fan, as I am, it might interest you to examine the etymology of the words J.K. Rowling uses in her books. Not all were coined by her; some have a long history in English. *Muggles,* non-wizard people in the Harry Potter world, is an old word dating back to the Middle Ages, probably deriving from *mug,* a term for face. In the 18th century, a bumblebee was sometimes known as a *dumbledore,* the name of Hogwarts' headmaster in the novels. And *howlers,* those flying, screeching telegrams of parental displeasure in the novels, once denoted people hired to wail loudly at funerals.

The idea that the earlier meaning of a word is somehow more correct is known as the **etymological fallacy**, for it is, indeed, a fallacy. As the world we live in changes, our words will change too, taking on new meanings or new grammatical functions. Change in word meaning or usage is, like all language change, natural, normal, and inevitable. Adding new words to a language's lexicon or shifting the meaning of old words is not a mark of corruption or decay. It is just change.

WORDS AND THEIR STRUCTURE

We've seen that words can enter a language in different ways; they are also structured in different ways. To understand how words are structured, we need to approach them from a **synchronic perspective**, one that examines language as it is used at a particular point in time. Using this perspective, we might ask how words are put together, the subject of **morphology**.

We've been talking about words as if they are unitary entities. A quick look reveals that's not true, that words are made up of smaller units. From a phonological perspective, words are made up of sounds in spoken languages and of primes in sign languages. Sounds or primes are combined to form words, which are then combined to form sentences. But there's a step between the sound unit and the word unit, what we might call the meaning unit. This meaning unit cannot be a sound because individual sounds don't have meaning by themselves. What does the sound "b" mean, for example? The smallest unit of meaning is not a word either, since as we've seen, some parts of words have meaning on their own; *preview*, *predate*, and *predawn* suggest that "*pre*" has a meaning of its own that stays the same even in different words.

Words, then, are made up of smaller units that have meaning, units we call **morphemes**. Technically, morphemes are the smallest unit of meaning in a language. In spoken languages, each individual morpheme has both a particular pronunciation (sound) and a particular meaning.

Some examples might help here. That [b] mentioned earlier has no meaning. But {bi} does. (Those squiggly brackets enclosing {bi} are a convention in linguistics to indicate we are talking about morphemes, not words or sounds.) That {bi}, therefore, is a morpheme, used in such words as *bilateral*, *bipolar*, *biennial*, and *bisexual*, which is sometimes clipped to become *bi*. All words have at least one morpheme; many have several. If a word cannot be divided into smaller units of meaning, it is comprised of only one morpheme and is called **monomorphemic**: *glass, list, love, they, pen, bottle, walk, token, friend, chalk*, to name but a few. Words comprising more than one morpheme can be divided into smaller units that contain meaning in themselves. *Preview*, for example, contains two morphemes: *pre*, which means before, and *view*.

We can analyze words into their constituent morphemes, for example:

preview	pre–view
impersonal	im–person–al
singing	sing–ing
girlish	girl–ish
unhelpful	un–help–ful
befriend	be–friend
glass	glass
toes	toe–s
chalky	chalk–y
friendship	friend–ship

You might be wondering right about now, what's the difference between a **syllable** and a morpheme? A syllable, usually defined as a phonological unit consisting of one or more sounds, refers to *sound*, to the grouping of sounds in how a word is pronounced; a morpheme refers to a unit of sound that carries *meaning*. A morpheme may contain one, two, or more syllables yet still be only one morpheme. Take the word *elephant*, for example. It contains three syllables but only one morpheme; it cannot be divided into any smaller units of meaning. What about {ant}? Doesn't it mean that small creature that invades picnics? *Ant* does indeed have that meaning on its own, but to determine if it is a separate morpheme in the word *elephant*, we need to ask if the meaning of "small black insect" is the meaning in *elephant*. No, even though it is pronounced the same, its meaning is different. *Ant*, then, is not a separate morpheme in this particular word.

Types of morphemes

Not all morphemes function in the same way. Linguists classify morphemes into different types in several different ways.

Free and bound morphemes

Free morphemes are those that can stand on their own as words and be combined with other morphemes. *Help*, for example, is a free morpheme that can be a word on its own or be combined with other morphemes, like {er}, {un}, or {ful}, in words such as *helper* and *unhelpful*. Free morphemes can be quite short (*play, run, table*) or long (*elephant, syllable*).

Some morphemes, however, cannot stand on their own, like {er} and {ful}. They are **bound morphemes:** {re}, {ness}, {un}, {er}, {ly}, and {dis} are all bound morphemes, unable to stand as a word on their own but still containing meaning. Free morphemes can be attached to other morphemes; bound morphemes must be attached to another morpheme.

Roots, affixes, and stems

The distinction between roots and affixes is related, but not identical, to the free or bound distinction. **Roots** carry the central meaning of words without any other morphemes. They are the form to which other morphemes can be attached. **Affixes** are bound morphemes that attach to a root. If we analyze the word *untimely* into its constituent morphemes, for example, we see that *time* is the root and {un} and {ly} are affixes, bound morphemes attached to the root: {un} is a prefix, {ly} a suffix, and *time* the root.

In English, affixes are almost always prefixes or suffixes. In other languages, however, we find different types. **Circumfixes** are affixes containing two parts, one occurring before the root, the other occurring after it. In Dutch, the past participle consists of a root and a circumfix (*ge-* and *-d*), as in *gewandeld* (*wandel* is a form of the verb *wandelen*, meaning *walk*; *ge-* and *-d* comprise the circumfix, which indicates a part participle; the whole thing, *gewandeld*, means *walked* as used in the sentence, *I've walked four miles today*).

Some languages have what is even stranger to English speakers' ears, **infixes,** morphemes inserted into a root rather than at the beginning or end. Bontoc, a language spoken in the Philippines, uses infixes to change nouns into verbs. For example, *fikas* means *strong*; adding an {um} in the middle of the word as an infix changes *fikas* to *fumikas* (*f-um-ikas*), which means *to be strong*. Although English does not make use of this type of affix as a rule, we do sometimes make use of the principle of infixing, generally in colloquial usage or slang. *Awholenother* results from inserting *whole* into *another* to give us *a-whole-nother*. This type of affixation is often used in English with obscenities, so we can say, *absofuckinlutely* (*abso-fuckin-lutely*), using *fucking* as an infix.

Generally, it's easy to tell the difference between free and bound morphemes; if the morpheme in question is not a word, it's a bound morpheme. There are some morphemes, however, that do not seem to fit easily into these categories. Take *huckleberry*, for example. Analyzing that word, we'd probably divide it into two morphemes: *huckle* and *berry*. *Berry* is clearly a free morpheme, but what is *huckle-*? It is bound, but it seems to have no clear meaning. Such morphemes are called **bound roots**. They convey meaning only when they are attached to other morphemes and cannot stand on their own. Linguists disagree about how to analyze such anomalies, which often occur in English words borrowed from Latin or Greek: *kempt* as in unkempt, *ept* as in inept, *chalant* as in nonchalant, and *gainly* as in ungainly are all bound roots.

Stems, like roots, are forms to which other morphemes can attach, but they differ from roots in that a stem is formed when an affix is combined with a root morpheme. Thus, *help* is a root to which the affix {ful} may be added. The resulting word, *helpful*, can then serve as a stem to which other morphemes may be added: *unhelpful*; *helpfulness*. *Help* remains the root; for *unhelpful* and *helpfulness*, *helpful* is the stem to which *un* or *ness* are added.

Derivational and inflectional morphemes

When we classify bound morphemes into suffixes and prefixes, we are doing so based on their *placement* in a word. We can also classify bound, but not free, morphemes according to their *function*: **derivational morphemes** or **inflectional morphemes**.

Derivational morphemes

The word formation process known as derivation (explained earlier in the chapter) derives new words by adding derivational affixes to a root or stem. As noted earlier, **derivational morphemes** change the meaning of an existing word in one of two ways: changing its meaning in some substantial way or changing its lexical category. To illustrate, let's look at an earlier example again, *untimely*: the affixes, {un} and {ly}, are both derivational morphemes. The suffix {ly} changes *time* from a noun to an adjective (*time* becomes *timely*), so it changes the lexical category. The prefix {un} changes the basic meaning of *timely* into its opposite, and the new word remains an adjective.

Let's take another example: *dehumidifier*, a device very useful in the hot, humid summers where I live. We can analyze it into the following morphemes:

- *humid* (root)
- {ify} (bound suffix, derivational morpheme changing lexical category, adjective to verb)
- {er} (bound suffix, derivational morpheme changing lexical category, verb to noun)
- {de} (bound prefix, changing meaning)

Such multi-morphemic words are very common in English.

It is important to remember that derivational morphemes are not attached randomly; they attach to specific lexical categories: some to nouns, some to verbs, and others to adjectives, as the list of derivational morphemes in Table 3.1 shows. The suffix {able} attaches to verbs,

One Big Happy / By Rick Detorie

By permission of Rick Detorie and Creators Syndicate, Inc.

FIGURE 3.1 It's unraining!

turning the verb into an adjective (*accept*, a verb, becomes an adjective *acceptable*). The suffixes {ful} and {ous} attach to nouns and make them adjectives (*glee*, a noun, becomes an adjective, *gleeful*, with the addition of {ful}; *monster*, a noun, becomes an adjective, *monstrous*, with the addition of {ous}). Many nouns can be made into verbs by adding suffixes such as {ize} or {ate} (*priority*, a noun, becomes a verb, *prioritize*, with the addition of {ize}; *vaccine*, a noun, becomes a verb, *vaccinate*, with the addition of {ate}), but one cannot add those suffixes to adjectives to make them verbs. One cannot, for instance, say, *prettyize* or *prettiate*. English does not allow it.

Derivational morphemes that change meaning but do not change lexical category also generally attach to one lexical category. {Ex}, for example, attaches to nouns or verbs but not adjectives. We can have an *ex-roommate* and we can *exfoliate*, but we cannot be *ex-happy*. {Re} and {de} attach to verbs, and the new words remain verbs (*refinance*, *deregulate*); {a}, {sub}, and {in} attach to adjectives; and the new words remain adjectives (*amoral*, *substandard*, *inhospitable*).

Inflectional morphemes

The concept of **inflectional morphemes** is sometimes hard for speakers of English to see as a distinct category because the English language has so few of them, only eight to be exact. They are, however, very common in other languages. Inflectional morphemes do not change the basic meaning of a word, nor do they change a word's lexical category. Instead, they indicate grammatical meanings like *past tense* or *plural*. An example might be the best way to understand this. I can say, *I walk to school every day*. But if I want to say that I did it yesterday, I have to add an inflectional morpheme, in this case {ed}, to indicate past tense: *I walked to school yesterday*. That {ed} does not change the meaning of *walk*, nor does it change its lexical category; *walk* and *walked* are both verbs. It occurs only because the grammatical rules of Standard English require it to express the meaning of past.

If it's my sister walking, I'd add a different inflectional morpheme, {s}: *She walks to school every day*. Again, the {s} is necessary because *she* is the subject, as it would be if the subject were *he* or *it* or *my grandmother* or *my dog*. It would not be necessary if the subject were *my dogs* or *my sisters* (*They walk to school every day*). And it would not be needed if the verb were future (*She will walk to school*) or past.

TABLE 3.2 English inflectional morphemes

Morpheme	Example	Grammatical meaning
Attach to verbs		
-s	She walks to school every day.	3rd person, singular, present tense
-ed	She walked to school yesterday.	Past tense
-ing	They are looking for it now.	Progressive or continuous
-en or ed	I've eaten too much already.	Past participle
	I've walked home every day this week.	
Attach to nouns		
-s	These books are way overdue.	Plural
-s	Mary's elephant is named Sue.	Possessive
Attach to adjectives		
-er	She is faster than I am.	Comparative
-est	She is the fastest runner I know.	Superlative

Table 3.2 lists the eight inflection morphemes used in Modern English. You'll notice that some inflectional morphemes attach to verbs {ed, ing, en, s}, some to nouns {s, and s}, and some to adjectives {er, est}. In English, inflectional morphemes always occur as the final morpheme in a word.

You may have noticed that {s} appears three times in this list. That's because there are three separate morphemes with three different meanings, all of which happen to be pronounced the same and indicated by {s}. The {s} we add to the end of verbs is a different morpheme than the one we add to the end of nouns; they just sound the same. And the {s} we add as a suffix to a noun to mean plural is a different morpheme from the one we add to a noun to mean possessive, even though they sound the same. Note that the apostrophe is not indicated when we list the possessive morpheme because it is not part of spoken language, merely a convention in writing.

Many morphemes, and not just inflectional ones, have **allomorphs**, variant pronunciations. That {s}, for example, has three allomorphs: it's either [s] as in *cuffs*, [z] as in *clowns*, or [Iz] as in *busses*. We'll discuss these variants again in Chapter 5 when we examine the phonological bases for them.

The English spoken a thousand years ago used many more inflectional morphemes to indicate grammatical meanings, but these gradually dropped out of the language, leaving only those eight. Modern English, thus, has a much-reduced set of inflectional morphemes. Some varieties of Modern English have an even more reduced set, omitting the {ed} or the {s} morpheme in certain situations. African American English does not require that {ed} nor the {s} plural morpheme in all situations; *she pass all the test yesterday* is grammatically correct in that variety, despite what many people think. In this way, AAE is similar to many languages, Mandarin Chinese, for example, in which the equivalent of {ed} is not needed; a time word or the context would suffice.

Grammatical meaning

One key principle in morphology is that all languages need to have a way of indicating relationships among words in a sentence. They need to be able to indicate, for instance, which word is the subject of a sentence, which noun a particular adjective refers to, when the action is taking place, what belongs to whom, things like that. Different languages express these **grammatical meanings** in different ways. Many languages use inflectional morphemes, which attach to nouns to indicate number, case, and gender, as described as follows.

Number

In English, we don't mark nouns for case, except for possessive, and nouns in English do not have a grammatical gender. We do, however, mark most nouns for number, that is, we add the inflectional morpheme suffix {s} to indicate plural, with a few exceptions like *mouse/mice*. We have no inflectional morpheme to indicate singular. Other languages, however, do. In Zulu, for example, an {um} is added to the beginning of nouns to indicate singular; a different prefix, {aba}, is added to indicate plural: *umfani* means boy; *abafani* means boys. Some languages have ways of marking not just singular and plural, but dual as well. Inuktitut, a language spoken in Northern Canada, has such a system: *iglu* means one house; *igluk* means two houses; and *iglut* means three or more houses. Some languages do not indicate number at all. Indonesian is one such language; *harimau* can mean tiger or tigers.

Case

More complex are the various systems for inflecting nouns for case; that is, for ways of indicating whether a noun is the subject, an object, or possessive. In English, we know whether a noun is the subject or the object in a sentence by the word order. Although it is sometimes a bit more complicated than this, the noun before the verb is usually the subject; the noun after the verb is usually an object. Many languages, including many closely related to English, use inflectional morphemes instead of word order to indicate case. Russian, for example, uses inflectional suffixes to indicate whether a noun is the subject of the sentence (nominative case), direct object (accusative case), indirect object (dative case), or possessive (genitive case) or if it has to do with location (locative case) or use (instrumental case). Each of the words in the list that follows means *house*:

Nominative (subject)	*dom*
Genitive (possessive)	*doma*
Accusative (direct object)	*dom*
Dative (indirect object)	*domu*
Locative (place)	*dome*
Instrumental (how)	*domom*

If we want to use the word *house* in Russia as the subject of a sentence, we say *dom*. In the sentence *That house belongs to Mary*, the word *house* is *dom*. If we want to use it as a possessive, we say *doma*, not *dom*; in the sentence *The house's trim needs painting*, the word *house* is *doma*. This all sounds very complicated to speakers of English, but many languages have a similar system (Finnish has 14 cases, not six cases like Russian), and their speakers get along just fine.

Grammatical gender

Some languages also inflect for **grammatical gender**; in French, Italian, and Spanish, all nouns are either masculine or feminine; in German, they are masculine, feminine, or neuter. Many of these languages inflect the article (*a* or *the*) to indicate that the noun is feminine or masculine or neuter. In Italian, both articles and adjectives must agree with the gender of the noun: *la machina rossa* (the red car) but *il piatto rosso* (the red plate). *La* is used with feminine nouns, *il* with masculine ones; both mean *the*. *Rossa* means red for feminine nouns like *machina*; *rosso* means red for masculine nouns like *piatto*. (In Italian, adjectives generally follow the noun.)

This concept of gender is not necessarily tied to the idea of male and female. For example, although *moon* is feminine in French (*la lune*), it is masculine in German (*der Mond*). *Sun*, which is masculine in French (*le soleil*), is feminine in German (*die Sonne*). And the German word for *girl*, *das Mädchen*, is actually neuter!

German inflects articles to mark case, gender, and number. The word *the* in German has six different forms, each indicating a different case, gender, and number of the noun as shown in Table 3.3.

TABLE 3.3 German articles

	Masculine	**Feminine**	**Neuter**
Nominative singular	der	die	das
Accusative singular	den	die	das
Genitive singular	des	der	des
Dative singular	dem	der	dem

In its plural form, *the* is *die* no matter the case or gender of the noun.

The boy saw the dog in German is *Der Knabe sah den Hund*. If you changed the word order of this sentence in English, you'd get a different meaning: *The dog saw the boy*. In German, however, you can change the word order and it means the same thing: *Den Hund saw der Knabe* also means *the boy saw the dog*. This more flexible word order is possible because the inflected articles, *der* and *den*, tell us which word is the subject and which word is the object no matter where in the sentence they occur. Languages with elaborate inflectional systems for nouns or articles like German and Russian allow a more flexible word order than English.

In Modern English, the only area where we have kept this type of inflection is in our pronoun system. *I, me,* and *my* all refer to the same thing; they differ in form to indicate differences in grammatical meaning: *I* indicates the subject, *my* indicates possessive, *me* indicates object (either direct or indirect). That is, English pronouns, except *you*, are inflected for case, just like *house* is in Russian. And although in English we do not inflect first or second person for gender, we do indicate gender in the third person: *he, she,* or *it*. Table 3.4 summarizes our pronoun system.

TABLE 3.4 English pronoun system

	First person	**Third person**		
		Masc	**Fem**	**Neuter**
Singular				
Subject	I	he	she	it
Possessive	my	his	her	its
Object	me	him	her	it
Plural				
Subject	we		they	
Possessive	our		their	
Object	us		them	

Linguistics in your world: He, she, and/or they

Pronouns have become a political issue in recent years, especially the lack of a non-gendered third-person singular pronoun. Other languages have one: Mandarin Chinese, Farsi, and Finish all use the same pronoun to refer to a man or a woman. Increasingly, English speakers have recognized the need for a third-person singular personal pronoun that does not assume there are only two genders and that allows individuals to identify as gender nonbinary or gender fluid.

Various solutions to this problem have been offered over the years, some centuries old: *ze*, *s/he*, *thon*, *ve*, *heer*, *e*, and *ey*, to name a few. Until recently, none has caught on. Today, *they* is used by many individuals, institutions, and media to respect those with nonbinary gender identities who wish not to be designated as either male or female. The *New York Times* now uses *they* for those who do not wish to be a he or she, without editorial comment or explanation; many people now regularly introduce themselves with not only their name but their pronoun of choice; you may have been asked for your pronoun of choice when introducing yourself at the beginning of a class.

Using *they* to refer to an individual is not new; English speakers have long used it when the gender of an individual is not known or is not relevant, even if the antecedent is singular. *Everyone* is technically singular, even though it has a plural meaning, so according to grammar books, it should take a singular pronoun, which again, according to those books, should be *he* or *he or she*. In everyday usage, though, speakers have long used *they*: *Everyone should wear their best clothes*. And if we don't know the gender of a person, we would use *they*: *Someone called but they didn't leave their name*. What is new now is its use for specific, known individuals. *Everyone has their secrets* has long been common, *their* referring to a plural sense of everyone. What is new is using *their* in sentences like the following: *Jan has their secrets*, where *their* refers to a known individual, Jan.

This use of *they* has met resistance. Sticklers complain that if we use *they* for both multiple people and one person, it will be confusing. Perhaps, but there are lots of possibly confusing things in English and every language (Does *bank* mean a financial institution or the edge of a river?) and people somehow figure it out. Others object to this use by claiming it is not grammatically or biologically correct; both arguments are bogus. Biologists tell us that there are individuals who exhibit both male and female sexual characteristics, and linguists tell us that what is considered grammatically correct changes over time.

English is not the only language changing in this way. Swedish and Hebrew are both going through changes. Swedish has a gendered pronoun system like that of English: for an individual, *han* (he) or *hon* (she) are used, *den* or *det* for *it*. In the last 20 years, it has become common to use a new word, *hen*, borrowed from Finnish, to refer to a person without indicating any gender. *Hen*, then, takes the place of both *han* (he) and *hon* (she). Although still a matter of debate (the Swedish Parliament ruled it should not be used in official documents but can be used by individual members of Parliament), *hen* seems to be catching on, becoming increasingly common in newspapers, journals, and on the street. In Hebrew, there are similar efforts to change the pronoun system. Because there are no gender-neutral pronouns in Hebrew, the masculine plural form is used when referring to a mixed gender group. Many want to change that and use both the masculine and feminine forms. Such a change is not as simple as it might seem; it would require changes to adjectives and verbs as well as to pronouns and might even require new Hebrew letters.

MORPHOLOGY IN LANGUAGES OTHER THAN ENGLISH

Other languages often do morphology quite differently from English. It might seem natural to English speakers that plural and past tense morphemes, for example, come at the end of the word, or that prepositions come before a noun. To speakers of other languages, such rules would not seem natural at all, but decidedly odd.

Turkish illustrates how languages differ in their morphology. Like English, Turkish indicates plurality in nouns through suffixes, not with an {s} but with {lar} or {ler}, two allomorphs whose distribution is dependent on the vowel in the root. *Mum* (candle) becomes *mumlar* in the plural, and *ip* (thread) becomes *ipler* in the plural. Other languages indicate plural not with a suffix but a prefix: Isthmus Zapotec, spoken in Mexico, uses the prefix {ka} to do so.

In English, location is often indicated with prepositions: <u>in</u> the house, <u>to</u> the house, <u>at</u> the house. In Turkish, the same meanings are indicated with suffixes attached to the noun, as shown in the following list:

house	ev
in the house	evde
from the house	evden
to the house	eve

Reduplication, a process uncommon in English, is used in Turkish to intensify adverbs: *iji* is well; *iji iji* is very well; *gyzel* is beautifully; *gyzel gyzel* is very beautifully. And Turkish has no need for some words we find necessary in English. Turkish, like Russian, has no articles: no *a*, *an*, or *the*.

In sign languages, although words have no sound, they are made up of the same types of morphemes as are spoken languages: roots, stems, bound morphemes, affixes, and derivational and inflectional morphemes. Instead of being sounds or combination of sounds added to a root, affixes in sign languages are particular gestures that precede or follow a root morpheme gesture, for example, particular movements of the hands toward or away from the signer.

HIERARCHICAL STRUCTURE IN WORDS

When we distinguish prefixes from suffixes, we are analyzing the **linear structure** of a word, the types of morphemes and the sequence in which they occur in a word—which comes first, second, etc. Root morphemes can occur anywhere in a word, but affixes cannot. The morphemes in a word like *disagreeable* cannot be put in a different linear order: *agree + dis + able* does not work. The linear structure rules of English do not allow it.

Words also have a **hierarchical structure**. That is, some units contain other units. We can see this hierarchical structure by analyzing the structure of *unworthy.* If we analyze its linear structure, we see that *unworthy* is made up of the prefix {un}, followed by a root morpheme, the noun *worth*, and the suffix {y}. To do a **hierarchical structural analysis**, we'd need to ask if we can identify units within units here. Is *unworthy* composed of *unworth + y* or of *un + worthy*?

A hierarchical structural analysis might go something like this. The root of *unworthy* is *worth*, a noun, which is the root to which the suffix {y} attaches, resulting in the adjective *worthy. Worthy* then functions as the stem to which the prefix {un} attaches, resulting in another adjective, *unworthy.* The hierarchical structure of *unworthy* must be {un} added to *worthy*, not {y} added to *unworth* not only because *unworth* is not a word but more importantly because {un} cannot be added to nouns, only to adjectives or verbs.

Linguists often use what are called **tree diagrams** to illustrate the hierarchical structure of a word. A tree diagram of *unworthy* is shown in Figure 3.2.

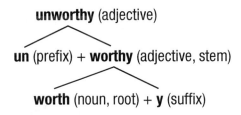

unworthy (adjective)

un (prefix) + **worthy** (adjective, stem)

worth (noun, root) + **y** (suffix)

FIGURE 3.2 Tree diagram for unworthy

Reading from the bottom up the diagram illustrates the following:

- The suffix {y} attaches to the root *worth* to derive the word *worthy*, changing the noun to an adjective.
- The prefix {un} then attaches to the stem *worthy* to derive the word *unworthy*, still an adjective.

It is important in these diagrams to indicate the lexical category of each word. Because certain affixes attach only to certain lexical categories, labeling the lexical category can help us determine the hierarchical structure of a word.

We analyzed the linear structure of *dehumidify* earlier, labeling each morpheme as prefix, root, and suffix. An analysis of the hierarchical structure is shown in Figure 3.3.

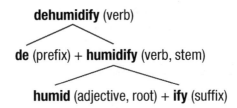

FIGURE 3.3 Tree diagram for dehumidify

In this analysis, the fact that {de} attaches to verbs, not adjectives, is important. We can't say *dehumid*, for example. Reading from the bottom up the diagram illustrates the following:

- The suffix {ify} attaches to the root *humid* to derive the word *humidify*, changing the adjective to a verb.
- The prefix {de} then attaches to the stem *humidify* to derive the word *dehumidify*, still a verb.

Let's take another example: *impoliteness*, made up of three morphemes: the root *polite* and two derivational morphemes, {im} and {ness}. Since both *impolite* and *politeness* are words, we need to pay attention to lexical categories and the affixes that can attach to them. We know that {im} attaches to adjectives and the resulting word is still an adjective. When {ness} attaches to *polite*, however, it changes the adjective into a noun. So {im} must attach to *polite*, not *politeness*. The suffix {ness} can attach to *impolite* because {ness} attaches to adjectives and makes them nouns. Figure 3.4 illustrates this structure:

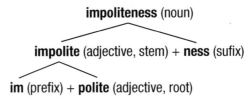

FIGURE 3.4 Tree diagram for impoliteness

Reading from the bottom up the diagram illustrates the following:

- The prefix {im} attaches to the root adjective *polite* to derive the word *impolite*, still an adjective.
- The suffix {ness} attaches to the stem *impolite* to derive the word *impoliteness*, changing the adjective into a noun.

Multi-morphemic words, then, like *unworthy*, *dehumidify*, or *impoliteness*, are not randomly put together; there is a linear order to them and a hierarchical order, a hierarchical structure in which one part contains other parts. Tree diagrams help us see that structure, as we will see again in Chapter 6 on syntax.

L1 ACQUISITION IN FOCUS: SHE COMED, THOSE MOUSES

You've probably heard children say things like *goed* or *foots* and wondered why they make such mistakes. Turns out, those utterances are not mistakes at all, but rather well-formed utterances for that child's internal grammar. It's just that her grammar has not yet developed to match the adult grammar of speakers of her language. How does she get to those utterances and how does she get from there to the adult grammar? We'll discuss part of that process here, focusing on how children learn the morphology of their language. What they learn, of course, varies as the languages they learn vary. The processes by which they acquire their language are, however, remarkably similar.

When we say children acquire the morphology of their language, what does that mean? Children learn first that words have meaning, an incredible feat in itself. They also learn that slight changes in the way those words are said or signed change that meaning. They learn that words are made up of parts that have meaning in themselves; that those parts (morphemes) are put together in a certain order; and that more than one can occur in a word. That's a lot to learn before they go to school.

Babies generally say their first words at around the age of one, when children begin consistently using a particular string of sounds or a sign to mean a particular thing. The meaning connected to these first words does not always match the adult meaning. As noted in Chapter 2, during the **one-word stage** (9–18 months), children use one word to mean what an adult would say in an entire sentence, *up* to mean *Pick me up*, for example. It's quite amazing that they can do this, given that adult speech does not usually consist of one word or one sign, even to small babies. Babies isolate, somehow, one word they need from that string of sounds or signs the adult aims at them. An adult might say to a child, *Look at the pretty bunny*, and the child might well repeat just *bunny*. These first words tend to be nouns or verbs, the words that convey the most meaning.

When they first learn words, children also often overgeneralize, using *doggie*, for example, for all four-legged creatures or *ball* for all round objects. This over-extension of meaning tends to disappear as children learn more words and narrow the meaning of words to more closely approximate adult meaning.

In acquiring their language, children form unconscious hypotheses about how the morphology or other aspects of language work. Let's look at that *goed* mentioned earlier. Adults do not use that word; it's not part of any dialect of English. Yet English-speaking children produce it regularly, just as they produce such oddities as *hitted*, *eated*, or *comed*. It seems clear they are applying a morphological rule they figured out—add the {ed} morpheme to the ends of verbs to make them past tense. The same thing happens with the plural morpheme {s}. They learn the rule: apply it to the ends of nouns to make the plural. At this stage, they haven't yet figured out the exceptions, so they produce words like *foots* or *mouses*. Eventually, they figure it all out.

There is a process that children go through in figuring it all out. For English-speaking children, for example, while learning the past tense {ed}, they usually first learn the past tense form of individual words like *came* or *saw*, storing them as separate units. At this stage, children don't seem to have learned the rule to add {ed}. Once they learn that rule, they apply it consistently across the board, including to those irregular verbs they used to say "correctly," producing forms like *comed* instead of *came*. Soon they figure out the entire system, the rules and the exceptions, as their internal grammar approximates the adult grammar. Utterances like *comed* and *goed* then disappear from their speech.

Children learning languages other than English must similarly learn the morphology of their language. By the age of two, children learning Italian have usually acquired the rules for grammatical gender, correctly using *la* for feminine nouns and *il* for masculine ones. (Both *la* and *il* correspond to *the* in English.) And they have mastered the system of inflectional morphemes for present tense verbs, a system more complex than ours. In English, we need only learn to add {s} to the ends of verbs for *he/she/it*; in Italian, children learn to add {o} for *I*; {i} for *you* (singular), {iamo} for *we*, and more. So they learn that *I speak* is *io parlo*, *you speak* is *tu parli*, *we speak* is *noi parliamo*.

CHAPTER SUMMARY

- The lexicon of a language changes over time, as do the meanings of words.
- Languages make use of word formation processes to add new words to their lexicon.
- Words have structure as well as histories. They are made up of smaller parts that have meaning (morphemes).
- Morphemes vary by function: roots and affixes, free or bound, inflectional or derivational.
- English uses many derivational morphemes but only eight inflectional morphemes.
- The English pronoun system retains inflection for gender (he/she/it), a fact that has led to efforts to change that system to be non-gendered.
- Words have both a linear and a hierarchical structure. Hierarchical structures are often illustrated with tree diagrams.
- Children learn early that words have meaning, that they are made up of morphemes, and that there are rules for combining morphemes.

KEY TERMS

lexical categories (aka parts of speech)
open classes, closed classes
word formation processes
compounding
borrowing
backformation
blending
acronym
abbreviation
clipping
coining
semantic shift
functional shift/conversion
derivation
eponym
reduplication
lexicalization
morpheme

derivational morpheme
inflectional morpheme
free morphemes
bound morphemes
affix
   prefix
   suffix
   infix
   circumfix
root and stem
inflection
diachronic perspective
synchronic perspective
productive
etymological fallacy
hierarchical structure
linear structure

EXPLORATIONS

Exploration 1: Word formation processes

Using an etymological or other good dictionary, find the origins of the following words and identify the word formation process involved (there may be more than one).

snafu	hangnail	netiquette
selfie-stick	giddy	apps
emoji	gerrymander	demo
televise	boycott	LOL
lynch	mall	howdy
thug	Zoom	NIMBY

Exploration 2: Morphemic analysis

Divide the following words into their morphemes, identifying the type of morpheme for each: bound or free, derivational or inflectional, root or affix.

One note: Don't get caught up in spelling. The affix {ify}, for example, changes its spelling to {ifi} when an {er} is attached. It's still the same morpheme, just a variant in spelling.

enlargements	predetermined	telecommute	improbably
fingered	teacher's	grandmotherly	forewarned
smaller	nonrefundable	deactivation	textbooks
dishonesty	reforming	disinclined	message
expansiveness	giraffe	unpredictability	untidiest

Exploration 3: Borrowing in everyday language

1. Make a list of some place names in your area, names of streets, towns, cities, states, neighborhoods, rivers, lakes, etc. Which ones are eponyms? Which are borrowed? From what languages? Why these languages?
2. Many of our names for foods are borrowed. Investigate the origin of the names of some of your favorite foods. Are any borrowed? From what languages?
3. Do you think the borrowing you found in 2 differs from the borrowing you identified in 1? How?

Exploration 4: Identifying hierarchical structure

Create a tree diagram for the following words that illustrates their hierarchical structure. Label the root, stem, affixes, and lexical categories for each level of the tree. You might want to first identify the morphemes as root, stem, or bound morpheme, then determine which affixes attach to which lexical categories.

Figure 3.5 offers an example.

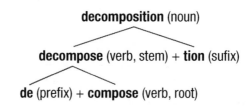

FIGURE 3.5 Tree diagram for decomposition

Words to diagram:

friendliness	unhelpful
priorities	reorganization
retouchable	nonrefundable
inexpensive	dispassionate

Exploration 5: Unforgivable curses, unbreakable vows

In English, we have a very productive prefix, [un], usually glossed as *not*. So *untrue* means *not true*. It has another meaning too, however: reversing an action. *Untie* means to reverse the action of tying. English, then, has two separate {un} morphemes; both are pronounced the same but each means something distinct. One attaches to adjectives and means *not* (*unhappy*, *unemotional*, *unlikely*); the other attaches to verbs and means reversal of the action (*unwrap*, *uncover*, *unpack*).

a) Think about the word *unlockable*. It has two possible meanings. Identify the two meanings and specify which {un} morpheme is involved in each meaning. Then draw a tree diagram for *each* meaning.

b) Several years ago, the makers of 7UP created a marketing campaign that heralded that drink as the "un-cola." Although perhaps successful as an ad campaign strategy (I still remember it), *un-cola* is definitely odd in English. Using what you know about the prefix {un}, why is it so odd?

c) Recently, a new term has entered the English language, *unfriend*, as in to unfriend someone on Facebook. We noted that {un} attaches to adjectives or verbs but not nouns. Is this an example of an exception to that rule or is something else going on? (Hint: Think about what *friend* means here.)

Exploration 6: Non-gendered pronouns

Discussion prompt: Some people decry the use of *they* as a non-gendered pronoun to replace or supplement *he* or *she*, saying that it is confusing, ugly, ungrammatical, or just plain wrong. How would you respond to these people? Do you use this pronoun? Do others around you? Why or why not?

Exploration 7: Grammatical gender

Do you know any language that marks nouns for grammatical gender (French, Italian, German, Spanish, Polish, for example)? Describe how gender is marked in this language: What inflectional morphemes are used? What lexical categories carry these inflections? Give examples.

Exploration 8: Just wiki it

Wikipedia has become a useful tool for many people today. Investigate the origins of its name. What does *wiki* mean? Where does it come from? How is it used now? What lexical categories can it be? Is it part of any compound words?

Exploration 9: Running it

In English, we have three {ing} morphemes, each meaning something different, as in these three phrases: *I was running*; *the running of the bulls in Pamploma*; *the running waters were loud*. How would you describe each morpheme: derivational or inflectional? What lexical categories can it attach to? What lexical categories does it derive through that attachment?

FURTHER READING

Baron, D. (2020). *What's your pronoun? Beyond he and she*. Liveright Publishing Co.

Bauer, L. (2003). *Introducing linguistic morphology* (2nd ed.). Edinburgh University Press. Accessible introduction with examples from many languages.

Bloomfield, L. (1993). *Language*. The University of Chicago Press. Classic in the field; good discussion of what makes a word a word.

CHAPTER 4

Phonetics

The sounds of English

....

First glance

International Phonetics Alphabet (IPA):
- Voice
- Consonants: place and manner of articulation
- Vowels
- Natural classes

Accents

Prosody

What's in a name?

Local acts of identity

Sign language phonetics

Phonetics in other languages

Acquiring language sounds

INTRODUCTION

Part of knowing any spoken language is knowing its sounds and how they are put together. We will begin here with the sound units of language, examining the meaningfully distinct sounds of English. In the next chapter on phonology, we will use that knowledge to examine how the sound system in English is structured.

To do so, we will need something besides letters to indicate sounds, since letters in English are poor at representing sounds. For one thing, one letter can represent more than one sound. How do you pronounce the letter *a*, for example? It depends; in the word *pat* it is pronounced differently than in *father* or *late*. The letter *t* can also be pronounced in several different ways—as in *pretty*, *late*, or *nation*. To make the whole thing even worse, one sound can be spelled in a variety of ways; the *ee* sound can be spelled *ee* (*seed*) or *ea* (*lead*) or *ey* (*key*), among other ways. And some letter combinations hide sound differences. Although we spell them the same, there are really two *th* sounds in English, the one in *think* and the one in *then*.

DOI: 10.4324/9780429269059-4

INTERNATIONAL PHONETIC ALPHABET

Because there is simply too much inconsistency in our alphabet, we will use a slightly modi-fied version of the International Phonetic Alphabet or IPA, an alphabet designed by linguists to designate a unique symbol for every sound in every language. (You can find and download the full IPA at internationalphoneticalphabet.org.) Here we will be concentrating on English, learning to use those symbols to represent the minimally distinct sounds of English. Other symbols are necessary to represent sounds in other languages, for many of the sounds in other languages differ from similar sounds in English or do not exist in English. We will learn what aspects of the vocal tract are involved in producing those sounds; that is, we'll be doing **pho-netics**, the study of sounds in human speech. Phonetics includes both **acoustic phonetics**, the study of the physical properties of speech as sound waves, and **articulatory phonetics**, which is our focus in this chapter—the study of how speech sounds are produced.

At some level, every language sound uttered is distinct from every other sound. The [p] sound in *pin* is slightly different from the [p] sound in *spin*. My [p] sound is slightly different from yours. Somehow, though, as English speakers, we hear all of the [p] sounds as the same; whether we hear your [p] or my [p], it's still a [p], not a [b] or a [d]. That is, [p] is meaningfully distinct from [b] or [d]. One way to tell if sounds are meaningfully distinct is to see if there are minimal pairs, two words that differ in only one sound. Minimal pairs for [p] and [b] are easy to find: *pit/bit, pain/bane, tap/tab*. Similarly, we can find them for [p] and [d] or [b] and [d] or for all three: *tap/tad/tap* or *bad/dad/pad*. When linguists say sounds are meaningfully distinct, this is what they mean: substitution of one sound for the other creates a different word in minimal pairs. Those meaningfully distinct sounds are usually represented in slashes //, but for now, we'll use brackets [] around the IPA symbols as we learn to use them and to classify those sounds. We'll discuss meaningfully distinct sounds and those slashes more in Chapter 5.

There are anywhere between 36 and 40 of these meaningfully distinct sounds in English, depending upon the variety. The variety we use here is what is known as General American. Generally associated with mass media and educated speech, General American is really a variety of accents spoken in several areas across the United States, most notably the Midwest and West. It is usually not associated with local, class, or ethnic differences, but regional, class, and ethnic variations do exist within General American; the usage described here may or may not match yours. Some of you, for example, will distinguish the vowel sound in *cot* from that in *caught*, others will not. Some pronunciations that are common across General American include the use of an alveolar flap (*ladder* and *latter* will sound the same) and what is called full rhoticity, pronouncing the [r] sound whether it precedes a vowel or not.

The symbols we will use to represent sounds are not the ones you may have used when learning to read, nor are they always the ones used in the dictionary. Some will be familiar to you because they look like letters; some will be totally new. The explorations at the end of the chapter are meant to help you learn the IPA; you'll need that knowledge in Chapter 5. As you learn these symbols, it helps to remember we are dealing with sounds, not letters, and to remember our purpose is descriptive: to use the symbols to represent our normal pronuncia-tion, not the pronunciation we think we should have.

As we classify sounds, it is useful to know what the vocal tract, the parts of the throat and mouth used in speech, looks like. Figure 4.1 shows the relevant parts of the vocal tract.

Language sounds are produced by expelling air through the vocal tract as we exhale. At each place along this tract, we can change the air flow slightly by changing the position of the vocal

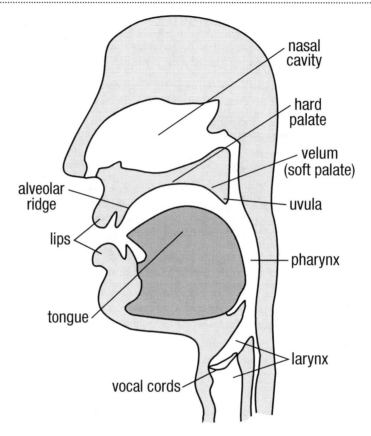

FIGURE 4.1 Diagram of human vocal tract

cords, the tongue, the lips, or other parts of the vocal tract, thereby producing different language sounds. As we expel the air from the lungs, it moves up to the larynx, an important place for producing different sounds. Here the vocal cords, which are inside the larynx, can be lax or taut, each way producing a different sort of sound, voiced or voiceless as described later. As the air moves up out of the larynx past the pharynx, the velum, hard palate, alveolar ridge, teeth, and lips, the movement of the tongue toward or away from those areas produces different sounds. We don't do this consciously; in fact, it is hard to do so consciously. But whenever we speak, we subtly change the position of parts of the vocal tract and thereby change the sound that emerges. Because of this, we can classify sounds according to where and how the vocal tract is being manipulated.

CLASSIFYING LANGUAGE SOUNDS

Consonants and vowels

Let's start with two basic classes of language sounds, classes you are already aware of: consonants and vowels. You probably learned that *a, e, i, o, u,* and sometimes *y* are vowels; the rest are consonants. You probably did not learn what constitutes vowels and consonants. Briefly, the difference between consonants and vowels is a matter of how much the air is constricted in the vocal tract when the sound is produced. With **consonants**, there is a constriction of the air flow; as air is pushed out through the vocal cords, throat, nose, and/or mouth, we constrict those areas so that there is friction, varying the consonant sound by changing the shape and place of that constriction. With **vowels**, there is little or no constriction of the air flow. Try saying the [s] sound and then the [a] or *ah* sound (as in *ma*). You should be able to feel some constriction of air with [s] and a relatively free flow of air with [a].

In addition to this large-scale distinction of consonants and vowels, we can classify sounds in terms of what are known as **articulatory properties**, where in the mouth they are produced (**place**) and how they are produced (**manner**). We will examine these properties as we introduce the IPA symbols for each sound, starting with what is known as **voice**, a key property in all human speech.

Voice

If you look at Figure 4.1, you'll notice the larynx midway down the throat. The larynx contains the vocal cords, which are key to speech production. There are two positions for the vocal cords, one in which the folds of the vocal cords vibrate and one in which they do not. When we force air through a narrow opening in the vocal cords, thus vibrating the cords, we get voiced sounds. You can feel this vibration if you place the tips of your first two fingers on the larynx, the lump on the front of your throat. While holding your fingertips there, say the [s] sound, the initial sound in *sing*. Hold it for a while. Then say the [z] sound, the initial sound in *zing*. You should feel a vibration with [z] but not [s]. That's because [z] is voiced and [s] is unvoiced or voiceless. This trick works with many consonants to determine if they are voiced or unvoiced. **Voiced sounds** are those that are produced when the vocal cords are vibrating; **unvoiced sounds** are those that are produced when the cords are not vibrating. This basic sound distinction is important not only in English but in most other languages as well.

All vowels are voiced in English, but not all consonants are, so it is especially important in learning consonants to pay attention to **voicing**. We will indicate the voicing of each consonant as we introduce the symbols for them.

Consonants

We continue our classification scheme with consonants. In addition to being sorted into voiced and unvoiced, they can be classified by their place of articulation and their manner of articulation. Each consonant can be uniquely described by its voicing, its place of articulation, and its manner of articulation.

Table 4.1 lists the meaningfully distinct consonant sounds in English, their IPA symbols, and words they are used in. We will describe each sound in more detail as we discuss the places and manner of articulation for English consonants.

Places of articulation

Each consonant is produced in a particular spot in your vocal tract, anywhere from the very front (the lips) to the very back (the pharynx). Languages can take advantage of all these places, but not all languages do so. In Arabic but not in English, for example, there are

TABLE 4.1 Consonant sounds

Phonetic symbol	Initial sound	Medial sound	Final sound
[p]	pun	lipid	shop
[b]	beet	rabid	tab
[m]	make	mommy	slim
[f]	five	lifer	tough
[v]	vine	mover	live
[θ]	thing	ether	bath
[ð]	this	either	bathe
[t]	take	city	cat
[d]	deal	Rodney	deed
[n]	know	bunny	man
[s]	sit	sissy	miss
[z]	zit	fuzzy	fizz
[l]	late	silly	tall
[r]	red	sorry	roar
[ʃ]	shun	masher	lash
[ʒ]	genre	vision	beige
[tʃ]	church	teacher	much
[dʒ]	judge	major	ledge
[y]	yes	mayor	
[w]	wink	bower	wow
[k]	cow	flicker	lick
[g]	gal	baggy	lag
[ŋ]		singer	rang
[h]	who	withhold	

pharyngeal sounds, those made at the pharynx. Here we will concentrate on the places of articulation used in English sounds.

Bilabials [b] [p] [m]

Sounds that are made with the upper and lower lips touching are called **bilabials**. In English we have three: [p], [b], and [m], the initial sounds in *pie*, *buy*, and *my*. Even though all three sounds are made in a similar place in the mouth, they are not identical sounds. The sounds [p] and [b] are very similar, but they differ in voice: [b] is a voiced bilabial; [p] is an unvoiced bilabial. The [m] sound is also a voiced bilabial. Bilabial sounds tend to be easy to identify because we can tell where our lips are as we say them.

Labiodentals [v] [f]

As you might have guessed from the name, **labiodental** sounds are those made with the top teeth (dental) touching the bottom lips (labio). The sounds [f] and [v] are labiodental sounds in English; [f] is unvoiced and [v] is voiced. So *fine* and *vine* both begin with labiodental sounds; and *leave* and *leaf* both end with them.

Interdentals [θ] [ð]

Interdental sounds are made by placing the tip of the tongue between the upper and lower teeth. There are two interdental sounds in English, one voiced and one unvoiced, both of which are spelled with the letters *th*. The symbols we use to represent these sounds will most likely be new to you: [θ] is the unvoiced sound that can be heard in the initial sound of *thigh* and *thin* and the final sound of *bath*; [ð] is the voiced sound that occurs at the beginning of *thy* or *then* and the final sound in *bathe*. If you're having difficulty differentiating the two sounds, try this trick. Say the sound and prolong it, without adding a vowel sound to it. If you can feel your lips vibrating while you do this, you are producing the voiced sound, [ð]. If they're not vibrating, you're producing the unvoiced sound, [θ].

Alveolars [t] [d] [s] [z] [n] [r] [l]

Alveolar sounds are made by placing some part of the tongue on or close to the ridge behind the upper teeth, the **alveolar ridge**. If you take your tongue and move it from the back of your upper front teeth upward toward the roof of your mouth, you'll feel a rough area close to your teeth. This is the alveolar ridge, which follows the line of teeth from one side of the mouth to the other. Try saying the [t] sound and you'll notice that the tip of your tongue touches this ridge. Try saying the [s] sound and you'll notice that it's not the tip of the tongue that touches the alveolar ridge but the edges of it as it curls up slightly and touches the ridge above your back teeth. We have several alveolar sounds in English: [t] and [d]; [s] and [z]; [n]; [r]; [l].

There are two pairs here distinguished by voice: [t] and [d] are similar alveolar sounds, but [d] is voiced and [t] is unvoiced. Similarly, [s] and [z] are similar, but [s] is unvoiced, and [z] is voiced.

The other alveolar sounds, [n], [r], and [l] are all voiced. The [n] sound is probably very familiar to you; it is the sound we hear at the beginning and end of *noon*. The [l] and [r] sounds vary greatly, depending on where in a word they occur. You can hear the [r] sound in words such as *red*, *tiger*, and *career*. In each word, it sounds slightly different. The same is true of the [l] sound: at the beginning of *life*, the middle of *jolly*, at the end of *pill*. This slight variation is common to all sounds, but it is especially noticeable with [r] and [l]. For ease of reference, the symbol we use for our [r] sound is different from that used in the IPA, where this symbol represents a slightly different sound.

Alveopalatals [ʃ] [ʒ]; [tʃ] [dʒ]; [y]

If you take your tongue and move it from the alveolar ridge back along the top of your mouth, you'll notice that you hit a hard, smooth area. This area is known as the **hard palate**. Sounds made with part of the tongue pushed up close to the hard palate are known as **alveopalatal** sounds. We have five alveopalatal sounds in English: [ʃ] and [ʒ]; [tʃ] and [dʒ]; and [y]. Some of these symbols will be unfamiliar to you so let's go through them one by one.

The sounds [ʃ] and [ʒ] constitute a pair: [ʃ] is voiceless; [ʒ] is voiced. The [ʃ] represents the unvoiced sound heard at the beginning of *shun*, at the end of *hush*, and in the middle of *mission*. The [ʒ] represents the voiced sound heard at the end of *beige* and in the middle of *pleasure* and *vision*. In English, this [ʒ] sound rarely occurs at the beginning of a word. If you're having difficulty distinguishing the two sounds, try saying *mission* (the middle sound here is unvoiced [ʃ]) and *vision* (the middle sound here is voiced [ʒ]) and see if that helps.

The sounds [dʒ] and [tʃ] also constitute a pair differentiated by voice: [tʃ] is the voiceless sound heard at both the beginning and end of *church*, and [dʒ] is the voiced sound heard at both the beginning and end of *judge*. The voiced [y] sound is a common one in English; it can be heard at the beginning of *you* and *yes* and in the middle of *mayor*.

Velars [k] and [g]; [ŋ]

If you take your tongue further back from the hard palate, you'll feel a soft spot. This area is known as the **velum** or **soft palate**; sounds made in this area are known as **velar sounds**. There are three velar sounds in English: [k] is the voiceless sound at the beginning and end of *kick*, and [g] is the voiced sound at the beginning and end of *gag*. It may be hard to feel your tongue rising toward the velum, but if you say [g] several times quickly, you can begin to feel movement there.

The [ŋ] symbol may be new to you, but the sound is not; it occurs at the end of *sing* or *dang*. It represents the voiced sound we discussed in chapter one: the n-like sound you hear in the word *finger*. If you say *fin* and then *finger*, you can hear and feel the difference between the two n-like sounds. In *fin*, you pronounce an alveolar [n]; you can feel the tip of your tongue against the alveolar ridge as you say it. But with *finger*, the sound between the vowel and the [g] sound is not alveolar; it is velar. In fact, that sound is called a **velar [n]**, symbolized by [ŋ]. This sound can be heard at the end of many words ending in *-ing* or *-ang*: *thing, ring, sang*. Note that there is no [g] sound at the end of these words despite the fact that they end with the letter *g*.

Labio-velars [w]

The voiced [w] sound, the sound heard at the beginning of *wink*, is a rather unusual one in terms of place. It is produced by raising the back of the tongue toward the velum and simultaneously rounding the lips. Hence the **labio-velar** label.

Glottal sounds [h] [ʔ]

The unvoiced [h] sound, the sound you produce at the beginning of *hold* or *horse*, is a **glottal** sound, that is, produced at the glottis, the space between the vocal cords in the larynx. This [h] sound is unusual in that it is made with an open glottis (so it is unvoiced), but neither the tongue nor other parts of the mouth manipulate the air flow. There is one other glottal sound, one that we usually don't notice as a separate sound because it is not meaningfully distinct: the unvoiced glottal stop, represented by [ʔ]. This is the sound you produce in the middle of the expression *uh-oh* and in the middle of *Latin* for many speakers. It is made by briefly closing the glottis tightly and then releasing it.

Table 4.2 summarizes places of articulation for English consonants.

Manner of articulation

In addition to classifying consonants by their place of articulation, we can classify them by their manner of articulation. Briefly, **manner of articulation** refers to the way sounds are produced rather than where they are produced.

TABLE 4.2 Places of articulation

	Voiceless	Voiced
Bilabials	[p]	[b] [m]
Interdentals	[θ]	[ð]
Alveolars	[t] [s]	[d] [z] [n] [r] [l]
Alveopalatals	[ʃ] [tʃ]	[ʒ] [dʒ] [y]
Velars	[k]	[g] [ŋ]
Labio-velars	[w]	
Glottals	[h] [ʔ]	

Nasal sounds

Nasals are sounds made by expelling some of the air out through both the nose and the mouth. With oral sounds the **velum** (see Figure 4.1) is in a raised position so that the air flows out through the mouth, not the nose. When making **nasal** sounds, we do **not** raise the velum, so some of the air flows out through the nose. We have only three nasals in English, all of which are voiced, each produced at a different place in the mouth:

- [m] a bilabial nasal
- [n] an alveolar nasal
- [ŋ] a velar nasal.

Oral sounds

Nasals are the exception in terms of language sound production; most sounds in languages of the world are **oral sounds**, made by blocking the air from escaping through the nose by raising the velum. Aside from the three nasal sounds, all sounds in English are oral. The following types of sounds are all oral sounds.

Stops, also called plosives, are made by blocking the air flow and then letting it all out at once in a sort of mini explosion of sound. We have seven in English:

- [p] and [b] bilabial stops (the complete blockage of air is at the lips)
- [t] and [d] alveolar stops (the complete blockage is at the alveolar ridge)
- [k] and [g] velar stops (the complete blockage is at the velum)
- [ʔ] a glottal stop (the complete blockage of air is at the glottis).

If you put your hand in front of your mouth as you say one of these sounds, especially [p] or [b], you can feel the sudden expulsion of air.

Flaps are similar to stops but not identical. We have only one in English, the voiced alveolar flap, [r], which is produced by briefly touching the tip of the tongue to the alveolar ridge behind the front teeth and then releasing the air, but with less plosive force than in a stop. It is heard in the middle of words like *ladder* and *pretty* in U.S. casual speech. It occurs mostly between vowels and is usually represented in spelling by *dd* or *tt*.

The glottal stop and the flap are not meaningfully distinct sounds in English, as we will see in Chapter 5. I include them here as they occur often in many people's speech.

Fricatives differ from stops in that we obstruct most, but not all, of the air by constricting some area of the vocal tract and then releasing it slowly through the narrow opening created. This constriction produces a kind of turbulence (which can feel or sound like a hissing sound) as the air is released. We have nine fricatives in English:

- [f] and [v] labiodental fricatives
- [θ] and [ð] interdental fricatives
- [s] and [z] alveolar fricatives
- [ʃ] and [ʒ] alveopalatal fricatives
- [h] a glottal fricative.

One noticeable difference between fricatives and stops is that you can pronounce fricatives for a long time. Try saying [p] for a long time. It can't be done. But try saying [s] or [v] for a long time; that can be done.

Affricates are a combination of a stop and a fricative. They are made by closing off the air and then immediately releasing it in a gradual manner like the release in a fricative. We have only two affricates in English: [tʃ] and [dʒ], both alveopalatal:

- [tʃ] unvoiced alveopalatal affricate
- [dʒ] voiced alveopalatal affricate.

Stops, fricatives, and affricates are **obstruents**; that is, they obstruct the air as it flows through the vocal tract.

Liquids are produced by obstructing the air flow only slightly. They are called liquids because they seem to move around in the mouth. We have two in English, both voiced and both alveolar: [l] and [r]. How do we distinguish them, then? The [l] sound is a lateral fricative in which the air escapes around the edges of the tongue as the tip of the tongue touches the top of the mouth near the alveolar ridge. The [r] sound, known as a retroflex [r], is produced by either bunching the tongue upward toward the hard palate or by curling the tip of the tongue back into the mouth.

Glides, [y] and [w], are also produced with little or no obstruction of the air flow. In English, they are always preceded or followed by a vowel. When making these sounds, our tongues move quickly either toward or away from the vowel sound, hence the name glides. In this way, glides are transitional sounds. They are sometimes called semi-vowels.

Glides and liquids are **approximants**; that is, the air flow is constricted slightly, but not enough to produce the friction found with obstruents.

Table 4.3 classifies English consonants by voice, place, and manner of articulation.

Vowels

When we turn our attention to vowels, the picture becomes less complicated in one sense and more complicated in another. Vowel classification is easier than consonant classification, but distinguishing vowel sounds and feeling them in your mouth can be tricky. Vowel sounds,

TABLE 4.3 Natural classes of consonants

Manner of articulation	Place of articulation						
Stops	**Bilabial**	**Labio-dental**	**Interdental**	**Alveolar**	**Alveo-palatal**	**Velar**	**Glottal**
Voiced	[b]			[d]		[g]	
Unvoiced	[p]			[t]		[k]	[ʔ]
Fricatives							
Voiced		[v]	[ð]	[z]	[ʒ]		
Unvoiced		[f]	[θ]	[s]	[ʃ]		[h]
Affricates							
Voiced					[dʒ]		
Unvoiced					[tʃ]		
Nasals							
Voiced	[m]			[n]		[ŋ]	
Liquids							
Voiced lateral				[l]			
Voiced retroflex				[r]			
Glides							
Voiced	[w]				[y]	[w]	
Flap							
Voiced				[ɾ]			

you remember, are different from consonants in that the air flow through the vocal tract has little or no constriction. When saying vowel sounds, then, it is harder to feel exactly where the tongue is. You can begin to feel the configuration of the vocal tract with vowels by saying the following pairs several times: *heat–hoot*. You may notice that the position of the tongue and the rounding of the lips vary between these two sounds. In *heat*, the tongue is high and in the front; in *hoot*, it is high but in the back. In *heat*, the lips are pulled back; in *hoot*, they are rounded.

Most of us were taught that there are five vowels in English. There are, indeed, five letters we use for vowel sounds, but there are between 12 to 14 vowel sounds in English, depending on the variety. It is sometimes difficult to distinguish vowel sounds that are often spelled with the same letter. Think of the letter *u*, for example, as it is used in *but* and *put*. The vowel sounds are different, yet we use the same letter to represent both. For some vowels sounds, we do not have a separate letter to represent them. The vowel sound in *bat* is common in English, but we do not have one letter to represent it.

There is also more variation in the pronunciation of any one vowel sound, both across groups and across individuals. My [a] sound, the sound in *hot*, for example, will be slightly different than yours, even if we come from the same region. If we come from different regions or speak different varieties, our vowel sounds may differ greatly. Those from the southern part of the United States have very different vowels than those from the Pacific Northwest. If we broaden our perspective to include Englishes spoken around the world, the variation is staggering.

TABLE 4.4 Vowels

Tongue height	Part of tongue		
	Front	**Central**	**Back**
High	[i] beet		[u] boot
	[ɪ] bit		[ʊ] book
Mid	[e] bait	[ə] but	[o] boat
	[ɛ] bet		[ɔ] caught
Low	[æ] bat		[a] cot

Vowel sounds are classified by the position (front, central, back) and height (high, mid, low) of the tongue in their pronunciation. We do not need to indicate voice with vowels since all vowels are voiced.

Table 4.4 lists the vowel sounds found in U.S. English, classified along these two axes, with examples of their use in words included to help you hear each sound.

In addition to these vowel sounds, English has three **diphthongs**: [aw], [ay], and [ɔy]. Diphthongs are vowel sounds where the tongue moves from one place to another as the sound is made. If you say the vowel sound [a] followed by the [w] glide, you will get a feeling for the tongue movement in the diphthong [aw], the sound in *lout* or *now*. It helps to say it slowly to feel this movement. The diphthong [ay] is the vowel sound [a] followed by the [y] glide, the sound in *buy* or *tide*. And the diphthong [ɔy] is the vowel sound [ɔ] followed by the [y] glide, to yield the sound in *boy* or *toil*.

Table 4.5 gives examples of each vowel sound used in different words.

Learning the symbols for vowel sounds takes practice. As you do the exercises at the end of this chapter, remember that you may pronounce some words differently than your classmates or your instructor. As mentioned previously, some speakers of American English do not use

TABLE 4.5 Vowel sounds

Phonetic symbol	Initial sound	Medial sound	Final sound
[i]	eel	meat	key
[ɪ]	it	hit	—
[e]	ate	grade	may
[ɛ]	elevate	tell	—
[æ]	at	math	—
[ə]	about	cup	sofa
[u]	ooze	groove	who
[ʊ]	—	could	—
[o]	open	mowed	hello
[ɔ]	awful	taught	—
[a]	operate	lot	ma
[aw]	out	loud	cow
[ay]	eye	writer	try
[ɔy]	oil	droid	toy

the vowel sound [ɔ]; instead, they use the [a] where others use [ɔ]. If you make a distinction between the vowel sounds in *cot* [a] and *caught* [ɔ], your speech does contain that sound. If you do not make that distinction, your vowels sound for both words will be [a].

The sounds [ʊ], [ə], and [a] are sometimes difficult to distinguish. If you find this is so, it helps to create a list of similar words in which the difference in the vowel sounds is easy to hear. Try these three: *good* [ʊ], *gut* [ə], and *got* [a]. Don't let the letters or spelling mess you up; listen for the sounds and you'll be able to hear the differences.

NATURAL CLASSES

Each category described earlier constitutes a **natural class**, a group of sounds that shares one or more articulatory features that are shared by no other sounds. Voiced sounds constitute one natural class, unvoiced sounds another, as do consonants and vowels. Bilabials form a natural class as do velars, alveolars, alveopalatals, and every place and every manner of articulation. Front vowels form a natural class, as do back vowels. We will discuss natural classes more in the next chapter when we examine phonological rules that are based on these classes.

Natural classes allow us to uniquely describe each of the sounds we learned in this chapter. That is, by listing the natural classes a sound belongs to, we describe it and it alone. So [b], for example, can be described as a voiced bilabial stop. Only one sound in English fits that description. Similarly, [s] can be uniquely described as an unvoiced alveolar fricative. Conversely, if I gave you a list of natural classes that a sound belongs to, you would be able to tell me what that sound is. Try it: What sound is a voiced labiodental fricative? Only [v] fits that description.

ACCENTS

We've been examining each sound in English as though it were always said the same by everyone. Of course, that's not true. Different people pronounce sounds differently, as we all know. Some of this variation is individual. Much, however, is related to accent.

What is an **accent**? In linguistics, there is no one meaning, but generally it refers to distinctive pronunciations of a spoken variety, whether it be in pronunciation of individual sounds or in use of prosodic features such as stress or intonation. Remember, varieties are distinguished by differences in morphology, lexicon, semantics, and grammar as well as accent.

Accents are often connected to region, in which case we call them regional accents. They are also connected to socioeconomic class (sociolects), ethnicity (ethnolects), religion, group affiliation, gender identity, sexual identity, or occupation. For non-native speakers, their accent may result from the influence of their first language, in which case we sometimes call it a foreign accent. It is not just non-native speakers who have an accent, though. We all do. Every native speaker of any language has an accent.

Studies have found that a particular variant of just one sound can be enough to indicate social identities to listeners. So how do listeners make use of these perceptions? For the dominant group, which generally believes itself not to have an accent, noticing a speaker's accent can mean more than, *Oh, they say that word differently.* It can come with all sorts of stereotypes about the group associated with that accent. French accents are seen in the United States as romantic, upper-class British ones are seen as sophisticated. Not all stereotypes are positive, however. British accents can also be seen as snobbish. And the English spoken by Latinx speakers too often evokes unfair and untrue stereotypes of laziness or illegality. None of these stereotypes are true.

In the preface, I wrote about living in London and being subtly encouraged to use the British pronunciation of [a] instead of [e] and [t] instead of an alveolar flap [ɾ] in *tomato*—an encouragement that felt more like pressure to be someone I'm not. As a speaker of white, middle-class North American English, that was a new and slightly unsettling experience for me. For many who speak a variety of English not considered standard, that sort of pressure to change their way of speaking happens often.

For those groups who speak what the dominant group considers a nonstandard accent, stereotyping can do real harm. One example: James Kahakua, a native speaker of Hawaiian Creole, a variety of English spoken by many in Hawaii, was denied a job reading the weather reports on the radio station where he worked because his accent—the way he pronounced his English—was deemed unacceptable for radio, even though it was easily comprehensible to listeners.

It is only some accents that are deemed unacceptable in official or formal situations and only some speakers who may be pressured to change that pronunciation in school or to get a professional job. The question for us here is—Whose accents are deemed unacceptable? Those who use the British pronunciation of *dance* rather than the American one? Probably not. In Chapter 2 we noted that when we discriminate against a particular variety of a language, it is the people who speak it that we are really discriminating against. The same goes for accents. It is generally the people in power, the dominant group, whose accent is perceived as normal, correct, and unaccented. Any speech that varies from that is called accented.

That perception is not true, but it sets up the expectation among many educators, politicians, broadcasters, business leaders, and others that there is only one correct way to speak, and everyone should speak that way. When we ask someone to change how they speak, we are asking them to change who they are, implying that who they are is not good enough. Gloria Anzaldua (1987), a native speaker of English, describes being required, along with all the other Latinx students, to take speech classes in college because her accent in English was deemed unacceptable. The message was not just that her English needed to be something other than it was, but that she herself needed to be something other than she was, something other than Latinx. This type of unfair stereotyping based on accents can have serious consequences: not being hired for a job, not being believed on the witness stand, not being allowed to rent an apartment because your accent indicated to others that you were African American or Latinx or Native American or a member of another marginalized group.

PROSODY

In addition to individual vowel and consonant sounds (known as segmentals), there are also prosodic or suprasegmental features that make up part of the sound system of a language: duration of individual sounds, pitch, stress, and intonation, all of which can be important to meaning. Prosody refers to how these features are used.

Duration or length refers to how long a sound is held. Although it makes no difference to meaning in English, we do have systematic differences in vowel length. The [i] is held longer in *bead* than in *beat*, for example. Try it and see if you can hear it. In many other languages, vowel length does make a difference to meaning: Japanese, Finnish, Czech, Arabic, and Vietnamese, among others. In Finnish, lengthening a vowel or consonant sound can produce a different word: [muta] means *mud*; if the [u] sound is held longer, as in [mu:ta], it means *other*. That colon indicates a long consonant or vowel sound. In Italian, lengthening a consonant can change meaning: [kasa] means *house*; if the [s] sound is held longer, as in [kas:a], it means *box*.

Pitch refers to how fast or slowly the vocal cords vibrate as we say a word: the faster the vibrations, the higher the pitch. Languages use differences in pitch in different ways. In **tone languages**, the pitch of a syllable, its **tone**, is used to distinguish between words. In English, which is not a tone language, we distinguish meaning by varying one sound: *hit* can become a different word, *heat*, by changing the vowel sound. In tone languages, changing the pitch of a word produces a different word, even when the individual sounds are the same. In Mandarin Chinese, which has four distinct tones, the word [ma] can have any of four different meanings depending on its tone: said with a high-level tone, it means *mother*; said with a high rising tone, it means *hemp*; said with a low falling tone, it means *horse*; said with a high falling tone, it means *scold*. In Mandarin, tones can vary through the course of a syllable, rising or falling along the way. These are contour tones. In other languages, such as Yoruba, spoken in West Africa, tones are constant, not rising or falling. Many, many languages around the world are tone languages: Thai, Vietnamese, Tibetan, Hmong, Cambodian, Yoruba, Zulu, Maasai, Somali, Cherokee, Hopi, Navajo, Apache, Mextec, and Ticuna, among others.

Stress refers to the relative prominence of syllables in a word or phrase; stressed syllables are generally said louder, at a higher pitch and/or held longer. In English, stress is not predictable, but it is in some other languages. In Italian and Polish, it tends to fall on the penultimate syllable; in Hungarian and Latvian, on the first; and in French, on the final syllable. English uses stress patterns to distinguish some pairs of words: *rebel* as a noun has the stress on the first syllable, as a verb on the second; similarly, *record* has stress on the first syllable when it is a noun, but on the second when it is a verb.

Intonation refers to changes in pitch across an utterance. Intonation patterns are used by all languages to mark differences in meaning; in conjunction with other prosodic features, they are used to express attitudes and emotions or to signal focus in an utterance. We can even see this in some one-word utterances in English: for example, *great* or *finally* spoken as an entire utterance. They can express either enthusiasm or sarcasm, depending on the intonation pattern. In English and many other languages, a rising intonation at the end of an utterance generally indicates a question; falling indicates a statement.

PHONETICS IN YOUR WORLD: WHAT'S IN A NAME?

A few years ago, when Sonia Sotomayor became a justice on the U.S. Supreme Court, some political media was aflutter with the question of how to pronounce her last name. She pronounces it as it is pronounced in Spanish, with the stress on the last syllable. Many English speakers put the stress on the penultimate syllable. Seems a simple difference, one not important to national politics, yes? Several commentators, however, objected to her pronunciation of her own name, calling it "unnatural in English" and "something we shouldn't be giving into" (Rosa, 2019, p. 146), implying that a particular pronunciation was being forced on others and was somehow dangerous. The real problem for the commentators was not the pronunciation per se; it was what that pronunciation evoked in listeners: a Latina identity, someone supposedly not quite American. Need we reiterate that such an assumption is based on ethnic and linguistic prejudice?

PHONETICS IN YOUR WORLD: LOCAL ACTS OF IDENTITY

Various studies have found that fine phonetic detail, detail we probably don't notice consciously, can be used to construct what might be called local social meanings. Eckert (1989), for example, in her study of jocks and burnouts in a U.S. high school, found that, among other phonetic variants, the pronunciation of the vowel sound [ay] was closely linked to the group the speaker belonged to: jocks pronounced it slightly differently than did burnouts. In other words, which variant a student used was closely linked to her social identity as a jock or a burnout.

The social meaning of a particular variant of a sound is not universal, of course. What a variant means in terms of social identity will vary across groups and contexts. Different pronunciations of [I], for example, have been found to predict membership in a particular gang among a group of Chicana/Mexicana high school girls (Mendoza-Denton, 2008). Pronouncing a variant of [æ] further to the front of the mouth has been shown to be associated with cheerfulness in Southern Michigan, doing so with [ay] is associated with toughness in Philadelphia (Hay & Drager, 2007). Speakers and listeners may not be consciously aware of these variants, but they nevertheless judge others based on small variation in how sounds are pronounced.

SIGN LANGUAGE PHONETICS

So far, we've been analyzing language sounds, how and where they're made in the mouth. Signs used as part of sign languages can be similarly analyzed by where and how they are made. For American Sign Language (ASL), for instance, we can think of hand shape, movement, and location as being three major articulatory features, all taking place within what is called the signing space, that area from head to waist and about forearm distance from the body. Hand shape refers to the configuration of the hand as it makes a sign: Are all five fingers spread? Does the thumb stick out? Is the hand in a fist? There are over 30 distinct handshapes in ASL. Movement refers to how the hand and arms move: Toward the body? Away from the body? Out and back again? Location refers to where the sign is produced: By the forehead? Shoulders? Chin?

In English, a change in manner or place of articulation can result in a new word. In ASL, a change in shape, movement, or location similarly results in a new word.

PHONETICS IN OTHER LANGUAGES

As we've seen, English has around 36 meaningfully distinct sounds; some languages have fewer, some many more. The smallest number seems to be 11 in Rotokas, spoken in the Indo-Pacific; the largest around 150 in !Xoon, spoken in the Kalahari Desert (Crystal, 2010). Generally, languages contain more consonants than vowels.

!Xoon is interesting in another aspect of its phonology; like several other Southern African languages, it uses several different clicks as consonants. **Clicks** are obstruents, though they are not produced by air being pushed through the vocal track. They are made by the lips or the tongue creating a suction sound. You can hear a dental click in English when we say *tsk, tsk,* or *tut tut*, made with the tongue against the top teeth. In !Xoon, there are five different clicks that are meaningfully distinct (substituting one for the other produces a different word): bilabial, dental, alveolar, palatal, and lateral. Each of these functions as do our consonants. Unlike our *tsk*, which is not used as a part of words, clicks are fully integrated into the sound system and function in combination with other sounds. You can hear clicks on YouTube in *Miriam Makeba's Qongqothwane (The Click Song)* or *How to pronounce Zulu clicks with Sakhile Dube.*

L1 ACQUISITION IN FOCUS: ACQUIRING LANGUAGE SOUNDS AND SIGNS

Children learning a language need to figure out the sounds or signs of that language. And the first year of children's lives is devoted to that task. Children are born with the ability and the propensity to pay attention to certain kinds of information, including language sounds or signs. Hearing children quickly learn to distinguish language sounds from other sounds in their environment, engine noises or animal sounds, for example. Children exposed to sign languages learn to distinguish language signs from other types of gesturing. During the **babbling stage**, from about 6 to 12 months of age, children appear to be practicing or playing with sounds or signs. In other words, they babble—a lot. This stage of language acquisition appears to be similar the world over. Early in this stage, hearing children rehearse not just sounds of the language they hear around them but a wide range of sounds, many of which are not used in their language. Soon, however, hearing children begin to hone their learning to focus on sounds present in their language, eventually diminishing or losing their ability to discriminate among and produce sounds not in their language.

Children first acquire those sounds that are common in languages in the world and only later acquire those that are rare but occur in their own language. Thus, an English-speaking child first learns [m, b, d, k] for they are common across languages, and only later masters [θ] and [ð], uncommon sounds. Natural class plays an important role in determining the order in which children acquire language sounds: nasals are acquired early, fricatives and affricates later; labials and velars are acquired early, alveolars and alveopalatals later.

CHAPTER SUMMARY

- Part of knowing any spoken language is knowing its sounds and how they are put together. Since letters in English are poor representations of sounds, linguists use the International Phonetic Alphabet to represent language sounds.
- Language sounds are produced by manipulating the vocal tract at various places and in various manners. Articulatory phonetics studies how these manipulations produce language sounds.
- Sounds can be classified according to natural classes; among those important in all languages are vowels/consonants and voiced/voiceless sounds.
- Consonants are further classified by the natural classes of voice, place of articulation, and manner of articulation. Each consonant can be uniquely described using voice, place, and manner.

- Vowels are classified by tongue height and position: front or back and high or low. All vowels are voiced.
- Prosody includes pitch, tone, duration, stress, and intonation, all of which are used by some languages to distinguish meaning.
- Accents are distinctive pronunciations of a spoken variety; we all speak with an accent.
- Our ways of speaking, including our accents, are emblematic of who we are, signaling our various social identities: our region of origin, socioeconomic class, race/ethnicity, gender identity, sexual identity, and other social factors.
- Too often people are judged by their accents, often in negative and unwarranted ways. These judgments are, in essence, a form of linguistic prejudice.
- Like sounds in spoken languages, signs in sign languages can be classified by their articulatory properties; for sign languages these are hand shape, movement, and location.
- The number of distinct sounds that occur in languages varies greatly, some as low as 11, some as high as 150. Nearly all languages contain more consonants than vowels.
- In the babbling stage, from 6 to 12 months, children first learn and practice a wide range of language sounds or signs, even those not used in their language; later they learn and practice the specific sounds or signs of their language.

KEY TERMS

voiced/unvoiced
consonant/vowel
front vowels

back vowels
diphthongs
natural classes

CONSONANTS: PLACES OF ARTICULATION

bilabial
labiodental
interdental
alveolar

alveopalatal
velar
glottal
labio-velar

CONSONANTS: MANNERS OF ARTICULATION

stop
fricative
affricate
nasal
liquid

glide
flap
obstruent
approximant

PROSODIC FEATURES

tone/tone languages
duration/length
intonation

pitch
stress

EXPLORATIONS

Exploration 1: Sounds not letters

For each word in the list, identify the number of different sounds involved. Remember, the number of sounds may not match the number of letters.

Examples: note (3 sounds); school (4 sounds)

charge	lamb
league	plant
thing	scarf
light	align
borough	ax
cough	schedule

Exploration 2: Natural classes

For each group of sounds listed, identify the feature that they all have in common. In other words, state the natural class each group comprises.

Example: [g] [p] [t] [d] [k] [b] [ʔ]   All are part of the natural class of stops.

1.   [t] [s] [ʃ] [k] [p] [f] [tʃ] [θ]
2.   [ɪ] [i] [ɛ] [e] [æ]
3.   [v] [ð] [z] [d] [b] [ʒ] [dʒ] [r] [l] [g] [m] [n] [ŋ]
4.   [k] [g] [ŋ]
5.   [m] [n] [ŋ]

Transcription practice

Answer keys for the transcription exercises are available online. It is usually best to say the word aloud as you would say it in casual conversation, then try to find the symbol that most accurately matches your pronunciation. Your pronunciation may differ from that in the answer key, which is based on my pronunciation. If you think your pronunciation is different from the answer key, ask in class. Remember to concentrate on sounds, not letters.

TABLE 4.6 Transcribing consonant sounds

Initial position	Middle position	Final position
1. pad [p]	1. added [d]	1. ache [k]
2. tad	2. about	2. these
3. cad	3. appear	3. cough
4. choose	4. other	4. ring
5. job	5. manor	5. shove
6. think	6. catcher	6. age
7. this	7. masher	7. garage
8. sure	8. singing	8. bash
9. sir	9. aging	9. loathe
10. use	10. ladder	10. beige

Exploration 3: Consonants

Transcribe the consonant sounds in the words in Table 4.6.

Exploration 4: Vowels

Transcribe the vowel sounds in the following pairs of words. You do not need to do the entire word (consonants and vowels), but you may if you wish.

1. sit	set	12. buck	book
2. sat	seat	13. bough	buy
3. let	late	14. met	mutt
4. mid	mud	15. key	cow
5. bait	bat	16. cub	cab
6. cap	cop	17. gist	just
7. hut	hot	18. said	sod
8. hot	height	19. gnaw	noise
9. who'd	hood	20. how	hoe
10. load	lewd	21. both	bother
11. took	tuck	22. font	front

Exploration 5: More vowels

Transcribe the vowel sounds in the following sets of words.

1. luck	luke	lack	lick	look	leak	lock	like	lake
2. fell	fool	foil	feel	full	fill	fail	fall	foul
file	fallow							

Exploration 6: Whole words

Transcribe each of the words as you would say them in *casual* speech. Do not be misled by orthography; listen for sounds not letters.

1. meat	11. flood	21. plied
2. great	12. game	22. grouch
3. they	13. sow	23. cough
4. fit	14. moon	24. through
5. whale	15. voice	25. speech
6. soup	16. size	
7. do	17. got	
8. don't	18. hat	
9. tough	19. through	
10. ploy	20. though	

Exploration 7: Transcription practice

Transcribe each of the words in the list as you would say them in *casual* speech. Do not be misled by orthography; listen for sounds not letters.

1. change	8. ache	15. laboratory
2. ouch	9. okay	16. freeze
3. tongue	10. penguin	17. face
4. muse	11. monkey	18. cringe
5. stood	12. language	19. played
6. doubt	13. chopped	20. crawled
7. rot	14. lies	

Exploration 8: Differing pronunciations

Fill in the blank with the correct phonetic transcription of a word that is spelled in one way but pronounced in two different ways.

    Example: The Olympic crew had a __[raw]__ about the correct way to __[ro]__ (row)

1. The dump was so full it had to _____ any more _____. (refuse)
2. If she wants to increase her _____ in the marathon, she'll have to get the _____ out. (lead)
3. After her illness, they discovered her insurance was _____ for the _____. (invalid)
4. The _____ quickly _____ into the bushes to avoid the cat. (dove)
5. She did not _____ to that _____ per se, just what it represented. (object)
6. They were too _____ to the door to _____ it. (close)
7. We must _____ the antique _____ furniture. (polish)
8. The _____ was too strong to _____ the sail. (wind)
9. The nurse _____ a strip of cloth around the _____. (wound)
10. It'll take me a _____ or two to get this _____ splinter out. (minute)

Exploration 9: From IPA to English

These words are in IPA; rewrite them in standard spelling.

1. [ðoz]	6. [baks]	11. [klawd]
2. [izi]	7. [ɪʃu]	12. [brɛθ]
3. [tʃiz]	8. [alðo]	13. [ken]
4. [tayt]	9. [kroke]	14. [ridʒ]
5. [ʃʊk]	10. [sin]	15. [prayd]

Exploration 10: Finding errors

In this transcription of a verse about a cat and a fiddle, there is one mistake in each line. Find the errors and correct them.

TRANSCRIPTION	ERROR
[he dɪrəl dɪrəl ðə cæt æn ðə fɪrəl]	[cæt] should be [kæt]
[ðə kaw dʒəmpt ovər ðə moon]	
[ðə lɪrəl dag (or [dɔg]) læfed tu si ʃətʃ ə sayt]	
[æn ðə dɪʃ ræn əwe wɪð ðə spun]	

Exploration 11: Advertising slogans

Find two or more slogans or jingles from an ad you hear on radio, TV, or other media; transcribe them into IPA. Share the transcriptions with your small group. Ask them to read them aloud to see if the transcription is accurate.

Exploration 12: Discussion prompt: Accents

Have you ever been told you speak with an accent? Where and when? Have others ever teased you about your accent or your way of pronouncing a particular word? What did they say? What was your reaction? Have you ever noticed another person's accent and commented on it, either directly to that person or to another person? What did you notice and what sort of comment did you make? Share your responses with your small group.

FURTHER READING

http://web.uvic.ca/ling/resources/ipa/charts/IPAlab/IPAlab.htm. A good interactive chart with clear recordings.

IPA website: www.internationalphoneticsassociation.org. Useful information about the discipline of phonetics.

Ladefoged, P. (2001). *A course in phonetics* (4th ed.). Harcourt. Classic in the field.

Ladefoged, P., & Maddieson, I. (1996). *The sounds of the world's languages*. Blackwell.

UCLA Phonetics Lab Archive: http://archive.phonetics.ucla.edu/

UCLA Phonetics Lab Data: www.phonetics.ucla.edu/course/chapter1/chapter1.html. To listen to speech sounds.

REFERENCES

Anzaldua, G. (1987). *Borderlands/La frontera*. Aunt Lute Press.

Crystal, D. (2010). *Language death*. Cambridge University Press.

Eckert, P. (1989). *Jocks & Burnouts: Social categories and identity in the high school*. Teachers College Press.

Hay, J., & Drager, K. (2007). Socio-phonetics. *Annual Review of Anthropology, 36*, 89–103.

Mendoza-Denton, N. (2008). *Homegirls: Language and cultural practice among Latina youth gangs*. Blackwell.

Rosa, J. (2019). *Looking like a language, sounding like a race: Raciolinguistic ideology and the learning of Latinidad*. Oxford University Press.

CHAPTER 5

Phonology

Why do we say it like that?

···

INTRODUCTION

As you transcribed words and phrases into IPA in the previous chapter, you may have noticed that sounds in the middle of a word do not sound the same as they do in isolation. And you may have concluded, quite rightly, that sounds influence one another when they are pronounced together, as they are in words and phrases. Take the [t] sound, for example. We probably pronounce the [t] at the end of *first* if that word is the last in an emphatic utterance, as in *I'm first*. But if we say *first grade*, the [t] seems to drop out, so we get [fərsgred]. There are other anomalies with [t]—what about the [t] in *city*? It's hardly a [t] at all. We pronounce it as the alveolar flap [ɾ], but we still see it as a [t]. What's going on here? Why is there so much variation? Is it lazy speech, mispronunciations, or just arbitrary individual differences from people who should know better? As you may have guessed already, it's none of the above. In fact, these so-called anomalies in the pronunciation of [t] are rule governed and systematic, as

DOI: 10.4324/9780429269059-5

is all language. It's clear that such variation is not the result of arbitrary individual differences because most of us make these same adjustments as we speak. We'll be examining this rule-governed sound system as we discuss phonology.

Phonology is often defined as the study of the systematic structuring of sounds in language. We could also say it is the study of how sounds are organized when not in isolation, that is, when we use them in speech. What does it mean for sounds to be structured or organized? For our purposes, it means that we can examine how sounds differ from one another, identifying which differences are important to meaning and which are not, and identifying the principles and processes that explain the variation we find within one sound, such as that within [t].

SYSTEMATIC STRUCTURING OF SOUNDS

Phonemes and allophones

Before we start investigating the regularities involved in the sound system, we will need some new concepts, including one that we hinted at earlier but did not really explain: meaningfully distinct sounds. Most of the sounds for which you learned symbols in Chapter 4 are meaningfully distinct in English, that is, they distinguish meaning. To explain what that means, we need to back up a minute and examine language sounds in general.

We could say that there are an infinite number of sounds in English—or in any language, for that matter. This variation occurs not just because of individual variation in pronouncing sounds. More importantly, it occurs because of variations of one sound that we all produce: the [p] in *pit*, for example, is slightly different from the [p] in *spit* for all of us. You can hear this difference by saying *pit* with your hand in front of your mouth. Can you feel a bit of air as part of the [p] sound? Now try saying *spit*, again with your hand in front of your mouth. Can you feel that there is less air? The [p] in *pit* is **aspirated**—that is, it has some extra air as part of its pronunciation—while the [p] in *spit* is not aspirated (no extra air).

We recognize that the variations in [p] do not make it a different sound the way that [b] or [f] or [r] are all different sounds. The fact that we have separate letters for [b], [f], and [r] but the same letter for the two [p] sounds helps us recognize that the latter are variations of one sound.

Having individual letters in an alphabet for a particular sound does not determine the status of that sound in the phonological system of a language. For example, we can recognize that /n/ is a different sound, a meaningfully distinct sound, from /ŋ/, even though the latter sound is not represented by its own letter. Think of *sin* [sɪn] and *sing* [sɪŋ], for example. It is the sound at the end that distinguishes the two words. We somehow know that those two sounds are different in some meaningful and important way.

Your brain organizes sounds at two levels: the **phonetic** level, the sound level itself, and the **phonemic** level, sound differences that make a difference in meaning. At the phonetic level, the [p] in *pit* is slightly different from the [p] in *spit*, and we easily pronounce them differently, even if we don't consciously recognize that they are different. At the phonemic level, we know that both [p]s are the same sound in some fundamental sense, just as we know that [n] and [ŋ] are different sounds in some fundamental sense.

When you learn a language, this is part of what you learn: the sounds that are part of your language and the patterns and rules about how to use those sounds in speech. Learning

English involves learning how to pronounce English sounds and learning which variety of a sound to use in what circumstances, the [p] with aspiration or the [p] without it, for example. And it involves learning which sound variation is important to meaning and which is not.

Another example might be helpful here, the [t] sound in English. Try this little experiment: say the following words as you would in casual conversation, paying attention to the [t] sound in each: *city, Latin, ton, stun*. The [t] in *city* is the alveolar flap [ɾ]; in *Latin*, it is a glottal stop [ʔ]; in *stun,* it is a [t] without aspiration, in *ton*, it is a [t] with slight aspiration. (We'll indicate this sound with aspiration by [tʰ]; that ʰ indicates aspiration.) In *kitten*, it is a [t] without aspiration and a glottal stop [tʔ] together. If we were to transcribe these words into the phonetic alphabet, they'd look like [sɪɾi], [laʔɪn], [tən], [stʰən], and [kɪtʔɪn]. All four sounds are /t/, but they are very different /t/s. We could say they are all variants of one basic /t/.

On one level all of the variants of /t/ are different; on another level, they are all the same. The two levels are the ones mentioned earlier: the phonetic (all different) and the phonemic (all the same). We use the term **phoneme** to refer to the abstract idea of a /t/, the way in which they are all the same. (In linguistics, phonemes are indicated with slashes; variants of phonemes, called **allophones**, are indicated with the brackets we used in Chapter 4.) For our example here, /t/ is a phoneme, and [ɾ], [ʔ], [tʰ], [tʔ], and [t] are allophones of this phoneme. Figure 5.1 models the situation.

What would happen if you substituted one allophone of /t/ for another allophone of /t/? Try it. Say *Latin* with the [t] allophone instead of the [ʔ] allophone. Still the same word? Sure. Try saying *city* with the [t] or with the [ʔ] instead of the [ɾ] allophone. Still the same word? Yes. The thing about allophone variation is that we can substitute one allophone of a particular phoneme for another allophone of the same phoneme, and doing so does not produce a new word.

Ok, so what exactly is a **phoneme**? Perhaps some formal definition will help. One way to understand a phoneme is as the minimal unit of sound that distinguishes meaning. In other words, the substitution of one phoneme for another phoneme changes meaning. Another way is as an abstract representation of a sound of which allophones are the actual pronunciations. This definition gets at the fact that phonemes are mental representations that exist as part of our knowledge of our language. How any phoneme is pronounced will depend on where it occurs in a word. If I say, how do you pronounce /t/, you'd certainly have some idea, but you couldn't say exactly without knowing the word it was in. In some words, it's pronounced [t], in some [ɾ], in some [ʔ], in some [tʰ].

How do we know which sounds are separate phonemes and which are merely variations of a phoneme? We can determine which sounds are different phonemes through the identification of **minimal pairs**: two words whose pronunciation differs by only one sound. *Fat* and *bat*

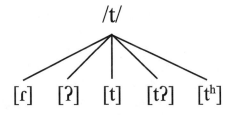

FIGURE 5.1 Diagram of allophones of phoneme /t/

are minimal pairs in that they differ only in the initial [f] and [b] sounds. *Fat* and *brat* are not minimal pairs because there is a difference of more than one sound: [f] and [br].

Minimal pairs are used to determine whether two sounds are separate phonemes. If we take the word *fat*, for example, and substitute a different consonant, say /b/, for the /f/, and thereby produce a different word, we know the two sounds, [f] and [b], are separate phonemes because they distinguish meaning. In other words, that one sound change creates a different word. Remember that substituting one allophone of /t/ for another allophone of /t/ does not create a new word: *city* can be pronounced with [ɾ] or [t] and it's still the same word, *city*. But if we substitute a different phoneme, say /l/, we do get another word: *silly* [sɪli] is a different word from [sɪɾi]. *City* and *silly* are minimal pairs, just as *fat* and *bat* are. From this we know that /t/ and /l/ are two separate phonemes just as /f/ and /b/ are two separate phonemes, and we indicate that by enclosing them in slashes: /f/, /b/, /t/, and /l/. Those slashes are important because they indicate a phoneme.

This system works because phonemes are always in what is called **contrastive distribution**; their distribution is unpredictable, and they contrast with one another: a [t] is not a [p]. Allophones, on the other hand, are predictable variants of a phoneme; they do not contrast as they are all variants of the same thing: [t], [ɾ], [ʔ], and [tʰ] are all /t/, not different things.

It's easy to find minimal pairs that distinguish most of the sounds we've learned so far. Look at the following series and list the phonemes you can identify from it:

fat, bat, sat, tat, mat, gnat, hat, cat, pat, rat, vat, that

To do this little exercise, you'll need to transcribe the words into the phonetic alphabet so that you can see the sounds, not the letters: the *gn* in *gnat*, for example, is pronounced as [n] so it is [næt].

From the list, we can see that /f/, /b/, /s/, /t/, /m/, /n/, /h/, /v/, /p/, /r/, and /ð/ are all separate phonemes in English. Once you have a minimal pair, that's it—the two sounds that distinguish the two words are two separate phonemes.

What about [w], [d], [θ], [g] and other consonants; are they separate phonemes? The only way to answer that is to look for minimal pairs that distinguish, say, [f] from [w], or [b] from [g], or [v] from [θ], and so on. Again, it's easy to find these pairs: *fall* [f] and *wall* [w], *burl* [b] and *girl* [g], *sink* /s/ and *think* /θ/. So, we now know that /f/ is a separate phoneme from /w/, /b/ is a separate phoneme from /g/, and /s/ is a separate phoneme from /θ/. We could go on listing minimal pairs and establish that the sounds we've studied so far represent different phonemes, except [ɾ] and [ʔ], which, as we've seen, are allophones of the phoneme /t/. The alveolar flap [ɾ] is unusual in that it can be an allophone of the phoneme /t/ or an allophone of the phoneme /d/, depending upon the word it is in. That is, /t/ and /d/ can both be pronounced as [ɾ], as in *letter* and *ladder*.

Much of this might seem obvious to you; after all, we know these are distinct sounds because we have letters for them, right? Well, letters can be misleading in any analysis of sounds, as we saw in Chapter 4. For example, what about [θ] and [ð]? They are both spelled the same, *th*. But are they allophones of the same phoneme, as the spelling might imply, or are they different phonemes? We can answer that by looking for minimal pairs. There are only a few in English, but we only need one: *thy* and *thigh*, for example. If you change the voiced [ð] of *thy* to the unvoiced [θ], you end up with a different word: *thigh*. That means that the two sounds are separate phonemes rather than allophones of the same phoneme, so we'll use slashes: /ð/ and /θ/.

How about two other sounds mentioned earlier, [n] and [ŋ]? Are they separate phonemes? We can easily find minimal pairs: *thin* and *thing* or *sin* and *sing*. The distinction between these two sounds makes a difference in meaning so they are separate phonemes: /n/ and /ŋ /.

So far, we've only looked at consonants in identifying phonemes; what about vowels? We can easily see that they are part of this system too by looking back at the chart of vowels in Chapter 4. Many of the sample words used there are minimal pairs: *beet, bit, bet, bait, bat, but, boot, boat*. We could add *bout* and *bite*. These minimal pairs show us that /i/, /ɪ/, /ɛ/, /e/, /æ/, /ə/, /u/, /o/, /aw/, and /ay/ are all separate phonemes. In fact, all the vowel sounds introduced in Chapter 4 are separate phonemes in English.

That doesn't mean that they are separate phonemes in other languages, however. The phonemes we've identified are in English; they are not necessarily phonemes in other languages. The system of phonemes as units of sound that distinguish meaning, and of allophones as variants of phonemes, holds true for all languages, but the details will vary from language to language. In English, /p/ and /b/ are separate phonemes; in Arabic they are allophones of the same phoneme. In English, *park* and *bark* are two separate words; in Arabic, if such words existed in that language, they would be heard as the same word, just as [sɪti] and [sɪɾi] are in English. In English, an aspirated [pʰ] and an unaspirated [p] are both allophones of the phoneme /p/; in Korean, they are separate phonemes. In Spanish, [b] and [v] are allophones of one phoneme, /v/; in English they are separate phonemes. In Turkish, [æ] and [E] are allophones of one phoneme; in English, they are separate phonemes. Which sounds are phonemes in any language is unpredictable, just as their distribution is unpredictable.

Allophonic variation: Complementary distribution and free variation

As we noted earlier, an allophone is a variant of a particular phoneme. One question usually arises here. Can we use allophones of a particular phoneme interchangeably, substituting one for the other at will? Well, in some ways, yes, we can. As we previously noted, substituting [t] for [ɾ] in the word *city* does not make it another word. It merely changes the word's pronunciation.

Although theoretically we can substitute one allophone for another, in actual speech we rarely do. We generally use one allophone in one phonetic environment and another in a different phonetic environment, so they occur in what is called **complementary distribution**. There are, in other words, rules for their use. To illustrate complementary distribution, let's do a simplified analysis of the allophonic distribution of /p/ and two of its allophones: an aspirated [pʰ] and an unaspirated one [p].

Complementary distribution relies on **phonetic environment,** so we need to examine the phonetic environment of each allophone. Phonetic environment refers to a sound's position in the word and its surrounding sounds. When allophones are in complementary distribution, there are rules or patterns that specify what type of phonetic environment we use them in. Let's go through the process of figuring out the rules for the distribution of the allophones of /p/, using the data in Table 5.1.

Even with this small amount of data, you can see that there is some regularity in their distribution. Although both appear before vowels, [pʰ] appears at the beginning of a word, while [p] appears after [s]. If we were to write a rule for the complementary distribution of these allophones based on these data, we would say that the phoneme /p/ is pronounced [pʰ] when

TABLE 5.1 Allophones of phoneme /p/

[pʰ]	[p]
pot [pʰat]	spot [spat]
pit [pʰɪt]	spit [spɪt]
pat [pʰæt]	spat [spæt]

appearing word initial and pronounced [p] following [s] and before a vowel. (With more data, we'd see that it is not word initial but syllable initial when the syllable is stressed. In the word *repair*, for example, /p/ is aspirated because it occurs syllable initial in a stressed syllable.) For /p/ allophones, then, the distribution is based on both their position in the word (word/syllable initial) and their neighboring sound /s/.

We can see the same regularity with allophones of /k/ and /t/, as shown in Table 5.2.

TABLE 5.2 Allophones of phonemes /k/ and /t/

[kʰ]	[k]
kit [kʰɪt]	skit [skɪt]
cool [kʰul]	school [skul]
kill [kʰɪl]	skill [skɪl]
kate [kʰet]	skate [sket]
[tʰ]	**[t]**
tack [tʰæk]	stack [stæk]
ton [tʰən]	stun [stən]
tamp [tʰæmp]	stamp [stæmp]
take [tʰek]	steak [stek]

From these data, we can see the following:

- /k/ is pronounced [kʰ] word/syllable initially and pronounced [k] following [s] and before a vowel
- /t/ is pronounced [tʰ] word/syllable initially and pronounced [t] following [s] and before a vowel.

To sum up, /t/ and /k/, like /p/, are aspirated when they are the first sound in a word or a stressed syllable, if not preceded by /s/.

We might ask ourselves if these regularities are the result of three separate rules or if there is some more basic rule. In other words, is there one rule for /p/, one for /t/, and one for /k/, or is there a single rule that applies to all of them? We might guess that there will be a more basic rule because the three phonemes involved are all voiceless stops. In fact, they are the only voiceless stops in English, and, as such, form a natural class. We can now rewrite our rule:

Voiceless stops are aspirated when they occur initially in a word or a stressed syllable and unaspirated when they occur directly after /s/.

Remember, a natural class is a group of sounds that share one or more features. It can be comprised of a large group of sounds; voiced consonants, for example, are one large natural class. Or it can be comprised of a small group of sounds; for example, nasals are a smaller natural class in English. What is important about natural classes is that the regularities governing our speech generally apply to natural classes rather than to individual sounds.

Let's look at two more examples of identifying phonemes and the distribution of their allophones, one in Hindi, a language spoken in India, and one in Italian. For each example, we want to know if the two sounds are separate phonemes or allophones of the same phoneme.

To determine that, we need to follow these basic steps:

1. Determine if they are phonemes. To do that, we first look for minimal pairs. If we find one, we know they are separate phonemes.
2. If we don't find one, we look at the distribution of the two sounds: What phonetic environments does each occur in? In other words, are they in complementary distribution? Look for natural classes here.
3. If they are in complementary distribution, we assume they are allophones of the same phoneme.
4. To complete the analysis, we must identify the rule that governs that distribution: Is it based on their position in a word or on their immediately surrounding sounds?

Let's start with Hindi, which has two voiced bilabial stops: [b] which is unaspirated and [bʰ] which is aspirated. Their use is illustrated in Table 5.3. Each Hindi word, written in IPA, is matched with its English meaning. Our question is this: Are these two separate phonemes or allophones of the same phoneme.

TABLE 5.3 Voiced bilabial stops in Hindi

[bitʃ]	middle	[abʰari]	grateful
[bar]	occasion	[bʰabʰi]	brother's wife
[baka]	crooked	[bʰar]	burden
[dʒeb]	pocket	[sebʰi]	all

1. First, we look for minimal pairs. And the data show us one: [bar] (which means occasion) and [bʰar] (which means burden). That means that the two sounds are separate phonemes, and we are finished with our analysis.

Let's look at some more data, this time from Italian. We know in English that /n/ and /ŋ/ are separate phonemes; we have lots of minimal pairs that indicate that. Is this the case for Italian too? Table 5.4 illustrates their use.

TABLE 5.4 [n] [ŋ] in Italian

[panda]	panda	[aŋke]	also
[dʒente]	people	[faŋgo]	mud
[nero]	black	[staŋko]	tired
[inalare]	inhale	[iŋkanto]	charm
[dʒenio]	genius	[veŋgo]	I go

1. There are no minimal pairs, so we need to move on to steps 2–4.
2. One way to determine the distribution is to put down all the sounds that immediately precede and follow each sound in question:

   e, i, a, [n] r, t, d, a, i
   e, i, a [ŋ] g, k

   As you do this, don't forget to note whether the sounds are word initial or word final; that makes it easier to see what's going on. We note that the sounds that precede our two sounds are the same. That means the complementary distribution is not based on the preceding phonetic environment. If we look at what sounds follow them, we see that there is a difference: only [g] and [k] follow [ŋ]; they never follow [n]. That means that [n] and [ŋ] are in complementary distribution: where we find [ŋ] (before [k] or [g]), we do not find [n] and vice versa.
3. We can now determine our rule. We know that that [g] and [k] are part of the same natural class, velar stops. Our rule then is that [ŋ] occurs before velar stops; [n] occurs elsewhere. If we have a rule like this, the two sounds are in complementary distribution and are allophones.
4. We have one more question to ask here: Which symbol do we use for the phoneme, [n] or [ŋ]? Since [n] occurs in more phonetic environments, we use that one, so the phoneme is /n/.

Free variation differs from complementary distribution; in free variation, the distribution of an allophone follows no pattern. Free variation is rarer than one might think. Most allophonic distribution is complementary, not free.

ARTICULATORY PROCESSES: CHANGING SOUNDS

Allophonic variation is not the only kind of phonological variation we find in spoken language. Some variation is the result of articulatory processes, which also have to do with the phonetic environment. I noted earlier, when we say *first* as the last word in a sentence, we tend to pronounce the [t], as in [aym fərst]. But when we say *first* in front of some other words, that [t] tends to disappear, so *first grade* becomes [fərsgred]. Why? To give another example, when we say *hand* alone or before a word that begins with a vowel as in *hand it to me*, we pronounce it [hænd]. But try putting *ball* after *hand*, as in *handball*, and what happens? If you're saying it in casual speech, you may pronounce it as [hænbal] or even [hæmbal]. Again, why? That's what we are about to find out. To do so, we need to examine the **articulatory processes** involved, the adjustments made during speech, of which we are, for the most part, unaware. **Ease of articulation** is often the impetus for these articulatory processes as they make it easier to pronounce words or word combinations.

Assimilation

One of the most common articulatory process in many languages is **assimilation**. Assimilation occurs when some feature (voice, nasalization, place of articulation) of one sound changes to become more like a neighboring sound.

Vowels often assimilate by becoming slightly **nasalized** when they occur before the nasal consonants [m, n, ŋ]. To hear this, say *back* [bæk]; then say *bank* [bæŋk]. You can probably hear the slight nasal quality in the vowel of *bank* that is not there in the vowel of *back*, although they are the same vowel /æ/. In [bæŋk], the vowel is assimilating to the nasal sound by becoming nasalized. We do this automatically and unconsciously, anticipating the nasal consonant by beginning the lowering of the velum during the production of the vowel sound. This nasalization occurs in English with all vowel sounds when preceding any of the natural class of nasals.

Consonants also undergo assimilation. They often assimilate to place, but they can assimilate to manner or voice. To illustrate assimilation to place, let's use the example of *bank* again. When we say *ban*, we pronounce the word as [bæn], using the alveolar [n] sound. When we say *bank*, however, the sound before [k] is not an [n], but an [ŋ]: [bæŋk]. Why? To understand, we need to look at place of articulation. The [n] sound is alveolar, said with the tongue on the alveolar ridge. The [k] sound, however, is velar, said at the velum in the back of the throat. And the [ŋ] sound? It too is a velar sound. When the "n" in *bank* is pronounced as a velar [ŋ], we see assimilation in action. The [n] sound assimilates to the velar [k] and becomes velar [ŋ] for ease of articulation. It's easier to say two velars in a row than an alveolar and a velar so we change the [n] to an [ŋ] when it occurs before a [k] or [g].

Nasal sounds, [m], [n] and [ŋ], are particularly apt to assimilate to sounds following them. We can see assimilation again in the following examples.

Fun [fən]   fungus [fəŋgəs]
in [ɪn]   input [ɪmpʊt]

The alveolar [n] assimilates to the following velar [g] in *fungus* and becomes [ŋ]. It assimilates to the following bilabial [p] in *input* and becomes [m], in both cases assimilating to place.

Dissimilation

Assimilation makes neighboring sounds more similar. Sometimes, however, sounds are too similar when put together and that makes them difficult to pronounce. Tongue twisters are based on this problem. *Sue sells seashells down by the seashore* is difficult to say because there are so many similar [s] type sounds, what are known as sibilants. The process of **dissimilation**, changing one sound to be less like a neighboring sound, occurs when two sounds are too much alike. It is rarer than assimilation but still common. For most speakers of English, for example, *fifths* becomes [fɪfts], changing the middle fricative, [θ], to a stop to break up the sequence of three fricatives.

Deletion

When several consonants occur together in what is known as a **consonant cluster**, especially if they are similar in some aspect, it is often difficult to pronounce them. Our response, unconscious of course, is to delete one or more of them. For example, we easily say *cup* [kəp], and we easily say *cupcake* [kəpkek], even though there are two consonants in a row in the middle of the word. But if we add *board* after *cup*, we do not usually get [kəpbord] but [kəbərd]. (Ignore the vowel change in *board* for now; it results from the common practice in

English of changing unstressed vowels to [ə].) Why do we delete the [p]? Because two bilabial stops are difficult to pronounce together. For ease of articulation, then, one is deleted. This process is known as **consonant cluster reduction**, a common one in English.

A similar thing happens with *friend* and *friendship*. *Friend* can be pronounced [frɛnd], especially if it precedes a vowel sound as in *a friend of mine*. When we add *ship* to it, however, the word becomes [frɛnʃIp}, and the [d] is deleted as part of consonant cluster reduction. Notice that of the three consonants, only the [d] can be deleted to remain English. We would not say [frɛdʃIp] nor [frɛndIp]; the rules of English phonology do not allow that.

Sometimes more than one of these processes occur in the pronunciation of a phrase or word. Let's look at the pronunciation of [hæmbal] for *handball*. How do we get there? Two processes occur: first deletion and then assimilation. In *handball*, we have three consonants in a row, something not so easy to pronounce. Try it and notice how you pause after the [d] before you say [b]. So, applying the articulatory process of deletion, the [d] is deleted and we get [hænbal], a perfectly normal pronunciation. Second, for some speakers, a further process is involved, assimilation, and [hænbal] becomes [hæmbal] when the [n] assimilates to bilabial [b] to become bilabial [m]. Assimilation follows deletion here; the [n] needs be next to the [b] to assimilate to it.

Epenthesis

Epenthesis, or insertion, is adding a sound to a word. The sound inserted in English is often the schwa, [ə]. We see epenthesis in action in such words as *realtor* when we pronounce it [rilətər] rather than [riltər] or in *athlete* when we pronounce it [æθəlit] rather than [æθlit]. We also see it used for special emphasis at times: saying *please* as puh-leeze [pɔːliz] instead of the more normal [pliz] to make our request more emphatic. Other sounds can be added too. *Warmth* is often pronounced [wɔrmpθ], adding a [p] after the [m]. Why might we do that? Think about place and voice here; [m] is a voiced bilabial; [θ] is a voiceless interdental. The [p] sound is a voiceless bilabial; it helps bridge the change from voiced to voiceless by having one feature of bilabial [m] and one of voiceless [θ].

Metathesis

Whereas epenthesis is adding a sound to a word to make it easier to say, **metathesis** reorders the sequence of sounds in a word for the same purpose. If you're a *Star Trek: The Next Generation* fan, you may remember the character Barcley [barkli], a bit of a nerd who was often referred to as *broccoli* [brakli] by the other members of the crew. That pronunciation of his name as a joke is an instance of metathesis, in this case switching the order of the [a] sound and the [r] sound. (For true fans, here's a case when the android Data was wrong. He quite rightly explained that saying [brakli] for *Barcley* was a type of metathesis, but he mispronounced the word, saying [metəθisIs] when it is usually pronounced [mətæθəsIs]). We can see examples of metathesis in other words. *Cavalry* is often pronounced [kælvəri] instead of [kævəlri], switching [l] and [ə]. *Irony* is often pronounced [ayərni] instead or [ayrəni], switching [r] and [ə].

These articulatory processes are part of our knowledge of our language. They are systematically applied, nearly always without any conscious attention on our part. Just like knowing which allophone of a phoneme to use in a particular phonetic environment, knowing how and when to use these articulatory processes marks us as native speakers of a language. In speaking a foreign language, it is often the small differences in pronunciation produced by these processes that mark us as non-native speakers.

PHONOLOGY IN YOUR WORLD: *ASK* VS *AKS* REVISITED

In the United States, the pronunciation of one word has been the focus of many negative stereotypes and much derision: the word *ask* and the pronunciation [æks]. Let's look at that phenomenon from the perspective of phonology and the articulatory processes we discussed to show how such derision is unwarranted.

While the pronunciation [æks] instead of [æsk] is sometimes perceived as an invention of African American speakers, it is shared by other English varieties, including one in Appalachia and several in Great Britain. This pronunciation is not a creation of these speakers, nor is it the result of laziness or ignorance, as some claim. It is a valid and correct pronunciation, just one that is different from that of Standard English. It is, in fact, a pronunciation descended from the Old English verb *acsian*, meaning *to ask*. In Old English, the word was variously spelled either *acsian* or *ascian;* in Middle English it was often spelled *axen* by Chaucer and other writers of the day. In fact, this variation in pronunciation and spelling were considered standard well into the 19th century. Although variation in its spelling has disappeared, variation in the pronunciation of this word continues today, with some varieties using [æks] and others [æsk].

The change from [æks] to [æsk] is an example of metathesis, a process many words went through as Old English became Middle and then Modern English. *Bird*, for example, used to be [brId] and *horse* used to be [hros]. The earlier pronunciations of *bird* and *horse* did not survive, but that of [æks] did, and because it is associated with oppressed groups, specifically African Americans, it is seen as wrong. Phonology may seem a long way from issues of social justice, but knowing the history of words and the facts about articulatory processes such as metathesis can perhaps help us more easily counter critics of [æks] and those who insist it is incorrect. And countering such critics may just move us a small step forward in reducing discrimination based on race.

MORPHOPHONOLOGY

Morphophonology sounds daunting, but it's not as difficult to understand as it sounds. Morphophonology, as you might guess, is an area of linguistics that investigates the interaction of morphology and phonology. We saw earlier that phonological analysis can help us understand how sounds are pronounced in casual speech. It can also help us understand variants in morphemes, what are known as **allomorphs**. That is, one morpheme may not always be pronounced the same way.

Many allomorphs are in complementary distribution; that is, there is a pattern for their use. This pattern is based on phonological rules, just like patterns of use for allophones: phonetic environments, natural classes, and articulatory processes all play key roles just as they do in phonological analysis.

We can use the past tense morpheme in English as an example for morphophonological analysis. In Chapter 3, we indicated the past tense morpheme as {ed}. That {ed} is pronounced in three different ways: [d], [t], or [Id], three separate allomorphs of the morpheme {ed}. Their

TABLE 5.5 Allomorphs of past tense morpheme in English

Words that add [t] as the past tense morpheme		Words that add [d] as the past tense morpheme	
miss–missed	[mɪst]	use–used	[yuzd]
talk–talked	[tɔkt]	follow–followed	[falod]
push–pushed	[pʊʃt]	nab–nabbed	[næbd]
cap–capped	[kæpt]	live–lived	[lɪvd]
lurch–lurched	[lərtʃt]	peg–pegged	[pegd]
laugh–laughed	[læft]	weigh–weighed	[wed]
look–looked	[lʊkt]	mime–mimed	[maymd]
rap–rapped	[ræpt]	lie–lied	[layd]

use is based on the phonetic environment they occur in, and there is a phonological rule that governs their use.

Table 5.5 lists verbs that add [t] and [d] as the past tense morpheme.

Following the steps set out with the Italian problem, we need to examine the phonetic environment. Here it is the final sound of each word that is important, so we list the final sound of each word. Doing so, we can determine what those sounds that add [t] have in common and what those that add [d] have in common.

[t] is used following [s, k, ʃ, p, tʃ, f]
[d] is used following [z, o, b, v, g, e, m, ay]

We need to identify natural classes here to determine the rule. Doing so, we see that [t] is used following unvoiced consonants and [d] is used following voiced consonants and vowels. We have thus determined the rules for the distribution of these two allomorphs. You've done your first bit of morphophonological analysis.

Let's go a bit further as we're not quite done. We still need to analyze words like *need* and *omit*. They add neither [t] nor [d] as the past tense morpheme; instead, they add [Id]. What's going on here? Some extra data will help us figure this out.

Words like those that follow add [Id] as the past tense morpheme:

need–needed	[nidId]
want–wanted	[wantId]
repeat–repeated	[ripitId]
plead–pleaded	[plidId]
omit–omitted	[omItId]

It seems that we need to add another part to our rule: when the final consonant is an alveolar stop ([t] or [d]), the past tense morpheme is pronounced as [Id].

The result of our morphophonological analysis looks like this: the past tense morpheme {ed} becomes

[t] following unvoiced consonants
[d] following voiced consonants and vowels
[Id] following alveolar stops /t/ or /d/.

The addition of [I] before [t] and [d] is a form of epenthesis. If we did not insert a sound, it would be hard, for example, to distinguish the present tense of need [nid] from the past tense [nidd]. And using [t] or [d] in the phonetic environments we noted earlier is a form of assimilation, in this case, assimilation to voice. Morphophonological rules, as we can see, follow general phonological rules.

L1 ACQUISITION IN FOCUS: LEARNING PHONEMES AND MORE

In Chapter 3, we noted that the first year of a hearing child's life is in some ways devoted to figuring out the sounds of their language. What they are really learning, of course, are the phonemes. They generally finish this task by around one year of age. In addition to mastering the phonemes, a child acquiring a spoken language must also acquire its phonological patterns, figuring out that those phonemes are pronounced differently in different phonetic environments, for example. That is, they need to learn the allophones of each phoneme and their distribution. Since that distribution is based on natural classes, they must figure those out as well. And they must learn the articulatory processes common for their language.

That's a tricky task, but children finish it successfully. In addition to figuring out allophones, they quickly learn that certain morphemes have allomorphs. They figure out, for example, that the [s] sound, the [z] sound, and the [Iz] sound are allomorphs of the plural {s} morpheme. It still takes them a while to figure out exactly when to apply which allomorph, but less time than you would imagine.

In an interesting experiment, Berko (1958) found that children figure out which plural allomorph to use with which word, sometimes as early as 2 years of age. In this study, children were shown an imaginary creature called a *wug* and asked what they would say if there were two of them. Most children correctly added the [s] allomorph. When presented with a *blick*, another imaginary creature, and asked about two of them, they correctly added the [z] allomorph. In Exploration 2 at the end of this chapter, you'll get an opportunity to figure out the rule English-speaking children have already unconsciously figured out by the time they're two or so.

CHAPTER SUMMARY

- In this chapter we've examined the systematic structuring of sounds. All spoken languages are made up of phonemes. Phonemes are the minimal units of sound that distinguish meaning; their various phonetic representations are allophones.
- Phonemes can be identified with minimal pairs, two words that differ by only one sound.
- Allophones are always of a particular phoneme. Most occur in complementary distribution; that is, their use is patterned, determined by the phonetic environment in which they occur.
- Speakers make use of various articulatory processes as they speak, usually for ease of articulation. Processes common in English include assimilation, dissimilation, deletion, epenthesis (insertion), and metathesis.

- Allomorphs, phonetic variants of morphemes, also often occur in complementary distribution. This distribution is based on phonological factors.
- Despite the disparagement of the pronunciation of [æks], that pronunciation is very old in English. The belief that [æks] is a mispronunciation of *ask* is erroneous and often discriminatory.
- Children learn the phonological system of their spoken language, not only the individual sounds but also how those sounds contrast and work together—the phonemes, allophones, and articulatory processes of their language.

KEY TERMS

phoneme	articulatory processes
allophone	assimilation
phonetic level	dissimilation
phonemic level	deletion
minimal pairs	epenthesis
contrastive distribution	metathesis
allophonic variation	consonant cluster reduction
complementary distribution	morphophonology
phonetic environment	allomorphs
free variation	

EXPLORATIONS

A note about "correct" pronunciation

As you do these phonology exercises, keep in mind that we are doing descriptive linguistics. We want to describe what people actually do, so we must recognize that pronunciation of a word can vary a great deal, depending on the phonetic environment and the casualness of the speech. Through our descriptions we can also recognize that this variation is not arbitrary or idiosyncratic; it is, like all language use, rule governed. These rules are not imposed on us by some authority; they are part of the structure of our language.

Some of us will be tempted to ask, "But what is the correct pronunciation?" We may feel, for example, that saying [aviəs] instead of [abviəs] for the word *obvious* is simply a mispronunciation or the result of lazy, careless speech. Such is not the case. There is an articulatory process we apply to *obvious*, deletion for consonant cluster reduction. When we say *obvious* in casual speech, we pronounce it differently than we do in formal speech, but that pronunciation is just as rule governed as its pronunciation in more formal speech. This does not mean that any pronunciation of any word is the result of phonological rules and thus common in English. There are no rules, for example, that would lead us to pronounce *obvious* as [obiəs].

Some of you may not pronounce words in quite the same way as indicated in these explorations. In all of these explorations, the data given is based on speech patterns of many people, so the rules we are looking for are indeed part of the language, even if one does not apply specifically to you.

Exploration 1: Allophonic variation: Dialects in English

In some dialects of English, the phoneme /ay/ has two allophones: [ay] and [əy]. Using the data in Table 5.6, state the phonetic environment in which each allophone is used.

TABLE 5.6 Allophones of /ay/—[ay] and [əy]

[əy] is used in the following	[ay] is used in the following	
light	lied	fly
pipe	dies	sigh
dice	bribe	tie
life	lives	buy
mike	file	
lithe*	mime	
	sign	

List all **sounds** preceding and following the vowel sounds in question.

_____ [əy] _____
_____ [ay] _____

Where should you be looking—at the sounds before or after the allophones? How do you know?

1. What natural classes do you see in each group?
2. State the rule for the distribution of these allophones in terms of natural classes. In other words, what phonetic environments does each allophone occur in?

    *   [əy] occurs _____
    *   [ay] occurs _____

*Note: lithe is pronounced [ləyθ] not [ləyð]. Why is it important to know this?

Exploration 2: Morphophonological analysis: Plurals in English

As noted earlier, there are three allomorphs for the plural morpheme {s}: [s], [z], and [ɪz]*. Using the data in Table 5.7, determine the phonological rule for the pronunciation of the plural morpheme {s}. You will first need to transcribe each word into IPA.

TABLE 5.7 Plural allomorphs in English

[s] is used with	[z] is used with		[ɪz] is used with
cat	dog	swallow	church
pick	king	play	bus
nap	boil	tie	lash
myth	litter	knee	buzz
lot	nib		judge
	limb		
	roar		

State the phonological rule for our use of the allomorphs of plural {s}:

[s] occurs _____

[z] occurs _____

[ɪz] occurs _____

* [əz] often occurs as a variant of [ɪz]. In your natural speech, you may use [əz] or you may use [ɪz]; the rule is the same for both.

Note: In order to do this exercise, you need to know that there is a natural class in English known as **sibilants**. This class includes most of the sounds that are produced with friction, that is, /s/, /z/, /ʃ/, /ʒ/, /tʃ/, and /dʒ/ (the alveolar and alveopalatal fricatives and affricates).

Exploration 3: Is that a pin or a pen?

In some dialects in the United States, there are two allophones of the phoneme /ɛ/—[ɪ] and [ɛ]. Using the data from Table 5.8, determine the phonological rule for when [ɪ] is used and when [ɛ] is used.

TABLE 5.8 Allophones of /ɛ/—[ɪ] and [ɛ]

[ɪ] is used in the following words	[ɛ] is used in the following words
pen	pet
lend	mesh
strength	ebb
(the <n> is said [ŋ] here)	
hem	heck
men	led
end	stretch

State the phonological rule for the distribution of these two allophones:

[ɪ] is used _____

[ɛ] is used _____

Exploration 4: Morphophonological analysis: Put it in there.

In English we have a morpheme, {in}, a prefix that makes words negative. It has three different allomorphs: [ɪn], [ɪm], and [ɪŋ]. The rules for the distribution of these allomorphs are phonological, so you will need to change the words into IPA. Using the data in Table 5.9, determine what those rules are.

TABLE 5.9 Allomorphs of {in}—[ɪn], [ɪm], and [ɪŋ]

[ɪn] is used with the following words	[ɪm] is used with the following words	[ɪŋ] is used with the following words
surmountable	partial	complete
animate	practical	consistent
ordinate	balance	glorious
eligible	material	considerate
dignity	perceptible	

TABLE 5.9 Continued

[ɪn] is used with the following words	[ɪm] is used with the following words	[ɪŋ] is used with the following words
voluntary		
terminable		
famous		

State the rule for when each allomorph is used.

[ɪn] is used before _____

[ɪm] is used before _____

[ɪŋ] is used before _____

What articulatory process can account for why {ɪn} becomes [ɪm] and [ɪŋ]?

Exploration 5: Identify the articulatory process involved in the following:

1. *Strength* is sometimes pronounced not [streŋθ] but [strɛnθ]. (Ignore the vowel sound change.) What's going on with the /ŋ/ change?
2. *Kindness* often becomes not [kayndnɛs] but [kaynɛs]. What's going on?
3. *Pumpkin* is pronounced in one of three ways:
   - [pəmpkɪn] in very formal, careful pronunciation
   - [pəmkɪn] in somewhat casual settings
   - [pəŋkɪn] for some in very casual settings.

   What's going on? Explain how we get to the final pronunciation through articulatory processes.
4) *Months* is regularly pronounced [məns]. What's going on?
5) *Have* is pronounced [hæv] in the phrase *I'll have a soda*, but as [hæf] in the phrase *He'll have to go*. What's going on?
6) *Won't you* is often pronounced as [wontʃyu]. What's going on?
7) *Mystery* is often pronounced as [mistri] rather than [mistəri]. What's going on?
8) *Handbag* is often pronounced [hæmbæg]. What's going on? Note: remember there may be more than one articulatory process involved.

Exploration 6: Spanish: Phonemes or allophones?

Spanish has two sounds, [s] and [z]. Those sounds happen to be phonemes in English. Our question here is this: Are these two sounds phonemes in Spanish or are they allophones of one phoneme? Use the data in Table 5.10 (adapted from Yule, 2017 and Justice, 2004) to answer this question.

TABLE 5.10 Spanish [s] [z]

[bezbal]	baseball	[dezde]	since
[peskado]	fish	[mizmo]	same
[vamos]	we go	[casa]	house
[sistema]	system	[izla]	island
[razgado]	torn	[resto]	rest
[hablas]	you speak	[riezgo]	risk

TABLE 5.10 Continued

| [espalda] | back | [sinko] | five |
| [dostapetes] | two rugs | [dozðeðos] | two fingers |

1. Identify any minimal pairs in the data. What does that tell you?
2. If there are no minimal pairs, determine whether [s] and [z] occur in complementary distribution. If they do, what phonetic environments does each occur in? State the rule for their distribution, referring to natural classes.
3. Given what you found, are [s] and [z] phonemes or allophones of the same phoneme? If they are allophones, how would you write the phoneme: /z/ or /s/? Why?

FURTHER READING

Davenport, M., & Hannahs, S. (2013). *Introducing phonetics and phonology* (3rd ed.). Routledge.
McMahon, A. (2002). *An introduction to English phonology.* Edinburgh University Press.

REFERENCES

Berko, J. (1958). The child's learning of English morphology. *Word, 14,* 150–177.
Justice, P. (2004). *Relevant linguistics.* Center for the Study of Language and Information Publications.
Yule, G. (2017). *The study of language.* Cambridge University Press.

CHAPTER 6

Syntax

Ordering words, making sentences

....

First glance

How do we put sentences together?

Surface structure and deep structure

Phrase structure rules and syntactic operations

Recursion

Structural ambiguity, synonymity, and relationships

Embedded sentences

Universal grammar

Do bird songs have syntax?

Acquiring syntax

INTRODUCTION

Syntax is about structure, specifically the structure of sentences. We saw in our study of morphology that we can analyze words structurally, looking at their linear structure, the order of morphemes (prefixes, suffixes, stems), and at their hierarchical structure, in which some morphemes are constituents of other morphemes. As we analyze sentences—the units that make them up and the rules for putting those units together—we'll see that these two levels of structure are even more important. As you no doubt remember, we drew trees to illustrate this hierarchical structure in words; we'll do the same with the hierarchical structure of sentences.

SYNTAX AND GRAMMAR

Before we move on to syntax proper, it might be helpful to differentiate syntax and grammar. When non-linguists talk about sentence structure, they often call it grammar and refer to things like subject–verb agreement or commas, dangling modifiers, or semi-colons. Syntax and grammar are related, of course, but for our purposes here, we need to differentiate them

DOI: 10.4324/9780429269059-6

clearly. Here we are not concerned with the aforementioned issues, which are mostly about stylistic preferences. Instead, we will be doing descriptive analysis, examining sentences to describe the way they are put together.

As we noted in Chapter 2, in linguistics grammar refers to a system of rules that governs how we put sounds or primes together to form words, put words together to form phrases, and put phrases together to form sentences. It is our knowledge of this system that allows us to speak, write, or sign. Syntax is the branch of linguistics that analyzes the structures and rules that allow for combining words into phrases and phrases into sentences to create meaningful utterances.

Syntactic theory seeks to describe the rules that allow us to construct and understand novel phrases and sentences, to create an infinite number of sentences, and to recognize grammatical and ungrammatical sentences in our language (that is, recognize any string of words as either being English sentences or not). It investigates our internal grammatical knowledge about sentences and phrases, about their structure, about the relationships of parts of a sentence to one another, and about the relationships of sentences to one another both in terms of meaning and structure.

One key to syntactic analysis is the idea of **generativity**. That is, we need a limited set of structures and a limited set of rules for putting those structures together, from which we can generate an infinite number of sentences. To that end, we need a way of looking at sentence structure that goes beyond the traditional grammar rules you may have learned in school. I'll summarize this approach now and then explain it in more detail.

We can analyze the structure of sentences in two ways. We can examine what is called their surface structure, the approach generally used in traditional grammar: here's the subject, here's the predicate, here's a direct object, here's an indirect object. We can also examine their deep structure, paying attention to how parts of a sentence relate to one another. In our approach, we will examine both the surface and deep structures of sentences, not only differentiating them but also showing how they are related.

Surface or linear structure is what we say or sign or write; it's called linear because our words come out like beads on a string, one after the other. Because it's impossible to say or sign all the words in a sentence at once, they have to be put together one after the other. The linear structure refers to those beads on a string and what order they are put in.

Deep structure offers us a different perspective on the structure of sentences, one that takes into account the hierarchical nature of that structure. We know from previous chapters that when we combine sounds, we get morphemes; when we combine morphemes, we get words. And when we combine words, do we get sentences? Well, yes and no. The next level up from words is not sentences, but phrases; and it is phrases, or **constituents**, that we combine to get meaningful sentences, following the syntactic rules of whatever language we are using. The key here is that those phrases are arranged hierarchically in the deep structure, as we will see. That is, some constituents contain other constituents within them.

Every sentence, then, has two structures simultaneously: a linear or surface structure (what we say or sign, word after word), and a deep structure that is made up of constituent phrases arranged hierarchically.

For any sentence, we can analyze its surface structure or its deep structure. We'll start with a somewhat simplified example to illustrate the two levels:

1. *The lazy dog sat in the shade under a tree.*

On the surface structure level, that sentence is made up of ten words. On the deep structure level, it is made up of four phrases that in turn contain those ten words:

2. *The lazy dog*
3. *In the shade*
4. *Under a tree*
5. *Sat in the shade under a tree.*

Although each phrase is made up of individual words, from a syntactic perspective, it is phrases or constituents, not individual words, that form the basic units of sentences. That's why another word for deep structure is **constituent structure**.

You'll notice that the last phrase contains two other phrases: *in the shade* and *under a tree*. That's because phrase 5 contains phrases 3 and 4 as part of it. That's an example of hierarchical structure where some constituents contain other constituents.

What we will examine in this chapter is that constituent, hierarchical structure: what rules create it and how it is related to the linear structure. We'll start with how that deep structure is created.

CONSTITUENTS OF A SENTENCE

To proceed with this analysis, we should clarify what the constituents of a sentence are and how they can be put together. Constituents are the units of a sentence put together in specific ways to create meaning. **Noun phrases (NP)** and **verb phrases (VP)** are the two constituents that make up every sentence. Some sentences also include other types of constituents, prepositional phrases (PP), for example.

Each phrase has a **head**, which is a particular lexical category, for example, a noun, a verb, a preposition, an adjective, or an adverb. In addition, there are sets of rules and a set of operations for combining words into phrases and phrases into sentences. These phrase structure rules create the deep structure of the sentence. **Syntactic operations**, discussed later, in turn derive the surface structure from that deep structure.

PHRASE STRUCTURE RULES

Phrase structure rules specify how sentences are put together; that is, they specify their constituent structure. To help us visualize this structure, we draw **tree diagrams** (or **trees**), a tool for illustrating the deep structure of a sentence.

Let's start with the phrase structure rule that specifies what a sentence is. This one will probably sound familiar: a sentence consists of an NP and a VP, what you may know as a subject and a predicate. We can state this rule succinctly:

S – NP VP

The dash has a specific meaning in syntax: whatever appears to the left of the dash consists of or can be rewritten as the elements that follow the dash. To put that rule into normal English, we'd say: a sentence consists of an NP and a VP.

That's true, even if the VP consists of only one word, a verb such as *sighed*, and the NP also consists of only one word, such as *John*. For a sentence, like *John sighed*, with only two constituents, the analysis is very simple. Of course, most sentences are a bit longer and more complex, so for those sentences we'll need to further specify what constitutes an NP and a VP.

As a way of beginning our discussion of NPs and VPs, let's look at the types of phrases we identified in *the lazy dog* sentence earlier.

- *the lazy dog*—an NP
- *in the shade*—a PP
- *under the tree*—also a PP
- *sat in the shade under the tree*—a VP containing two PPs

You might be asking about now, What's the difference between a noun and an NP or a verb and a VP? Here the distinction is between two different types of categories: a syntactic category and a lexical category. **Lexical categories** are terms we apply to individual words to identify their role within a phrase: noun (N), verb (V), preposition (prep), adjective (adj), or adverb (adv)—what you may know as parts of speech. **Syntactic categories** are terms we apply to types of constituents in a sentence: NP is a syntactic category that includes a noun; VP is a syntactic category that includes a verb. Both may include other syntactic categories, as we'll see later. Together they function syntactically as the constituents of a sentence.

How do we know whether a group of words is a constituent? There are a few tests we can use.

- First, we can use a **proform**: any word that substitutes for an entire phrase is a proform. If we wanted to use a pronoun, which is one type of proform, to refer to our lazy dog, we'd say *she*. That *she* would substitute for *the lazy dog*, the entire NP, not just for *dog* or *the dog*. The proform substituting for the entire phrase is evidence that *the lazy dog* is a constituent phrase. We can use proforms with verb phrases too: *The lazy dog sat under the tree and so did the cat.* That *did* is a proform. It substitutes for the entire VP, *sat in the shade under the tree*, not just the verb *sat*, because we wouldn't say, *and so did the cat under the tree in the shade.*
- Another test relies on the fact that if we move a phrase to a different position within a sentence, we must move the entire phrase, not just one or two of its words. For example, we could say, *In the shade under the tree, the lazy dog sat* but not *In the, the lazy dog sat shade under the tree.* The latter is simply not English.
- Still another test relies on asking questions. If we ask where the dog sat, we'd answer with an entire phrase, either *in the shade* or *under the tree* or *in the shade under the tree*, but not just *shade* or *tree*.

These tests are good tests for determining if a particular group of words is a constituent within a sentence.

Let's continue our analysis by describing the constituents that make up a sentence as well as the rules for putting those constituents together.

Noun phrases

To examine the noun phrases in our lazy dog sentence, we will write our first phrase structure rule:

NP – (det) (adj) N

Let's put that equation into normal English: NP consists of a determiner (det), in this case *the*; an adjective phrase (AdjP), in this case, *lazy*, and an N, in this case, *dog*. We'll look at (det) and (AdjP) in more detail later.

Our NP rule defines what must be present for the phrase to be considered an NP. The parentheses mean that whatever category is written inside them is optional. It can either be present or not and can appear more than once. In our rule, for example, the parentheses mean that you can have an adjective (or more than one adjective) but having an adjective in a noun phrase isn't required.

Our NP rule, then, tells us that every NP must have a noun (the head word in a noun phrase) and can have a determiner and an adjective or adjectives.

There's one other lexical category that can be part of an NP: a prepositional phrase or PP. We might say, for example, *The lazy dog with brown spots*. That NP now includes a PP, *with brown spots*. We must, then, expand our NP rule by adding PP as a possible optional unit.

NP – (det) (AdjP) N (PP)

That is, an NP can consist of an optional det, an optional AdjP, and an N, as well as an optional PP (in this case, *with brown spots*). We put the PP in parentheses to indicate that an NP may include a PP or it may not. We put the PP after the N because, in English, PPs generally occur after the N in an NP.

One point about adjectives: we've labeled them as **adjective phrases** (**AdjP**) in our rule. That's because they can be more than one word: *very tall, a bit hot, rather silly*. Adjective phrases consist of adjectives and optional **degree words** like *very, rather, somewhat, too,* labelled (deg) in our rules. AdjPs must have an adjective and can have an optional degree word. We can write the rule for AdjP as follows:

AdjP – (deg) Adjective

Let's come back to that **determiner**, the **det** in our rule. A determiner can be any one of several different types: articles (*a, an, the*); demonstratives (*this, that, these, those*); possessive pronouns (*my, your, her, his, its, our, their*); or count words like *many, some, several, a few*. Try substituting one of those words in the sentence and you'll see that they take the place of the determiner *the*. Generally, you don't have two determiners before a noun in English, though you do in some other languages.

One other point about determiners. A simple look around shows us that not all NPs consist of a determiner and an N. Instead of *the lazy dog*, for example, I might say *Jasmine* or *she*. And if I'm talking about the species in general, I would probably say just *dogs*. *Jasmine* and *she* and *dogs* are still NPs. So, an NP can be a phrase specified by our rule, or it can just consist of a proper noun (*Jasmine*) or a pronoun (*she*). With proper nouns and pronouns, we do not use determiners or adjectives or PPs. And we can omit the determiner when the N is plural if we mean dogs in general rather than a specific group of dogs: *Dogs are sweet animals* vs *Those dogs are sweet animals*.

Here are our final phrase structure rules for NPs:

NP – (det) (AdjP) N (PP)
NP – PropN
NP – Pro

where **PropN** stands for proper noun (a name) and **Pro** stands for pronoun (*she, it, he, they*, etc.).

You can read these three rules together as a single definition: a noun phrase may be formed in one of three ways. It can consist of a determiner, a noun, an optional adjective, and an optional prepositional phrase; it can consist of a proper noun; or it can consist of a pronoun.

Prepositional phrases

Prepositional phrases (**PPs**) are phrases such as *in the shade* and *under the tree*. (If you're not sure what prepositions are, check the online resources, where you'll find them explained along with a list of common English prepositions.) We can write the rule for PPs as follows:

PP – Prep NP

In other words, PPs must consist of a preposition (Prep) and an NP. We've already seen what an NP consists of, so there is no need to rewrite that part here. The phrase structure rule for NPs applies to any NP, including those in a PP.

Prepositional phrases are extremely common in English, more so than in some other languages: *in the morning, over the hill, around the house, for our sakes, under the stairs, behind the closet, after the war, before the flood, around the corner*—all are PPs and thus consist of a Prep and an NP. They can appear in many different places in a sentence: at the beginning, middle, or end; they can occur in NPs or in VPs. They are very handy little structures for getting a lot of information into a sentence.

We can illustrate the NP and PP rules with tree diagrams, as in Figure 6.1 and Figure 6.2.

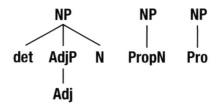

FIGURE 6.1 Phrase structure rules for NPs

FIGURE 6.2 Phrase structure rule for PPs

Verb phrases

The verb phrase is often the most complex part of a sentence because a VP can contain several elements. Let's start with a simple sentence: *The dog sat.* Here the VP consists of just a verb (V), what you may have been taught as being the predicate of a sentence. All VPs must consist of at least one verb. We can write the rule like this: **VP – V**. For this sentence, then, we have a VP that consists of a V (*sat*). (The NP, of course, consists of a det and an N, *the dog*.)

Most sentences are not so simple, however. If we use the VP from our lazy dog sentence, *sat in the shade under the tree*, we recognize that a VP can also have one or more PPs. If we added a word such as *quietly* to our sentence, we'd have the following sentence: *The dog sat quietly in the shade under the tree*, and we would know that a VP can also contain an adverb phrase, AdvP, in this case *quietly*. We'll come back to that AdvP later. So, our rule for a VP now looks like this:

VP – V (PP) (AdvP)

Here's how you would read this rule: A VP must consist of a V and can also consist of one or more PPs or AdvPs.

If we examine a different sentence, we learn that one more element can also be present in a VP. *The cow ate the corn* will illustrate our purpose. Here our VP consists of a verb, *ate*, and an NP, *the corn*. A VP, then, can contain an NP as well as a PP and an AdvP.

In fact, a VP can consist of all those constituents, as the following sentences show:

- *The cow ate the corn in the field hungrily*. (Here the VP consists of a V, an NP, a PP, and an AdvP.)
- *The cow gave the farmer a kiss*. (Here the VP consists of two NPs.)
- *The cow kissed the farmer sweetly on the cheek*. (Here the VP consists of an NP, an AdvP, and a PP.)

We can summarize our examples with this phrase structure rule:

VP – V (NP) (PP) (AdvP)

To express that in plain English, a VP must contain a V and may also contain an NP, a PP, and/ or an AdvP, each of which may occur more than once.

We know what NP and PP are already, but **AdvP** is new. We use **adverb phrase** because, like an AdjP, an adverb phrase can consist of a degree word as well as an adverb: *too quickly*, *rather slowly*, *very happily*, all of which consist of an adverb and an optional degree word: *too*, *rather*, *slowly* (there are many others). The rule then is as follows:

AdvP – (deg) Adv

We can illustrate the rule for VP with a tree diagram as in Figure 6.3.

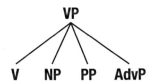

FIGURE 6.3 Phrase structure rule for VPs

Tree diagrams

As we've discussed, phrase structure rules generate the deep structure of all sentences. What follows is the set of phrase structure rules:

S – NP VP
NP – (det) N (AdjP) (PP) (S)
NP – Prop N
NP – Pro
VP – V (AdvP) (NP) (PP) (S)
PP – Prep NP
AdjP – (deg) Adjective
AdvP – (deg) Adverb

You may have noticed that (**S**) in both the NP and the VP. It simply indicates that we can embed sentences into other sentences by putting them in either the NP or the VP. We'll discuss embedded sentences in more detail later.

Using our phrase structure rules, we can draw tree diagrams to help us visualize the deep structure of sentences. And in illustrating that deep structure with a tree diagram, we can identify the hierarchical nature of that deep structure.

We can use the following sentence to illustrate how to draw a tree diagram:

The dish eloped with the spoon.

In drawing trees, we always start with S – NP VP. For our sample sentence, we would draw the tree illustrated in Figure 6.4.

Then we further specify the NP and the VP and, if necessary, do further analysis with the PP or other phrases. Thus, our expanded tree diagram would look like Figure 6.5.

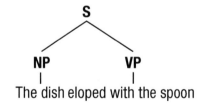

FIGURE 6.4 First step for tree diagram for The dish eloped with the spoon

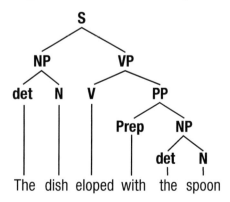

FIGURE 6.5 Final tree diagram for The dish eloped with the spoon

This diagram reveals how the entire sentence is structured, including which elements are part of the NP (a det and an N) and which are part of the VP (a V and a PP).

In all sentences, there is an NP and a VP that are directly under an S, meaning that they are **immediate constituents** of the top S node. In this case, the NP, *the dish*, is directly under the S, so it is an immediate constituent of S; in traditional grammar, this would be called the subject. The VP, *eloped with the spoon*, is also directly under the S, so it is an immediate constituent of S as well; in traditional grammar, this would be called the predicate.

Not all NPs are immediate constituents of the S, however. Some NPs are part of the VP or part of a PP, which is then part of a VP or an NP. In Figure 6.5, the NP, *the spoon*, is part of the PP, which itself is part of the VP.

The four sentences that follow are diagrammed to further illustrate the phrase structure rules. You might try doing them yourself first if you like. Start with S – NP VP and go from there. Remember, there can be more than one PP or NP in a VP. Notice how many places NPs show up in our trees.

Figure 6.6 shows the tree diagram for sentence 1, and Figure 6.7 shows the tree diagram for sentence 2.

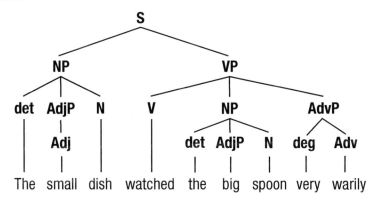

FIGURE 6.6 Tree diagram for sentence 1

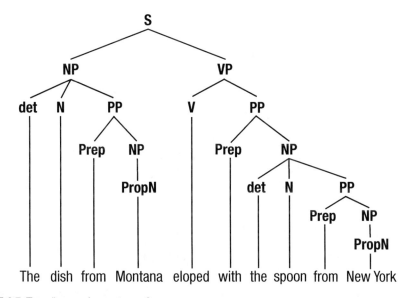

FIGURE 6.7 Tree diagram for sentence 2

1. *The small dish watched the big spoon very warily.*
2. *The dish from Montana eloped with the spoon from New York.*

Notice the two PPs here. One is part of the NP *the dish*. The other is part of the VP, but it does not come directly off the VP. That is because it does not modify or belong to the VP directly. It modifies and belongs to the NP, *the spoon*. It is thus a part of that NP, and that NP in turn is part of the VP.

Figure 6.8 shows the tree diagram for sentence 3.

3. *The dish saw the spoon through the fence.*

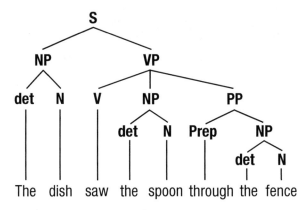

FIGURE 6.8 Tree diagram for sentence 3

Note that the PP here, *through the fence* is part of the VP directly, not part of the NP *the spoon*. That's because the seeing takes place through the fence; the spoon is not through the fence the way it is from New York in the previous sentence.

Figure 6.9 shows the tree diagram for sentence 4.

4. *The dish gave the spoon a book.*

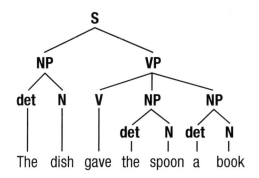

FIGURE 6.9 Tree diagram for sentence 4

In this sentence, there are two NPs in the VP, what in traditional grammar are called the direct object (a book) and indirect object (the spoon).

From these sentences, we can see in how many different places NPs can appear: directly under the S, in the VP, or in a PP that is part of the VP or part of an NP.

RECURSION

Using tree diagrams to illustrate a sentence's deep structure also enables us to illustrate a principle called **recursion**, which permits phrase structure rules to produce phrases of infinite length by embedding one phrase within another of the same type. This crucial property of all languages allows identical elements in a sentence to be used repeatedly. To put it another way, it allows us to embed phrases within phrases over and over. For example:

The boy played on the swing in the yard near the campus of the school for wayward boys.

Here PPs are involved in the recursion, one within the other, as shown in Figure 6.10.

It is not just parts of a sentence that can occur over and over; entire sentences can also be embedded in other sentences ad infinitum. The children's rhyme about the house that Jack built relies on embedding one sentence within another sentence within yet another sentence, connecting them all with *that*.

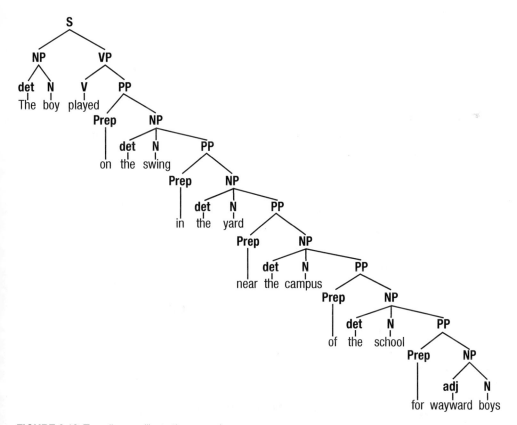

FIGURE 6.10 Tree diagram illustrating recursion

This is the cow that kicked the cat that chased the rat that ate the corn that lay in the house that Jack built.

There are five sentences embedded in the main sentence *This is the cow*:

1. *The cow kicked the cat.*
2. *The cat chased the rat.*
3. *The rat ate the corn.*
4. *The corn lay in the house.*
5. *Jack built the house.*

STRUCTURAL AMBIGUITY

Earlier we noted that any syntactic theory needs to be able to account for one sentence having two or more meanings. Let's examine now how that happens. How does our syntactic theory help us account for the ambiguity around Hermione, the wizard, and the tower in this sentence?

Hermione watched the wizard from the tower.

The ambiguity in this sentence does not lie in any one word; the meaning of each word is clear. It is not **lexical ambiguity** that is at issue here. Lexical ambiguity refers to ambiguity that is caused by one word having more than one possible meaning—*tie* or *bank*, for example. For this sentence, what is at issue is not lexical ambiguity but **structural ambiguity**. That is, the ambiguity lies in the relationships among the parts of the sentence: the PP *from the tower* could belong to the NP the wizard (he's from the tower), or it could belong to the VP (the watching is being done from the tower). Where that PP belongs is the crux of the ambiguity.

Because there are two possible relationships among *watch*, *wizard*, and *tower*, there must be two deep structures, each one having a different meaning that reflects one of those relationships. The two deep structures associated with those two different meanings are illustrated in Figure 6.11 and Figure 6.12.

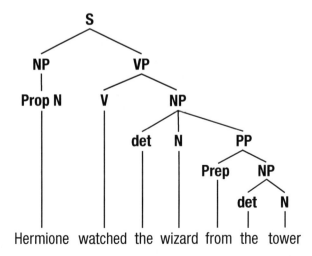

FIGURE 6.11 One tree diagram for Hermione watched the wizard from the tower

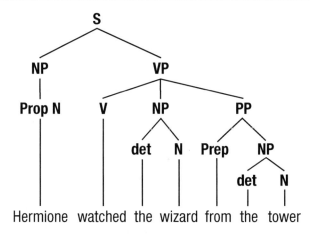

FIGURE 6.12 Second tree diagram for Hermione watched the wizard from the tower

The tree diagram in Figure 6.11 illustrates the deep structure of the sentence that means it is the wizard who is from the tower because the PP (*from the tower*) comes directly off the NP (*the wizard*).

The tree diagram in Figure 6.12 illustrates the deep structure of the sentence that means the watching is being done from the tower because the PP (*from the tower*) comes *directly* off the VP (*watched*).

What causes the ambiguity is that the two deep structures happen to appear the same in the surface structure. In fact, structural ambiguity is defined as two different deep structures that are realized as the same surface structure.

STRUCTURAL RELATIONSHIPS AMONG SENTENCES

It may seem odd to talk about sentences being related, but they are. In fact, they can be related in several ways. We can see this relationship with declarative statements and their corresponding questions, for example, or positive statements and their corresponding negatives. The following pairs of sentences, though not synonymous, are clearly related somehow:

1a. *Sally will win that race.*
1b. *Will Sally win that race?*
2a. *Sally aced the exam.*
2b. *Sally didn't ace the exam.*

Our theory of syntax needs to be able to account for these relationships. To do so, we posit that both sentences in the pair are derived from the same deep structure. Our theory can account for this phenomenon, but we'll need a new concept to explain it: syntactic operations.

SYNTACTIC OPERATIONS

So far, we've been focusing on the constituent structure of sentences, gliding over how that structure is related to the surface structure. The concept of syntactic operations helps fill in that gap. **Syntactic operations** are a set of rules that derive surface structures from deep structures. The basic assumption here is that related sentences derive from a common deep structure, and it is syntactic operations that derive those related sentences from that common deep structure. Deriving a surface structure from a deep structure may produce a surface structure that does not resemble that deep structure or one that looks very much like it. It is this aspect of our theory that accounts for structural synonymity and sheds light on other structural relationships, as we shall see.

Our knowledge of the syntax of our language extends beyond knowing phrase structure rules; it also includes knowledge of these syntactic operations and the ways that they can move constituents around, delete constituents, add elements, and do even more complicated maneuvers, like embedding sentences. There are unique rules for each operation and constraints on which constituents they can be applied to. We won't go into detail about these operations (there are hundreds of them); instead, we will briefly examine a few common ones.

Structural synonymity

Just as there are two types of ambiguity, there are two types of synonymity, lexical and structural. **Lexical synonymity** refers to two words that mean the same thing. **Structural synonymity** refers to two sentences that mean the same thing. Ambiguous sentences occur when one surface structure represents more than one deep structure. Synonymous sentences occur when the opposite happens, when one deep structure can be realized in more than one surface structure, as illustrated in the following sentences:

1. *The wizards approached cautiously.*
2. *Cautiously, the wizards approached.*

Although the emphasis may differ slightly, these two sentences are structurally synonymous; that is, the two surface structures derive from a common deep structure. The deep structure has gone through a specific syntactic operation to derive sentence 2, whose surface structure looks different from sentence 1 but whose meaning is the same.

Active and passive sentences can serve as another example of structural synonymity, as illustrated with these two sentences:

3. *A wizard threw his wand at the dementor.*
4. *The wand was thrown at the dementor by a wizard.*

The first sentence is active; the second passive. Granted, there is again a difference in emphasis between the two sentences, but in essence they are synonymous. That is, they share a common deep structure. The deep structure of sentence 3 has gone through a syntactic operation, in this case the passive operation, to derive the surface structure of the second sentence.

Movement operations

Movement operations are among the most common of syntactic operations. We find them in many, if not all, languages in the world. They move phrases around, sometimes from the VP to the NP as in sentence 2 and sometimes from the NP to the VP as in sentence 4. (There is more to the syntactic operation that derives passive sentences from their active deep structures that we won't go into here.)

Adverb movement

One common syntactic operation is called **adverb movement**, which allows certain AdvPs in the VP to move to different parts of the sentence, including the very beginning. If it is placed at the beginning of a sentence, the AdvP might appear to be part of the NP, but it is not. It is still part of the VP in the deep structure, no matter where it appears in the surface structure because it modifies the verb, not an NP.

5.   *The wizards entered the cave fearfully.*
6.   *Fearfully, the wizards entered the cave.*

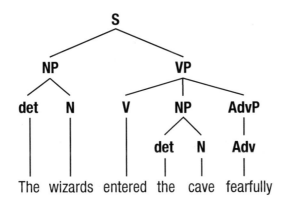

FIGURE 6.13 Tree diagram for sentences 5 and 6

Applying the adverb movement operation moves *fearfully* from the end of the sentence to the beginning, as in sentence 6. This creates a difference between the deep structure and the surface structure. It does not, however, change the meaning of the sentence. Those two sentences are synonymous and share an identical deep structure as illustrated in Figure 6.13.

This operation can occur with some PPs in the VP as well, as shown in sentences 7 and 8.

7.   *All muggles take their final exams on Friday.*
8.   *On Friday, all muggles take their final exams.*

Here again, the PP appears to be part of the NP, but in the deep structure for both sentences it is part of the VP.

Yes/no question formation

As noted earlier, related sentences derive from a common deep structure. Questions, then, have the same underlying structure as the declarative sentences from which they are derived.

The yes/no question syntactic operation derives the surface structure of these questions. Let's look at two statements and their corresponding questions:

9. *Mary is playing her guitar.*
   Is Mary playing her guitar?
10. *Mark should leave now.*
    Should Mark leave now?

We can see that forming these questions involves moving part of the VP to a position in front of the subject NP, but what part is it that moves? To answer that, we need to revise our phrase structure rules slightly and posit the inclusion of what is known as **AUX**, an **auxiliary verb**. Auxiliary verbs are *have, be, do*, or modals, verbs like *should, can, must, will, may, might, could, shall*. Auxiliary verbs usually occur with another verb: *can read, must work, is playing, has eaten, should apologize, will succeed. Have, be*, and *do*, but not modals, can function as main verbs or as auxiliaries in the following sentences:

11. Mary has a guitar.   Mary has borrowed a guitar.
12. Mark is hungry.   Mark is eating.

In the first of each pair of sentences, the verb (*has* or *is*) functions as the main verb in the sentence. In the second, *has* and *is* are auxiliary verbs, functioning as part of the main verbs *borrow* or *eat*.

Our theory posits an AUX as part of the deep structure of all sentences, whether or not it appears in the surface structure. Our revised phrase structure rules then become this:

S – NP AUX VP

AUX – (modal) (have) (be) or (do)

We can now describe the syntactic operation for forming yes/no questions; it even has a name, **subject-auxiliary inversion**. In plain English, we move the AUX verb from its usual place before the main verb to a position in front of the subject NP.

For the sentence, *Mark should leave now*, the tree diagram would look like Figure 6.14.

The subject-auxiliary inversion would then take the AUX *should* and move it to the beginning of the sentence, creating *Should Mark leave now?* as the surface structure.

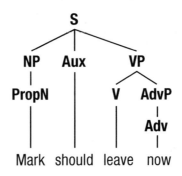

FIGURE 6.14 Tree diagram for sentence 10

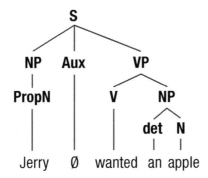

FIGURE 6.15 Tree diagram for sentence 13

If there is no AUX in the surface structure, we insert a different auxiliary: *do*, what is sometimes called a *dummy do*. Thus, for sentence 13, we insert a dummy do to make a question and get sentence 14.

13. *Jerry wanted an apple.*
14. *Did Jerry want an apple?*

Figure 6.15 illustrates the deep structure for sentence 13. The AUX does not appear in the surface structure, but it is present in the deep structure, as evidenced by its appearance when we turn that declarative sentence into a question, as in sentence 14.

Auxiliary verbs are the only ones that undergo subject-auxiliary inversions; they are also the verbs that show up in tag questions and occur to the left of *not* in negative sentences. *You haven't eaten yet, have you?* illustrates both occurrences of an auxiliary.

Embedded sentences

You may be thinking about now, this is all well and good but most of the sentences I read or hear or see are a lot more complex than the examples you've used here. Very true. One way that sentences become complex is having other sentences embedded within them. In fact, the syntactic definition of a complex sentence is one that contains another sentence within it. There are several ways this can happen. Two sentences can be joined through coordination, using conjunctions like *and* or *but* or other coordinators. One of the first ways children learn to join sentences is by stringing them together in a linear sequence with *ands*: *I went to the store and I saw a doggie and he licked me and I petted him*—sentences like that. When we do this, we're joining what are called two independent clauses; that is, each could stand on its own as a sentence. A **clause** is a unit that contains a subject and a predicate, in our terms, an NP and VP together.

As children get older, they learn to embed sentences, putting a dependent clause, one that cannot stand on its own as a sentence, within an independent clause, creating adverb clauses, complement clauses, or relative clauses. We'll examine the latter two types here.

As our phrase structure rules show, one constituent that can occur within NPs or VPs is a sentence (S). That is, we can embed sentences within sentences by placing them within NPs or VPs. Let's look at two similar sentences to illustrate an embedded sentence.

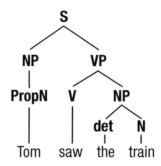

FIGURE 6.16 Tree diagram for sentence 15

15. *Tom saw the train.*
16. *Tom saw that the train was late.*

Figure 6.16 illustrates the deep structure for sentence 15:

If we want to diagram sentence 16, a question immediately arises. What should we do with *the train was late*? It's neither an NP nor a VP but both as one unit; in other words, a clause or sentence (S).

That S takes the place of the NP after *saw*; that is, it is a **complement clause**, a clause that functions as an NP in a VP or PP. We place that complement clause within the VP because it is related to the verb *saw*, as shown in Figure 6.17.

You'll notice there's a new element in Figure 6.17, a **COMP**, which stands for complementizer. It is there as a sort of place holder, indicating that the S that follows is embedded in the main clause. In the surface structure, it can appear as *that*, in which case we would say, *Tom saw that the train was late*. Sometimes it does not appear at all, as in *Tom saw the train was late*.

Let's look at another type of embedded sentences, **relative clauses**. Here the embedded sentence does not function as an NP but rather as part of an NP, functioning as a modifier of the noun that it follows, known as its head noun. When two NPs with the same referent occur in the deep structure of the main sentence, a relative clause can occur, embedding one clause

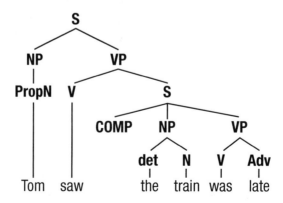

FIGURE 6.17 Tree diagram for sentence 16

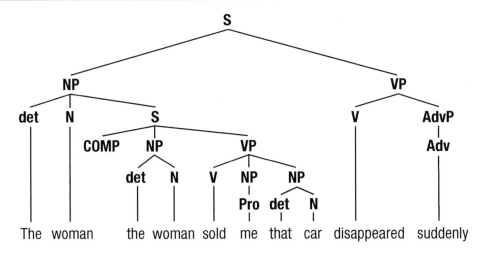

FIGURE 6.18 Tree diagram for sentence 17

within the other. Relative clauses always occur within NPs, never directly under the VP node; they are usually introduced in the surface structure with a **relative pronoun**: *who, which, whom, whose, that.*

17. *The woman who sold me that car disappeared suddenly.*

Here, *who sold me that car* is a relative clause. It contains an NP and a VP, so it is a clause; it modifies the NP *the woman*, so it is a relative clause not a complement clause. Diagramming the sentence as shown in Figure 6.18, we can see that there are two NPs with the same referent, that is, two NPs that refer to the same thing, *the woman*. In the surface structure, one of them becomes part of a relative clause modifying the other through the relative clause syntactic operation.

The main clause here is *the woman disappeared suddenly* as indicated in the tree with the NP *the woman* and the VP *disappeared suddenly* directly under the top S node. The deep structure of the embedded sentence again contains a COMP, but in this case, it serves as a place holder for the relative pronoun *who* that appears in the surface structure. That relative pronoun takes the place of the repeated NP, *the woman*, which does not show up again in the surface structure. You'll notice that the embedded sentence S comes under the NP *the woman* in the main sentence because it modifies that NP.

Under some circumstances, the relative pronoun may be omitted, as the following sentence indicates.

18. *The book that I lent you is due at the library.*
19. *The book I lent you is due at the library.*

We can use these diagrams to help us differentiate what, in the terminology of traditional grammar, are called **dependent clauses** and **independent clauses**. If an S (a sentence) occurs within another constituent, an NP or VP, rather than as the top node, it is a dependent clause. Independent clauses are only dominated by the S node.

USING SYNTAX IN WRITING

We've examined only a few of the many syntactic operations possible. It is these syntactic operations that allow for the same underlying structure to have many surface forms, a phenomenon that is particularly helpful to writers as it allows them many ways to say something.

A man who was wearing a blue hat stole the pies from the cart yesterday.
The pies were stolen from the cart by a man who was wearing a blue hat yesterday.
Yesterday, a man wearing a blue hat stole the pies from the cart.
A man wearing a blue hat stole the pies from the cart yesterday.
The pies were stolen from the cart yesterday by a man wearing a blue hat.
It was a man wearing a blue hat who stole the pies from the cart yesterday.
It was yesterday that the pies from the cart were stolen by a man wearing a blue hat.

I could go on, but you get the picture: Although not all are particularly graceful sentences, they all mean the same thing. For writers, this is particularly useful when they want to foreground a word, put a phrase at the beginning of a sentence for cohesion or as a transition, or move it to the end of a sentence for emphasis.

UNIVERSAL GRAMMAR

Obviously, there is a lot of variation among different languages on the surface level; anyone who has studied a language other than their native language is aware of that. But what about at the deeper level? It turns out that there are some aspects of structure that apply across all languages; linguists call those aspects **principles** of Universal Grammar (UG). There are also areas of structure in which there is variation among languages; linguists call those aspects **parameters**. NPs can serve as a somewhat simplified example. All languages have NPs that contain a noun and may contain other elements such as determiners, adjectives, or prepositional phrases. That is a principle of UG. The order of those elements in the surface structure varies greatly across languages. In English, as we saw, the usual order is det Adj N. If there is a numeral, it comes directly after the determiner: *the four little pigs*, for example. In some languages, the determiner and numeral would come before the noun, but the adjective would come after it; in other languages, that numeral would come last; in still others, all those elements would follow the noun. The order of these elements, then, is a parameter that can vary across languages, but the constituent NP occurs in all languages and is thus a principle of UG.

L1 ACQUISITION IN FOCUS: ACQUIRING SYNTAX

Acquiring a first language entails not only learning that language's sounds or signs and the ways in which they can be put together into morphemes and words, but also how those words can be put together to form sentences. That task entails learning the underlying system we have been examining in this chapter. Children learn the permissible and impermissible word orders for sentences and allowable variations (questions or negations, for example); the rules for embedding phrases and sentences (what constituents can go inside other constituents); and all the many syntactic operations that allow us to manipulate the deep structure of a sentence. One key aspect of that system, you'll recall, is its ability to produce novel sentences; in learning that underlying system, children learn to not only produce novel sentences but understand them as well.

Seems like a lot to ask small children to do, but children do so easily and quickly. By the age of three, children have mastered most of the complex set of rules and syntactic operations required to form questions and negations and to embed sentences. This ability shows that children clearly understand that sentences possess a structure that is distinct from the surface linear order of words. There is a great deal of evidence for this; we'll discuss only a small part of that evidence here. As we noted in Chapter 2, at the age of two, children begin to form two-word utterances that are not just two words randomly joined. Instead, those two words have clear syntactic relations: two NPs, for example, that are subject and object in adult speech, *Daddy shoe* used to mean *Daddy is putting on his shoe*.

They also rarely make errors in word order; their utterances, though not adult-like, still follow the word order rules of whatever language they are learning. English-speaking children, for example, put NPs that are subjects before the verb and NPs that are objects after it, as required by English syntax. If we examine sentences typically uttered by young children, such as *Molly play new game*, we can see that although there are no inflectional morphemes to indicate tense on the verb, the sentence clearly consists of an NP and VP, and the NP after the verb clearly consists of AdjP and N.

SYNTAX IN YOUR (NATURAL) WORLD: DO BIRDS HAVE SYNTAX?

We've seen that syntax is about how the combination and order of phrases create meaningful utterances. For many years, linguists believed that syntax was unique to human communication. That may not be true, however, as new research has shown. Birds, it turns out, may have a syntax of their own. That is, they may combine different sounds or notes to communicate complex meanings.

Researchers in Japan wondered if some bird songs were composed of different elements with distinct meanings, as human language is, and if reordering their notes allows for the creation of compound meanings. What these researchers concluded was that the Japanese great tit, a species related to chickadees, may indeed have a sort of syntax that uses note-ordering rules to combine different meanings into one compound meaning. Though not quite syntax as we have discussed it here, the study provides evidence that these birds pay attention to how notes are put together in specific combinations.

SYNTAX IN OTHER LANGUAGES

Like all aspects of language, syntax varies greatly across languages and at all levels. We'll examine a small part of this variety in the word order of sentences and noun phrases. Though all languages have NPs and VPs, they do not all put them in the same order. In English, the usual word order for sentences is SVO, subject–verb–object. We indicate that in our phrase structure rules: S – NP VP and VP – V (NP). In Maori, spoken in New Zealand, and in Scots Gaelic, spoken in Scotland, the usual order is VSO, verb–subject–object. The usual word order in Japanese is SOV, subject–object–verb. In Fiji, it is VOS, verb–object–subject.

The order of elements in an NP also varies across languages. In English, we usually put the article before the noun: *the boy, a dog*. In Ewe, spoken in West Africa, the article comes after the noun. In Ewe, *the dog* would be *avu la* (literally, *dog the*). If we add a number and adjective, in English, we usually have det–number–adjective–noun: *these four red apples*. In Basque, the order would be number–noun–adjective–determiner: *Lau sagar gorri hauek* (four apples red these). In Spanish, the order would be det–number–noun–adjective: *estas cuatro manzanas rojas* (these four apples red).

We can see differences from English in both sentence order and noun phrase order in the following sentence from Scots Gaelic: *chummaic an duine more an cu beag* (literally, saw the man big the dog small) or in English, *the big man saw the small dog*.

A NOTE ABOUT THEORY

The syntax theory we have used here was originally proposed by Noam Chomsky, perhaps the most influential linguist of the 20th century. In his 1957 book *Syntactic Structures*, he revolutionized the field of linguistics when he introduced the theory of generative grammar, a theory that seeks to describe a set of rules and operations that allows us to produce and understand the infinite number of possible sentences in a language. In the years since then, several newer theories have evolved within generative grammar (lexical functional grammar, relational grammar, head-driven phrase structure grammar), all of which differ from the original formulation in significant ways. What they all have in common with that original theory, however, is a realization that syntactic relationships among phrases in a sentence cannot be accounted for by examining only the linear surface structure. Instead, to represent how sentences are put together, we need to examine what we have called the deep structure.

CHAPTER SUMMARY

- Syntax is the branch of linguistics that analyzes the structures and rules that allow for combining words into phrases and phrases into sentences to create meaningful utterances. It investigates the structure of sentences, the relationship of parts of the sentence to one another, and the relationship of sentences to one another in terms of both meaning and structure. It seeks to describe the rules that underlie the generativity that is present in all languages.
- All sentences have a surface structure, which is the linear word order, and a deep structure, which is composed of hierarchically arranged constituents (noun phrases [NP], prepositional phrases [PP], and verb phrases [VP], among others).
- A finite set of phrase structure rules describes this deep constituent structure, indicating which elements make up each constituent and which constituents can be part of other constituents. The deep structure of any sentence can be illustrated with a tree diagram using these phrase structure rules.
- Syntactic operations can be applied to that deep structure to derive different surface structures. Some common syntactic operations include adverb movement and yes/no question formation.

- These syntactic operations help us account for how some sentences are related: structurally synonymous sentences or declarative statements and questions, for example.
- There is a set of syntactic principles that all languages share, what linguists call Universal Grammar, and parameters that are variations of these principles across languages.
- In acquiring their first language, children learn the structure of that language as they also learn its words.

KEY TERMS

syntax	structural relationships
grammar	syntactic operations
generativity	movement operations
surface structure/linear structure	adverb movement
deep structure/constituent structure/hierar-	auxiliary (AUX)
chical structure	subject-auxiliary inversion
constituents: NP, VP, PP, AdjP, AdvP, S	embedded sentences
phrase structure rules	complementizer (COMP)
determiner (det)	complement clause
syntactic categories	relative clause
immediate constituent	relative pronoun
recursion	principles and parameters of
structural and lexical ambiguity	Universal Grammar
structural and lexical synonymity	

EXPLORATIONS

Exploration 1: Write a phrase that conforms to each structure:

Noun phrases

1. Det + N
2. Det + AdjP + N
3. Det + AdjP + AdjP + N
4. Det + AdjP + N + PP
5. Det + AdjP + N + S

Verb phrases

1. V
2. V + AdvP
3. V + NP
4. V + NP + PP

5.   V + AdvP + NP + NP + PP
6.   V + AdvP + S

Exploration 2: Identifying NPs

Identify the NPs in the following sentences:

The girl on the red swing pumped her legs as though her life depended on it, but she couldn't get that swing to go any higher than the top of the fence in the yard nearby.

My neighbor plays the French horn for a well-known orchestra that recently went on strike to protest their treatment by the management of the organization.

Exploration 3: Practice using phrase structure rules

Using the phrase structure rules listed in the chapter, draw a tree diagram of the deep structure of each phrase or sentence. Not all are complete sentences.

1. The angry child
2. A difficult theoretical book about linguistics
3. Into the fog in the dead of night
4. Sat on the chair on the porch
5. Enjoys chocolate at any time of the day
6. The puppy found a bone.
7. My guitar gently weeps.
8. The ice cream melted in her hand.
9. She wanted another cone immediately.
10. The fierce wind destroyed the potato crop.
11. A fabulous old castle appeared in the mist.
12. A demented passenger drove the train into the tunnel at high speed.
13. The school for gifted children collapsed in the storm.
14. The children put the toys from their aunt in the box.

Exploration 4: More practice

Using our phrase structure rules, draw a tree diagram of the deep structure of each sentence.

1. The committee awarded the cup to the winner of the race.
2. The senator apologized for his mistake.
3. The linguistics professor challenged her students with an extremely difficult test.
4. The reporter realized that the interviewee had lied.
5. A stranger cleverly observed that a dangerous spy lurked in the alley by the old shipyards.
6. The spy met his contact, who was a double agent in disguise.
7. Yesterday, our student was given the prize for the best new essay by the faculty committee.

Exploration 5: Structural ambiguity

The sentences that follow are ambiguous. First determine the two possible meanings for each, then explain the ambiguity in terms of the relationships among the constituents in the sentence. Finally, choose one sentence to diagram, noting which diagram reflects which meaning (remember, if it is ambiguous, there will be at least two diagrams).

1. Annie called the monster from Minneapolis.
2. My living room has several small tables and chairs.
3. The president announced they would leave on Friday.
4. She attacked the thief with the umbrella.
5. The commission finally decided on the train.

Exploration 6: How many ways can you say it?

Choose one of the example sentences in this chapter or create one of your own; then see how many ways you can rewrite it without changing the meaning. That is, write as many surface structures for your sentence as you can without changing its deep structure.

FURTHER READING

Larson, R. (2010). *Grammar as science*. MIT Press. Further discussion of concepts from this chapter.

phpSyntaxTree: http://ironcreek.net/phpsyntaxtree. This site helps you produce trees.

Tallerman, M. (2020). *Understanding syntax* (5th ed.). Routledge.

CHAPTER 7

Semantics

Relationships among words

···

First glance

How do we mean things with words?

Reference, sense, and meaning

Semantic relations:

- Synonymity, slurs, and euphemisms
- Antonymity, complementarity
- Hyponymy

- Homonymy and polysemy

Figurative language:

- Metaphors: Do tables have legs?
- Metonymy: Can a House, even a White one, talk?
- Idioms: Who's pushing up what daisies?

Semantic fields, semantic roles

INTRODUCTION

In this chapter, we'll turn our attention to **semantics**, the study of how we construct and understand the meanings of words and sentences. For a word, that might seem like a straightforward endeavor: Just look it up in the dictionary; that'll tell you what a word means. Well, yes and no. The dictionary definition never tells the whole story of a word's meaning. And words help construct the meaning of a sentence by the roles they play in it.

MEANING AND MEANINGS

We can start by asking what it is we know when we know a word. Clearly, we know how to pronounce or sign it; how to use it in a sentence; how to use it appropriately in discourse; how to use it non-literally (*freeze* to mean *stop* as well as to make something frozen). What is not so obvious is that our knowledge includes much more than that: what other words it is related to; what affective connotations it has; what social meaning it carries, and more.

DOI: 10.4324/9780429269059-7

The concepts of reference and sense can help us begin to differentiate various aspects of word meaning. **Reference** (also called **referential meaning**) is the association of the word with the object or concept it refers to; that object or concept is the word's **referent**. This type of meaning is most easily seen in words that refer to objects or individuals: *the car, her cat, that sandwich, Michelle Obama, my teacher in fifth grade.* Not all words, not even all nouns, refer to specific objects or individuals, however. Take the following sentence: *Preparing to become a teacher takes years.* In that sentence, *teacher* has a related but not identical meaning to its meaning in the phrase, *my teacher in fifth grade.* In the former, there is an additional element to the meaning, something broader and more abstract, not referring to any one teacher. **Sense** is the term used to refer to the additional elements of meaning beyond reference.

The distinction between sense and reference does not exhaust our ideas of meaning, by any means. We know that certain words and phrases carry what is called **affective meaning**, meaning about the speaker's attitudes or emotions toward what is said. *The idiot who banged into my car hadn't a clue how to drive* has a different affective meaning from *the driver who accidentally hit my car seemed to be unsure of how to maneuver his vehicle*, even though their sense is about the same.

Words and utterances also carry **social meaning**: information about social identities of the speaker and information about the relationship between the speaker and listeners. Take the following utterances, for example. *Thanks for the grub, Jake; it was great* and *Thank you so much for dinner, Mr. Jackson. It was delicious.* We can probably guess that the relationship between the speaker and listener in the first utterance is closer and more equal and in the second is more distant. Again, it's partly the word choice that carries that information. We will discuss social meaning in more detail throughout Chapters 8 through 13.

Connotation is the suggested or implied meaning commonly associated with a word; **denotation** is the explicit or literal meaning. Affective or social meanings are often expressed through connotation, which can be positive or negative. Roses connote romance or love; rain often connotes sorrow. Calling someone rigid connotes disapproval of his actions; calling him determined connotes approval. Connotative meanings are not universal; they are ones that are commonly associated with a term in a particular culture or society. The heart is seen as the seat of emotions in English-speaking cultures, for example, so its use connotes emotions for English speakers. The liver is seen as the seat of emotion in Indian culture, so heart would not carry the same associations for Hindi speakers.

SEMANTIC RELATIONS: IS SALT THE OPPOSITE OF PEPPER?

Word meanings exist in relationship with other word meanings. That relationship may be one of similar meanings or opposite meanings; it may be a part/whole relationship, or a "kind of" relationship; it may be a matter of multiple meanings, some figurative, some literal; or a matter of being part of a semantic field, a relationship discussed later. Knowing the meaning of a word also means knowing the ways a particular word relates to other words. Not only are those relationships an important part of lexical semantics; an understanding of them can help us examine certain social issues as well.

Synonyms

Synonyms are perhaps the best known of semantic relations. As you probably learned in school, synonyms are words that mean generally the same thing: *attorney/lawyer* or *bush/shrub*, for example. Writers often use a thesaurus to find synonyms. As any thesaurus user knows, however, synonymous words are not always interchangeable; in fact, there are no synonyms that mean exactly the same thing. *Doctor* and *physician* are often listed as synonyms, but their meanings do not exactly overlap. I am a doctor, for example, as I have a Ph.D., but I'm not a physician, as I do not practice medicine. Even words that mean generally the same thing can vary by how formal or casual they are: *intelligent* means about the same as *smart* but is less casual in tone. And the use of the two terms is different; we talk about *street smarts*, but not about *street intelligences*. That is, synonyms differ by how they collocate.

A **collocation** is a set of words that seem to native speakers to naturally belong together. They can be combinations of adjective and noun, verb and object, or other types of combinations: *salt* and *pepper* collocate, for example. They belong together. In the earlier example, we can say that *smart* collocates with *street* (*street smarts*) but *intelligence* doesn't. *Strong* and *powerful* are synonyms, to examine another example, but they collocate differently. We generally say *strong tea* but not *powerful tea*. It's not that *powerful tea* is wrong; it's just odd in English. Similarly, some nouns collocate with certain verbs and not others. We use the phrase *commit* murder, for example, rather than *make* murder or *do* murder, which seem logically possible. We use *make* and *do* for other actions: *make* a proposal and *do* research. We use still other verbs for other actions: we say *catch* (not find) a bus and we talk about snow *falling*, not *dropping* or *descending*.

Synonyms can differ in social meaning as well as usage. *Purse* and *pocketbook* are often listed as synonyms, but one, *pocketbook*, indicates that the speaker is probably older than 50; its synonym, *purse*, does not. Use of *hot dish*, a synonym for *casserole*, carries the additional social meaning of being from the Midwest, a social meaning *casserole* does not carry.

Semantics in your world: slurs and euphemisms

Euphemisms are synonyms used to make a concept sound less offensive or more acceptable. These can be common and unremarkable: *the john* for the bathroom, which in itself is a euphemism for *toilet*; *make love* for sexual intercourse; *knocked up* for pregnant; *lose your lunch* for vomiting. Many euphemisms replace either religious terms or swear words: *jeez* for Jesus, *darn* for damn, or *the f-word* for fuck. These common euphemisms can offer insight into what a society deems unacceptable to discuss: sex, excretion, vomit, obscenities, for example. It is a bit hard for me to see why society deems pregnancy in need of euphemisms, but it does; there are lots of them: *bun in the oven, in the family way, with child, preggers*. Euphemisms can also be used to hide some disturbing activities, as the following military euphemisms demonstrate: *anti-personnel device* for bomb, *neutralize* for kill, *friendly fire* for fire coming from one's own side that causes injury or death to one's own forces.

Slurs are offensive synonyms for more neutral terms, usually for groups of people. *Towel head* is an offensive term or slur used to refer to Arabs, for example; *bitch* an offensive term for women. *Dago* and *greaser* were slurs my father remembers being aimed at him as an Italian immigrant to the United States. I remember him telling me how he and most Italians he knew also felt the pronunciation of *Italian* as [aytælyɔn] was a slur. When I tell my students that, many react with concern, knowing that they and their families use that pronunciation without meaning it to be derogatory. They bring up the question of who gets to decide whether a particular term is a slur, a question that can lead to heated debates.

A few years ago, for example, Arizona decided to rename a mountain near Tucson. What had been called Squaw Peak became Piestewa Peak, named after a Hopi woman from the area who had been killed on combat duty in Iraq, the first Native American woman killed while a U.S. soldier in combat. The debate centered around whether or not the term *squaw* was a slur and around who gets to decide that question. Some claimed it was just a term for a young American Indian woman. Others pointed out, quite correctly, that it had long been used derogatorily, at least since the early 1800s, a time when a general belief system that Whites were superior to other groups necessitated different terms to refer to men, women, and children who were not White. Thus *buck*, *squaw*, and *papoose* became a common way of referring to Native Americans, but not to Whites. *Squaw* seems to have been borrowed into English from Massachusett, an Algonquin language in which it did indeed mean a young woman, with no pejorative connotation. That fact, however, has little or no bearing on the question of whether it is a slur today in English. To determine whether a word is a slur, we need to examine the historical context not just of that individual word, but also of any history of oppression, whether it be of Native Americans and their cultures or other oppressed groups. And we need to ask: who gets to decide if a word is offensive? To me, the answer to that question belongs to those to whom the term refers.

Antonyms

Antonyms are pairs of words that are opposite in some way. *Good/bad, dead/alive, teacher/student* are all antonym pairs, but they differ in significant ways in their "oppositeness." The clearest type of antonyms are **gradable antonyms**: *big/small, young/old, up/down, long/short, wide/narrow*. These antonyms express two ends of a scale with gradations: a thing can be smaller or bigger, the biggest or smallest, or very small or extremely big. Thus, with gradable antonyms, what counts as the meaning of any one term is relative; my dog, for example, is considered big compared to the dog down the street, a Scottie, but small when compared to the one next door, a Great Pyrenees.

Relational (or converse) antonyms are not really opposites at all but pairs of words that describe a certain relationship: *parent/child, above/below, teacher/student*, or *lend/borrow*, for example. Although they are often seen as opposite ends of a relationship, these terms describe what is called **converseness**: *parent* is not the opposite of *child*; instead, they have a converse relationship such that if A is the parent of B, then B must be the child of A. Similarly, *above* and *below* have a converse relationship: if X is above Y, then Y must be below X.

Complementary antonyms are in a binary relationship: if you are one, you cannot be the other. They are sometimes defined as absolute opposites—something is either *legal* or *illegal*, someone is either *dead* or *alive*, you either *passed* that test or you *failed* it, you're either *single* or *married*, at least legally.

Semantics in your world: Complementarity

Some introductory linguistics textbooks use *male* and *female* as examples of complementary antonyms. We noted in Chapter 3 that the terms man and woman are not complementary antonyms because transgender or intersex individuals have attributes of both. If we see *man* as the opposite of *woman*, we run the risk both of seeing people as belonging to opposing camps (people still talk about *the opposite sex*) and of seeing all people as either one or the other. Defining men and women as binary categories can have consequences in many fields of life. Recently, the International Olympic Commission decided that an athlete who had competed as a woman for years could no longer do so without taking drugs that lowered her unusually high level of testosterone. This athlete, who is intersex and identifies as female, has naturally, not drug-induced, high levels of testosterone, higher than many other female athletes. The commission basically decided that people needed to fall into one of the binary categories of man or woman; there was no room for an in-between classification.

Semantics in your world: Markedness

Although antonyms are opposites, they are not always equal opposites. Or to be more precise, they do not sit on equivalent ends of a scale. **Markedness** refers to this phenomenon, one in which one term, the **unmarked** term, is seen as neutral or the norm, a sort of default mode, and its opposite or related term, the **marked** term, is seen as an abnorm, somehow out of the ordinary. Generally, for example, *big* is unmarked and *small* is marked. That is, if we want to know something's size, we ask, *How big is it?* That *big* is unmarked, no special meaning attached. We could ask, *How small is it?* If we do so, however, we've used a marked term and thus indicated that something is unusual, perhaps the object is especially small. Many pairs of gradable antonyms have marked and unmarked words: *tall* is unmarked, *short* is marked (we ask how tall someone is, not how short); *wide* is unmarked, *narrow* is marked.

We can see markedness at work in other ways too. The term *bird*, for example, includes various types of birds, but birds that fly are the unmarked type. We generally mark those birds that do not fly by adding the adjective *flightless* before the noun. We have *birds* (unmarked for flight) and *flightless birds* (marked for lack of flight).

This markedness with birds is innocuous. It is not so innocuous with terms about social relations. If we constantly mark certain terms for race, as we do with Black History or Asian-American History, the implication is that the norm, the unmarked form, of history is White, for we do not mark history for whiteness by saying White History. If we consistently mark certain professions for gender, as we do when we say *female astronaut* or *female engineer*, or *male nurse* or *male kindergarten teacher*, the implication is that the unmarked, normal situation is that astronauts and engineers are male, and nurses and kindergarten teachers are female. Using *male* or *White* as unmarked terms sets up in people's minds a view of reality in which history is the history of White people and where women are not astronauts or engineers, a view of reality which does not conform to the world we live in.

Hyponymy and part/whole relationships

Hyponyms are specific terms that are part of a more general **superordinate term**: *roses, lilacs,* and *peonies* are all hyponyms of the superordinate term *flower*; *chair, sofa,* and *table* are hyponyms of the superordinate term *furniture*; *tigers, lions, bears, raccoons, snakes,* and *birds* are hyponyms of the superordinate term *animal*. Hyponyms have a "kind of" relationship with their superordinate term: *lilacs* are a kind of *flower*; lions are a kind of *animal*.

Each term may have other terms which are its hyponyms: *insect* is a hyponym of *animal*, and *mosquito*, *gnat*, and *butterfly* are hyponyms of *insect*.

The term hyponym simply refers to words and their relationship to other words, but how we see that relationship gives us insight into how we see the world. Cultural anthropologists, for example, study hyponyms as a window into how different languages conceptualize the world. Color terms are notorious for varying across cultures and languages. Ancient Greek and Biblical Hebrew had no word for blue or green; objects that we call blue or green were a kind of black in those languages. Ancient Egyptian, however, did have words for blue and green. The Meriam language, spoken on Murray Island, has names for black, white, and red, but no separate name for blue; like Greek and Hebrew, the name used for something blue is the same as that used for something black. Modern Russian, on the other hand, has two words for our word blue: *siney*, which means dark blue, and *goluboy*, which means light blue. To us, light blue and dark blue are both hyponyms of blue; to Russian speakers, they are not. They are separate colors.

A **part/whole relationship** is like hyponymy in that it is hierarchical but different in that it does not consist of a "kind of" relationship. Body parts are good examples: toes are in a part/whole relationship to foot, for example, but toes are not a kind of foot. Rather, the term foot includes the idea of toes, for toes are part of the foot.

Homonymy and polysemy

Words can carry more than one meaning in various ways. **Homonyms** are words that have the same spoken or written forms but different meanings. They can be **homophones**, words that are pronounced the same but have different meanings (*bank*—a financial institution or the edge of a river) or **homographs**, words that are spelled the same, but are pronounced differently and have different meanings: *row* (moving a boat with oars) and *row* (an argument). A **polysemous word** is one that has multiple meanings that are related either historically or conceptually: *rich* is polysemous in that it does not mean the same thing in describing a person or soil. In one case it refers to quantity (amount of money); in the other, quality. But the meanings are related conceptually in a way that the two meanings of *row*, for example, are not. Thus, *rich* is considered a polysemous word.

FIGURATIVE LANGUAGE

So far, we've been discussing word meaning as if it is always literal, but much of our language use is non-literal or figurative. Phrases like *keep an eye out for her* or *getting hitched*, for example, are figurative in that no eye is really out, nor is anyone being physically yoked to another person. **Non-literal** or **figurative language** expressions, whose meanings do not conform to their primary meaning, are an important part of the meaning of words and expressions. There are various types of figurative language, including metaphors, metonymy, and idioms.

Metaphors

Metaphors make use of or create figurative meanings by extending the meaning of a word beyond its primary sense to describe something not originally part of its primary reference.

Thus, two dissimilar things are presented as having a type of resemblance, which can be implied or directly stated. Metaphors work by referring to one domain of meaning using language usually associated with another domain. Metaphorical language is often seen as a rhetorical device found in poetic language, but it is extremely common in our everyday discourse. For example, the manager of a company is described as its *head*, a metaphorical use of a body part to describe company relationships. Using body parts or body functions metaphorically, we talk about *the leg of a chair, the foot of the table, the eye of a needle, pulling someone's leg, the neck of a bottle, having a heart-to-heart, seeing through an argument, having a long face, lending a hand, seeing eye-to-eye, the long arm of the law*, and more. Each of these expressions, which probably do not seem like metaphors to most of us, take one domain, the body, and apply terms from that domain to another domain: furniture, objects, activities, etc.

Some metaphorical use is so widespread it seems to be woven into the language itself. For example, in English, time is talked about metaphorically as money, as we can see in the following expressions: *waste time, spend time, live on borrowed time, save time, budget one's time*. Similarly, arguments are often metaphorically a type of war: *attack her argument, be right on target in her arguments, win or lose an argument, shoot down an argument*. Lakoff and Johnson (1980) argue that some metaphors are such an integral part of language that they provide a structured way of mapping the world onto a language. As such they are a fundamental part of our thinking and can influence how we see the world and behave in it. We will come back to this claim in Chapter 14 when we discuss ecolinguistics and the metaphors we use about nature.

Metonymy

Metonymy, a type of figurative language similar to metaphor, involves extending the meaning of one word to refer to something commonly associated with it. The distinction between metaphor and metonymy is not always clear cut, but generally metaphors extend the meaning of a word to areas not usually associated with it while metonyms extend it to areas related to that word. Like metaphors, metonyms are common in everyday language. It's not unusual to hear utterances like the following: *The White House imposed tariffs on China today* or *The Pentagon responded to claims of corruption*. The Pentagon and the White House are buildings so they cannot literally do anything (except perhaps stand there). Using the name of a building to refer to either an institution or a person is a form of metonymy. We similarly use names of countries or cities metonymically to refer to sports teams: *The United States has never won a world championship in men's soccer, but they have in women's soccer* or *Baltimore won the final game of the World Series*. We can use the material an object is made of to refer to it metonymically: *plastic* for credit cards. We can even use ourselves to refer to our cars at times: *I'm parked three blocks away* uses *I* metonymically to refer to my car.

Like metaphors, metonymic expressions structure not just our language but our thoughts, attitudes, and actions. Metonyms, for example, can hide certain features of a situation. Using an expression like *boots on the ground*, a metonym for combat troops, disguises the fact that actual people, the soldiers, are involved. They have become merely a piece of clothing, *boots*, rather than individuals who can be killed or wounded.

Idioms

Still another type of figurative language is idioms, conventionalized phrases whose meaning cannot be predicted by examining the literal meaning of the words themselves, phrases like *putting your foot in your mouth, sawing wood, pushing up daisies, flying by the seat of your pants, a fly in the ointment, a cross to bear, a rotten egg, the squeaky wheel* (the one that gets the grease), *one's heartstrings* (the ones pulled by a sad story), and more. We can see the difference between idioms and non-idiomatic phrases by examining a common idiom: *going out on a limb* (taking a chance). *Limb* has a synonym, *branch*, but *going out on a branch* has a different meaning altogether, only a literal one. Idioms, then, tend to function as phrases in which one cannot substitute different words.

SEMANTIC FIELDS

Semantic fields are sets of related words that denote or connote something about the same general phenomenon. Sports is a semantic field, one containing terms like baseball, basketball, soccer, team, field, equipment, fans, leagues, win, lose, and many more. Terms in a semantic field may be in a hyponymic relation to the superordinate term (soccer is a kind of sport); some may be synonyms (football is synonym for soccer, at least in some countries), and some may be antonyms (win/lose). There is evidence that we mentally store word meanings by semantic field so that one term in the field may evoke another.

What's interesting, at least to me, about semantic fields is that they help us see how different languages and cultures divide the world up differently. Anthropologists have long been interested in these differences, often citing kinship terms as examples of them. All cultures and languages have ways of referring to the semantic field of kin relations; they just divide up that field differently. The Yanomamo Indians in Brazil, for example, make no distinction between one's brother and one's male cousins, as long as those cousins are sons of paternal uncles or maternal aunts! Both are [ɛiwǝ]. There is a different term for son of a maternal uncle or paternal aunt: [tʃoriw] (Deutscher, 2010). The semantic field for English contains the terms *brother* and *cousin*; that for Yanomamo contains the terms [ɛiwǝ] and [tʃoriw], neither of which quite matches up with brother and cousin.

SEMANTIC ROLES AND SENTENCE MEANING

It's clear that we rely on word meanings in creating sentences. But knowing the meaning of individual words in a sentence does not tell us the meaning of the sentence itself. We also need to understand what roles those words, especially the NPs, play in the sentences. Those roles are referred to as **semantic** (or thematic) **roles**. Each sentence consists of a verb and one or more NPs that relate to that verb. Each NP in a sentence plays a different semantic role vis-à-vis the verb; that is, it contributes to the action, situation, or state described by the verb in different ways.

This rather abstract theory may be easier to understand with a simple example. Let's look at two sentences:

1) *The dog gnawed the bone.*
2) *The bone was gnawed by the dog.*

In sentence 1, the NP *the dog* is the doer of the action of the verb, gnawing. We call that role the **agent**. The bone has a different role in the sentence; it is being acted upon; we call that role the **patient** (I know, a rather odd term, but that's what we have).

The syntactic roles of the dog and the bone are different in sentences 1 and 2: in 1, *the dog* is the subject; in 2, *the bone* is the subject. The semantic roles of the NPs *the dog* and *the bone* are still the same, however: *the dog* is the agent; *the bone* is the patient in both 1 and 2 because the dog is still doing the action of the verb, gnawing, and the bone is still being acted upon.

The important point here is that the semantic roles have not changed because the meaning has not changed. Semantic roles, then, are a way of characterizing the meaning relationship between NPs and the verb, no matter how they show up in the surface structure of the sentence.

The major semantic roles include the following. The noun playing the listed role is italicized.

1. **Agent**: the one who does the action: *The dog* gnawed the bone.
2. **Patient**: the entity that is acted upon: The dog gnawed *the bone*.
3. **Experiencer**: the noun that experiences emotional or sensory input: *The dog* was hungry.
4. **Instrument**: the means through which an action occurs: The dog was groomed *with a special comb*.
5. **Locative** and **temporal**: nouns that show time or place: We brought the dog *home* in *October*.
6. **Recipient**: something that receives a physical object: The vet gave *our dog* a shot.
7. **Beneficiary**: someone or thing for which an action is done: She gave us some treats *for our dog*.
8. **Cause**: a natural force that causes a change: *The storm* ruined our plans for a walk with the dog.

We can see from all this that one important factor in how meaning is constructed in sentences is the semantic role each NP plays.

CORPUS LINGUISTICS

Corpus linguistics has given linguists a powerful tool for examining semantics questions. Suppose you want to know what words most often collocate with other particular words in American English or what adverbs are most often used in sports reporting. Those would be difficult things to ascertain as just one individual. With the help of databases, however, it is easily done.

A corpus is a database, a machine-readable collection of texts. Corpus linguistics uses these databases to analyze language. As a field, corpus linguistics has been around for decades; with recent advances in technology, its use has expanded greatly. The assumption underlying computer analysis of these databases is that by examining a large number of texts, we can detect patterns that otherwise might not be apparent.

And these corpora are large. The first one was the Brown Corpus in 1967, which consisted of about a million words. That's peanuts nowadays. One current corpus, the Corpus of Contemporary American English, consists of about 450 million words. Many of these databases contain not just texts from today, but ones from hundreds of years ago as well. Such large databases are being used in all sorts of ways today: speech synthesis, speech recognition, machine translation, and more.

As you may have noticed if you've been on the phone with a machine lately, using computers to emulate speech is not an easy matter. Computers must first break the stream of sound into words (phonology and morphology), then ascertain the relationship among those words and determine what it all means (syntax and semantics). Each of those steps, of course, involves numerous smaller steps; if a word can be both a noun and a verb, determining which it is in a specific case, for example. The human brain does so easily; computers have to work a bit harder at it.

CHAPTER SUMMARY

- Semantics is the study of meaning, of how we construct and understand the words and sentences in our language. Meaning includes not only referential meaning but sense, affective meaning, and social meaning.
- Word meanings are part of a network of semantic relations that include synonyms, antonyms, hyponyms, part/whole relationships, and homophones.
- Figurative language, which includes metaphors, metonyms, and idioms, is an important part of our everyday language and offers insight into the ways we view the world.
- Examining semantic relations and concepts such as slurs, markedness, and complementarity can help us analyze and understand social issues.
- Semantic fields are sets of related words that denote or connote something about the same general phenomenon.
- The meaning of words in sentences includes the semantic role they play in a sentence: agent, patient, experiencer, instrument, locative, temporal, recipient, beneficiary, and cause.

KEY TERMS

reference/referential meaning/referent
sense
connotation and denotation
semantic relations
synonyms
collocation
slurs
euphemisms
antonyms: gradable, relational, complementary
markedness: marked and unmarked terms
hyponymy

part/whole relationship
homonymy: homophones, homographs
polysemy
figurative language
metaphors
metonymy
idioms
semantic fields
semantic roles
corpus linguistics

EXPLORATIONS

Exploration 1: Synonyms

How do the following synonyms differ in terms of their affective and/or social meanings or their collocations? Think about level of formality, gender, age, ethnicity, things like that. Then identify a context in which one synonym would work but another would not. Can you add any terms to each list?

* Idiot, ass, jerk, airhead, bastard, punk, fool, nincompoop
* Talk, converse, gossip, swap stories, chat, chitchat, gab, yak, discuss, parley, have a heart-to-heart, have a conversation
* Friend, bud, pal, mate, chum, comrade, BFF, colleague, associate, bestie, kindred spirit

Exploration 2: Antonyms

Identify **antonyms** for each term and mark each pair as gradable, relational, or complementary. Identify any pairs which have an unmarked and marked form and explain your reasoning. Compare your answers and discuss any differences.

1. High
2. Beginning
3. Inside
4. Question
5. Day
6. Cheap
7. Sad
8. Hero
9. In front of
10. Poor
11. Polite

Exploration 3: Euphemisms

Choose one term or phrase from the list provided and provide as many euphemisms (words or phrases) as you can. When might such euphemisms be used?

1. Tell a lie
2. Have sex
3. Defecate
4. Be drunk
5. Die/be dead

Exploration 4: Which nym is it?

Identify the type of semantic relationship in each group of words. If it is antonymic, identify which type of antonym. If it is hyponymic, identify the superordinate term.

1. Elm, oak, maple, sycamore, pine, cedar

2. Pester, annoy, bother, harass
3. Gigantic, minuscule
4. Sister, brother
5. Sister, brother, parent, aunt, uncle
6. Asleep, awake
7. Foot, knee, thigh, calf, leg

Exploration 5: Euphemisms in war

For each euphemism, identify the non-euphemistic meaning. What do you think of the use of such terms in discussions of war?

1. Air campaign
2. Extraordinary rendition
3. Surgical strike
4. Collateral damage
5. Detainees
6. Use of force

Exploration 6: Collocations

Quick and *fast* are often listed as synonyms but they collocate very differently. Which term would you use with each of the words provided? How does it sound to use the other term? For example, we generally say *fast lane*, not *quick lane*, as *fast* and *lane* collocate but *quick* and *lane* do not.

Food   meal   bite   train   learner   shower   glance   fix   wit

Exploration 7: Markedness

We noted earlier that certain terms are marked for gender. Recently on Facebook, I came across a site selling T-shirts with sayings such as *male architect, male astronaut,* and *male president*. What makes such phrases odd and worthy of being sold on Facebook? Can you come up with similar phrases playing on the marked/unmarked language around gender and professions that could be used on T-shirts?

Exploration 8: Body parts

Words for body parts are particularly susceptible to being used figuratively: *heart-to-heart conversation* or *pain in the butt*, for example. Come up with other phrases that use *heart* or *butt* figuratively; then identify what type of figurative language is involved: metaphor, metonymy, or idiom.

Exploration 9: Semantic roles

Identify the semantic role of each italicized noun in the following sentences:

1. *We* were exhausted flying back *from New Zealand last week*.
2. *The gardeners* worked *the soil with a backhoe*.
3. *The final game* of the World Cup was postponed because of *a hurricane*.

FURTHER READING

British National Corpus: http://natcorp.ox.ac.uk.
Corpus of Contemporary American English: www.americancorpus.org.
Saeed, J. (2009). *Semantics* (3rd ed.). Wiley-Blackwell. A broad introduction to the field.
WordNet: http://wordnet.princeton.edu/, A lexical database of English where you can investigate related words.

REFERENCES

Deutscher, G. (2010). *Through the looking glass: Why the world looks different in other languages*. Picador.
Lakoff, G., & Johnson, M. (1980). *Metaphors we live by*. University of Chicago Press.

CHAPTER 8

Language in everyday interaction

....

INTRODUCTION

We start our investigation of language in everyday interaction by examining how we actually use language throughout our day: in conversations with family, small talk at the office, gab fests with friends, or the little snippets of interaction we might have with a stranger on the elevator. Those conversations and snippets can seem natural and random. A casual conversation with friends probably doesn't look like the language presented in grammar books. We don't use complete sentences; we overlap and interrupt; we use phonological forms (*wanna*, *gonna*) not considered proper; our pronouns do not have clear antecedents. It's all a chaotic mess from one perspective. From another, it's highly structured, following certain patterns. It's those patterns that we'll examine in this chapter.

There is, as in all language use, variation in those patterns. Quite a bit of it sometimes. If, for example, I wanted you to pick up the shoes you'd left in the doorway for me to trip over, I might say any of the following, all meaning the same thing:

DOI: 10.4324/9780429269059-8

Pick up your shoes!
Shoes?
You left your shoes there, again!
Ahem! (with a slightly guttural sound and a nod toward the shoes)
Your name (with a similar nod).

That's a lot of variation for such a small request. Why are there so many ways to say that same thing? An examination of phonological, morphological, and syntactic structures would not provide much help here. To understand how language works in everyday interaction, we need to move beyond a focus on form and begin asking questions about discourse and other social factors.

DISCOURSE

Discourse is a term used by linguists to refer to several different concepts, all related but slightly different. At its most basic, discourse is any unit of language beyond the sentence, so a friendly conversation, an interaction between doctor and patient, an extended anecdote, a college lecture, and a political speech are examples of different types of discourse. Discourse analysis examines these units for their structure; conversations are not put together the same way as lectures, for example. Discourse need not be oral or signed; written texts are also discourse: college essays, leases, newspaper articles, and online blogs can all be examined as discourse. For any discourse, we can ask how it is structured and how people make sense of it. We can also ask how our discourse interacts with the social, political, and cultural lives we lead and how we construct our world through language. We will discuss the latter two questions in subsequent chapters; here we begin by examining a common type of discourse: conversations. We then turn our attention to **pragmatics**, a subfield of linguistics that focuses on everyday interaction and our attempts to make sense of what others say.

CONVERSATION PATTERNS AND ORGANIZATION

Conversations are, perhaps, the quintessential type of verbal interaction; for most of us, it's probably hard to imagine a day when no conversation occurs. It may also be hard to imagine that our conversations are organized. Don't we just talk? Well, no, we don't. Rather than a free-for-all, there are ground rules for conversations that we generally follow, if mostly without conscious attention: ground rules for openings, turn-taking, holding the floor, closings, among other aspects. In the following sections, we examine some of these patterns. One bit of terminology before we start; the term **interlocutors** refers to persons involved in a conversation through speaking or signing to one another.

Opening and closing sequences

The beginnings and ends of conversations are nearly always marked somehow. Rarely do we just walk up to someone, except perhaps a good friend we see often, and jump into a topic; nor do we just stop in the middle of an interaction and walk away. We ease our way in and out of conversational interactions.

Opening sequences tend to be fairly formulaic, with people choosing from a limited number of ways to greet someone and initiate a conversation: *Good morning, nice day isn't it?* or *Hey, Jude, ready for break?* or *Hello, Dr. Lennon. How was your vacation?* or *Sally, I haven't seen you in ages* or *Hi, Ben. What's up?* Opening sequences usually involve more than just greetings. Often, we follow a greeting with a question, as in the examples, giving our interlocutor a chance to offer a comment. After a greeting, we also sometimes indicate that we're about to jump into the conversation with such phrases as *You'll never guess what just happened to me* or *The weirdest thing just happened* or *Have you heard about . . . ?* These types of phrases can be used as part of an opening sequence or in the middle of a conversation to introduce a new topic. What we do in an opening sequence can depend on who we're interacting with; with strangers, for example, a phrase such as *Excuse me* is often used not so much to greet but to open an interaction.

Closing sequences are sometimes quite protracted and negotiated, with one interlocutor testing the waters to see if the other concurs that it's time to end the conversation. Sometimes they are quite brief and simple, as in *Gotta go, see you in class.* The following is an example of an elaborate, negotiated closing:

A: *Well, I've got to get going.*
B: *It's been good to talk to you.*
A: *You too. We should get together more often.*
B: *Yeah, I miss talking to you.*
A: *Me too.*
B: *OK, see you soon. Take care.*
A: *You too. Bye.*

Whether short or protracted, the end of a conversation is nearly always marked somehow, usually with a conclusion to the topic at hand, slightly longer pauses between utterances, some preparation for the actual closing (*I've got to get going*) and of course, some sort of farewell (*Bye, now*).

Linguistics in your world: Just saying hello

The example of leave-taking in the last section comes from the area I live in, the U.S. state of Minnesota. In fact, people in the Midwest often joke about how long Minnesotans take to say good-bye. Other parts of the United States and other cultures throughout the world have different conventions for opening and closing conversations. In many cultures, it's not the closing but the opening sequence that is expected to be lengthy and formulaic.

Such lengthy and formulaic greetings seemed to be the norm in Sudan when I was traveling there several years ago. Their greetings were more than just *hello* or *hey*; they were elaborate exchanges of blessings and good wishes. From what I could work out, opening sequences included an overt greeting, *Salaam aleikum*, a response of *Aleikum salaam*, several question-and-answer sequences about the other's wellbeing, and usually blessings on their family. This ritual took place even if one met someone several times a day or in an official setting. Only after this greeting could the conversation begin. To me, it seemed to take forever; I'm sure to them my greetings seemed curt and rude.

What is considered appropriate in telephone call greetings can also vary greatly across cultures. In France, for example, the caller generally apologizes for interrupting whoever answers, not to do so is impolite. In the United States, no such apology is expected; indeed, to do so can seem unnecessarily formal.

Turn-taking

Once the opening sequence has been accomplished, the tricky part of managing the interaction begins. In any conversation, interlocutors must manage turn-taking and topic-raising: who gets to speak when and about what. Such management includes negotiations about taking the floor, raising topics, picking up on other's topics, keeping the floor, relinquishing the floor, inviting others to speak, among other moves.

One important aspect of any conversational interaction is managing **the floor**. The person speaking or signing at any one time is said to have the floor. When we have the floor, we follow certain patterns to indicate to our interlocutors either that we want to keep it or that we are finished. If we want to keep the floor, when we need to pause, we'll do so in the middle of a sentence or thought, perhaps after a preposition: *We're going on . . . uh . . . Friday.* We also use fillers, terms like *um* or *kinda* or *you know* to indicate we've paused but still have the floor. When we're finished, we can indicate that in various ways: by matching our pauses with the end of a sentence or thought; by using a tag question and/or nominating someone else to take the floor (*Isn't that right, Sally?*); or by changing our pitch (in spoken languages), raising or lowering it sharply.

When one speaker is finished with her turn, if no one is nominated, confusion can sometimes occur as to who will take the floor next. More than one interlocutor can start, in which case interlocutors may try to work it out (*Sorry, you go ahead . . . That's all right, you go ahead . . . No, that's okay. You go.*), each apologizing and trying to smooth out the transition. In some cultures, if more than one person speaks at once, each keeps going, raising their volume to gain the floor until one backs off.

Linguistics in your world: Stop interrupting me!

What constitutes an interruption is sometimes difficult to determine. Some interruptions result from one person trying to take the floor or trying to dominate the conversation. Others are inadvertent interruptions, a result of misjudging cues from the speaker. Still other interruptions are not interruptions at all but what is called **overlapping**, when two interlocutors contribute to the conversation at the same time.

Turn-taking mishaps such as interrupting or overlapping can be a source of misunderstanding, especially when those conversing come from different cultures or subcultures. Some cultures, for example, expect the pause that marks the end of one person's turn to be quite short; other cultures expect it to be longer. For most Euro-Americans, a pause of a second is an indication that the speaker is finished with her turn and someone else may now safely take the floor. In other cultures, Athabaskan for example, a pause of a second-and-a-half is the norm. Shorter than that means *I still have the floor.* That half second may not seem like much, but in the middle of a conversation, it can be important.

Misunderstandings occur when interlocutors interpret those pauses differently. The addressee may interpret that second-long pause as permission to now take the floor, while the speaker might mean he's pausing but not ready to give up the floor. These types of mis-understandings are common across cultures, even when all are speaking the same language, and can be a source of stereotypes. If I'm from a long-pause culture, I would wait, politely, for a long pause before I started talking. My interlocutor might assume that, because I don't join in after her short pause, I have nothing to say and so continue talking. To her, I might seem unresponsive, not engaged, a bit aloof. The opposite interpretation can also occur. If I'm from a culture that expects short pauses between turns, it would be perfectly polite for me to start talking after a second. If my interlocutor, however, comes from a culture that expects longer pauses, she might think that I'm rude, interrupting her and dominating the conversation. You can see the potential for misunderstandings and misjudgments of others, especially as these patterns generally occur below the level of consciousness.

Silence

Although not usually thought of as meaningful, silence can carry a lot of meaning in an interaction: it can be awkward, companionable, polite, respectful; its social meaning depends on the situation. In many English-speaking communities, silence, especially if it goes on for more than a very short while, is seen as something negative, a gap to be filled. In other cul-tures, this is not so. According to Meshrie et al. (2000), in Athabaskan communities, certain interactions require a lengthy period of silence: when first interacting with strangers, when meeting again with friends or relatives after a period of separation, or when initiating court-ing, in other words when the relationship is ambiguous in some way. Rather than engaging in small talk to get to know the other person, as many English speakers might do, Athabaskans will remain together in silence until they feel they have become acquainted or reacquainted with the other enough to then talk.

PRAGMATICS

Pragmatics deals with analyzing language in context, especially how we interpret possible meanings of others' utterances. **Pragmatics**, then, is the study of how context shapes our use and interpretation of utterances: the when, why, where, how, and who of language use. It is concerned with questions like the following:

- How do we understand what others say or sign?
- What do context, power, and solidarity have to do with this meaning-making?
- Why are we so often indirect when directness is so much clearer?
- What exactly is politeness?

As the questions indicate, pragmatics focuses on how people use language to do things in spe-cific contexts. It is concerned with the distinction between what is said and what is meant, with intentions, and with interpretations.

One key concept in pragmatics is the fact that we do things with words. That may seem like a strange concept; we are used to thinking of words as meaning things, not doing things. Part of their meaning, though, is what they are doing. If you think about it, it's not so odd to say we do things through language. We even have words for these actions: promise, suggest, threaten, compliment, insult, to name but a few. For some of these, it is hard to imagine doing them without using language—complimenting, for example. You might give a thumbs up to indicate *Well done!*, but generally compliments are expressed through language.

Language is used to do more abstract, less immediate, less concrete things too: to signal and establish our social identities, to signal and establish our relationships to others, to be polite or impolite, to negotiate power relations, to increase or decrease solidarity, and much more. Take, for example, the seemingly simple decision of how to greet someone: *Hi? Hello? Hey? Good morning? What's up girl? Stella?* That decision is influenced by such factors as the relative status of the individual we're greeting, our closeness or distance, the context in which we encounter each other, and a host of other factors. I might greet a colleague with *Hi*, a student with *Hey*, a dean with *Hello*, and my neighbor with *Good morning*. All of this is influenced by who I am: my personal characteristics (how formal I am generally), my social standing (a student, a professor, a dean), and who I'm greeting. Each greeting does more than just greet; it signals my relationship to the other person in some way.

We can use greetings to illustrate other concepts in pragmatics. When someone passes you in the corridor, nods and says, "*Hi. How are you?*" what does that utterance mean? It looks like a question, but we all know what can happen if we respond to it as a question and start relating our latest troubles. We're often met with a blank stare and subtle efforts to end the conversation. If that and similar questions (*How's it going? What's up?)* are not real questions, what are they?

Instead of asking what does *How's it going?* mean, we might more productively ask, what is the speaker doing by saying it? Put that way, it's easy to answer—she's greeting us, of course. That's the meaning; it's a greeting. Similarly, *Could you pass the salt?* is not a yes/no question, even though it looks like one, but a polite request. And we know this because if we answer *yes* instead of just passing the salt, we're considered at worst odd or rude and at best lamely humorous.

So, we have utterances that look like questions but aren't really questions, and greetings and requests that don't look like greetings or requests at all. We usually understand the meaning intended with no problem, but how do we do so? In other words, how we do know what an utterance means?

It would seem to make sense that to analyze meaning, we should focus on the words, for they carry the meaning, don't they? Although words do indeed have meaning, or perhaps constellations of possible meanings, those meanings do not carry the entire meaning of an utterance. In fact, sometimes the meaning of an utterance does not seem to lie in the words at all. Take a phrase like, *Oh, yeah*. The words have virtually no referential meaning at all: they don't refer to a particular thing or concept. But that simple phrase can have multiple meanings: agreement (*Oh, yeah, I see what you mean*), disagreement (*Oh, yeah? I don't think so*), sarcasm (*Oh, yeah. I'm sure!*), threat (*Oh, yeah? just try it*), expression of recall or recognition (*Oh, yeah, I almost forgot*), or expression of joy (*Oh yeah!* with raised fist). How do we figure out the meaning?

Speech acts

One way is to figure out the **pragmatic intent**: what the speakers intends her utterance to do. As we saw with *Oh, yeah*, one phrase can serve various pragmatic intents: to threaten, to disagree, to agree, to name a few. The meaning, then, depends on what the speaker intends the utterance to do. If she intends it to threaten, then that is what it means. The meaning of the utterance thus includes the action it is meant to accomplish, or to put it in more linguistic terms, the speech act or pragmatic intent it is meant to accomplish.

Speech acts are actions that we perform through language. We often think of language as a tool to inform others. It is, but when we speak, we are usually doing more than just informing. We can be disagreeing, agreeing, threatening, questioning, suggesting, reminding, advising, promising, greeting, taking leave, apologizing, complimenting, lying, bullying, flirting, replying, insulting, and many more. All of these are speech acts.

We cannot do everything with words, of course. Borrowing, for example, is not a speech act. It is not *borrowing* until the object changes hands. The speech act involved, then, is requesting, in this case, requesting to borrow something. Similarly, being grateful is not a speech act. Gratitude is a feeling; you can be grateful and not express it. It's the expression of gratitude that is a speech act.

Each speech act consists of three components: locution, illocution, and perlocution. The **locution** of a speech act refers to the form it takes, the utterance that is spoken, written, or signed. For every utterance, the speaker has some intention in uttering it. This aspect of a speech act is referred to as its **illocution**: what the speaker intends the utterance to do. Illocution can be thought of as the pragmatic intent of the speaker. **Perlocution,** not an actual part of the utterance itself, refers to what is called the uptake of a speech act: what the hearer takes the utterance to mean.

We can see the distinction between locution and illocution more clearly with an example: *Could you hold this for me*? The locution or form of that utterance is a question, in this case a yes/no question. As such, a simple yes or no answer should suffice. Such an answer does not suffice in real life, however, because the illocution of the utterance is not a question but a request for action: *hold this*. The illocution, the pragmatic intent, is a request, so that is the speech act being performed.

The perlocution may or may not match the illocution of a particular utterance. In fact, many misunderstandings are the result of a mismatch between the illocution, the pragmatic intent of the speaker, and the perlocution, what the addressee takes as the intent. Many jokes too are based on this mismatch, as shown in Figure 8.1.

In some cases, one locution can serve more than one function, as we saw previously with *Oh, yeah*. The opposite is true too. Any illocution can be expressed with more than one

BEETLE BAILEY   By MORT WALKER

Beetle Bailey © 1996 Comicana Inc., Distributed by King Features Syndicate, Inc.

FIGURE 8.1 Mismatch between Sarge's illocution and Beetle's perlocution

locution; that is, we can perform the same speech act with very different utterances. Look at how many ways we have to make a request. Even such an everyday request as passing the salt can be done with numerous locutions: *Could you pass the salt?*, *Would you pass the salt?*, *Can you pass the salt?*, *Would you mind passing the salt?*, *Send the salt down this way*, *We need the salt down here*, *Salt?*, and many more. Each of these has the same illocution but different locutions.

Most of those examples are easily recognizable as requests because they are so commonly used to ask people to do things. But what about an utterance like *This food needs salt*, uttered while eating dinner? How do we interpret the speech act meant here? It could be a request, a complaint, or an evaluative judgment of the quality of the food, all different illocutions. How do we work out which one is meant? One explanation of how we do so involves a principle we all unconsciously agree to when conversing: the cooperative principle and its attendant maxims of conversation.

Cooperative principle and maxims of conversation

The **cooperative principle** posits that generally we try to be cooperative in interacting with others, and we assume that others try to be cooperative too. This seems like a simple idea, but there are some important ways in which this simple idea can help us account for seemingly aberrant expressions, as we shall see. The cooperative principle has four maxims attached to it.

Maxim of quantity

We expect speakers to be as informative as, but no more or less than, is necessary. If, for example, we ask a new acquaintance whether he has any kids and he answers "Two girls," using the maxim of quantity, we would assume that he has only two girls. If we found out later that he also had a boy, we might feel deceived. He would have broken the maxim of quantity by giving too little information.

Maxim of relevance

We expect speakers to offer utterances that are relevant to the ongoing context. If we ask someone whether he is ready to go and he replies, "I can't remember the capital of Albania," he has broken the maxim of relevance, for his answer has nothing to do with the question.

Maxim of manner

We expect speakers to be clear and orderly in their utterances, not opaque and rambling. That is, we expect those we converse with to speak in such a way that it is easy to follow. Not all conversational contributions are clear and orderly, of course, but our general expectation is that they should be.

Maxim of quality

We expect speakers to say what they believe to be true and to have some reason to believe what they say to be true. In other words, we generally expect people not to lie. Obviously, people do lie, but we see lies as exceptions to the rule, not the norm. This maxim only applies to statements; questions cannot be said to be true or false in any meaningful sense, though their implications can be.

As we are conversing with our friends, we don't consciously think, *OK, be sure to follow the maxims here.* How do they help us understand conversations, then? For one thing, they help us understand the function of such phrases as *to make a long story short* or *bear with me* or *not to change the subject, but . . .*, each of which signals we're about to follow or violate a maxim: quantity, manner, or relevance, respectively. Hedges, those little phrases like *sort of* or *kind of* can sometimes indicate we are violating the maxim of quality. Saying *It was kind of purple* allows us to follow the maxim of quality by indicating we're not totally sure about the color.

And we certainly notice when someone violates these principles egregiously or too often. If someone gives us too much information, thus violating the maxim of quantity, we might say, *TMI.* If someone gives too little information, we might call her secretive or aloof. If someone breaks the maxim of quality, we call her a liar. Conversing with someone who consistently breaks the maxim of manner or relevance might evoke the thought, *What is she on about?*

People do routinely violate these maxims, yet these violations do not seem to disrupt communication. The question becomes, then, how do we interpret these seemingly non-cooperative utterances? We use the cooperative principle and our knowledge of these maxims to help us figure it out. As an illustrative example, let's look at a conversation taking place at home between partners.

George: *Someone's at the door.*
Martha: *I'm on the phone.*
George: *Okay, I'll get it.*

Now we might say that Martha's reply to George's utterance breaks the maxim of relevance. What does being on the phone have to do with the doorbell ringing? That's exactly the question that leads George to his response. He must go through an unconscious reasoning process that goes something like this: *I assume Martha is being cooperative (the cooperative principle), so although her response literally breaks the maxim of relevance, I'll look for an alternative interpretation. Using my knowledge about the context and about the real world, I deduce that being on the phone precludes her from answering the door, and her mention of it is meant to indicate that.*

Indirectness

As we can see from that little interaction, we often don't say directly what we mean. In fact, in everyday conversations, much of what we say is indirect. We rely on the addressee's willingness and ability to figure out what we mean when we state something indirectly. Three questions arise here: What is indirectness? How do we figure it out? Why is it so common, especially given that it requires more work on the part of addressees since they must figure out what the speaker means?

Let's start with what it is. An utterance can be indirect in any one of several ways:

1. It can seem to violate one or more maxims of the cooperative principle. Martha's response earlier seems to break the maxim of relevance, so it is indirect.
2. It can also be indirect because its form does not match its function, a request phrased as a question, for example. You may have noticed that George's statement in the first place is indirect as well. He says *Someone's at the door*, literally a statement, but his pragmatic intent is a question, *Will you answer it or should I?* (We can also say it is indirect because it violates the maxim of quantity by stating the obvious.) To respond to George's initial statement, Martha needs to go through an inference process to determine that its meaning is a question. We know she went through such a process from her response, not a response to a statement of the obvious, but an indirect response to an indirect question.
3. When the literal meaning of an utterance differs from its intended meaning, it can also be indirect. Some humorous responses, such as *Is the Pope Catholic?* to mean *yes*, are indirect in this way.

Speech acts are considered indirect if they do any of the aforementioned acts. These **indirect speech acts**, as we saw with George, require some additional reasoning to figure out. We can summarize the reasoning a hearer goes through to interpret indirect speech acts as follows:

1. Recognizing an apparent violation of a maxim or recognizing that the form of an utterance does not match its function, and assuming the speaker is trying to be cooperative, the hearer identifies the utterance as indirect in some way. Thus, we use the theoretical concept of the cooperative principle and its maxims to help us understand indirect speech acts.
2. The addressee works out its intended meaning using knowledge of the context and **real-world knowledge**, what we know or believe about the world around us, including the social world.

Continuum of indirectness

Indirect speech acts are not all equally indirect, of course. There is a continuum of indirectness from conventionally indirect, to indirect, to very indirect.

Conventional indirectness

As mentioned earlier, some expressions are so conventionally used that they barely seem indirect at all; indeed, they seem like direct speech acts. *Could you pass the salt?*, the example used earlier, is a conventionally indirect request that most people would see as a direct request, easily interpreted. Utterances like *could you possibly . . ., would you mind . . ., would you be so kind as to . . ., if it's not too much trouble, could you . . .*, and many more are also conventionally indirect.

Indirectness

Other utterances seem a little more indirect and thus a little harder to interpret. Martha's response to George's statement falls in this category; it is simply indirect. It takes a little unconscious interpretation to work out Martha's meaning but not so much that the answer calls attention to itself by its indirectness or is incomprehensible because of its indirectness. George probably did not consciously scratch his head and say, *What the heck does she mean by that?*

Extreme indirectness

When utterances are extremely indirect, we often do scratch out heads and say, *What the heck does he mean by that?* And we can get it wrong sometimes, misinterpreting the speaker's intent. The following interaction happened at the university where I teach, though I've changed some details and names. The president, who has her own parking spot and who usually drives a Honda, walked into her office one morning and said to her secretary, "Tell Pete [the head of parking] that there's an Oldsmobile in my parking spot." Her secretary, trying to interpret what the president's pragmatic intent was, assumed she meant that the Oldsmobile was illegally parked there, called Pete, and asked him to have the car towed. You may have guessed that the president had a very different pragmatic intent. She had borrowed an Oldsmobile for the day and wanted to alert Pete so that he would not tow it.

Functions of indirectness

As noted in the previous section, indirectness is very common in all sorts of situations. Why should this be so? If it's harder to interpret indirect utterances, you'd expect them to be rather rare, but they're not. They must, then, serve some purposes important enough to override the cognitive difficulties they can cause.

Politeness

One of the most obvious functions of indirectness is to be polite. In many English-speaking societies, indirectness is considered polite. You would probably not ask a stranger to open a window by saying, *Open the window!* though you might use such an expression to a close friend or family member. With a stranger or acquaintance, you'd probably be more likely to phrase the request more indirectly to be polite: *Would it be too much trouble to open the window?* Such conventionalized indirect forms are considered much more polite in many cultures but not all. In Moroccan culture, directness is generally more polite than indirectness. We return to indirectness, including questions of the variability of what is seen as polite, in the section on politeness later.

Avoiding overt markers of power

Indirectness also allows speakers to avoid overt expressions of power through seeming to offer options. A boss might, for example, say to her secretary, *If you have time, could you send this out for me today?* Such an indirect request implies that the secretary has a choice here. That may be true, but it also may not. Chances are the indirect request is really an order: this needs to be done today. The appearance of choice implied by the indirectness politely masks the fact that it's an order.

Creating solidarity

Earlier we mentioned the importance of context in interpreting indirect utterances. The point about such contextual knowledge is that it must be *shared* knowledge. That is, for an indirect utterance to be successful, interlocutors must share the contextual knowledge necessary to interpret the utterance. Let's look at an example here. If a friend asks you, *Coming to the party tonight?* and you reply, *Got a test tomorrow*, you are both using shared background knowledge about the interaction itself (questions demand answers), about each other (you are a serious student who cares about your learning), and about the real world (tests require that one study the night before, thus precluding a party). When you reply to his question, you rely on the fact that he has this knowledge; when interpreting your answer, he relies on the fact that you do too. The whole thing only works smoothly if you both share the necessary contextual knowledge and both know (however unconsciously) that you share it.

This is all rather a round-about way of getting to another function of indirectness, that of creating closeness or solidarity. Indirectness can be used to create closeness because it signals that you and I share this knowledge to such an extent that it need not even be stated explicitly.

Indirectness can also be used to create distance, the opposite of solidarity. When one person does not share the knowledge necessary to interpret an indirect utterance, it can create social distance in that it implies, *You don't get it*.

Language and social meaning: Context and identity

Earlier I noted that one definition of pragmatics is the study of language in context. In some ways, it is redundant to say *language in context*, for language is always in some context, even if that context is a linguistics textbook or a cheer at a ball game. The context of interest here is not a linguistics textbook, of course, but language as it is used by people in everyday interaction. Context includes much more than the physical location in which we interact. It includes aspects of the social setting as well: the relationship among interlocutors, the speech event, the purpose of the interaction, and other social factors. One aim of our analysis here is to illuminate the role these contextual factors play in the construction of social meanings, including social identities and relationships.

Register

We all know that we talk or sign differently depending on where we are, who else is there, and what we're there for; we don't talk the same at dinner with our families as we do in a job interview, for example. We adapt our language use, our discourse, to the situation or context in which it occurs. The term we use for language variation that relates to social situations is **register**. As we learn to be communicatively competent, we learn to use different registers, that is, to adapt our language to different speech situations. Some research has shown that quite young children, as young as four, have an understanding of register, and they adapt their way of speaking to reflect that understanding. Kids can often quite accurately mimic the register of doctors or nurses, for example. Registers can differ in vocabulary, pronunciation, grammar, politeness, eye contact, proxemics (how close you might stand to another), and other aspects of communication. In one situation, for example, we might say *Would you like* *to leave now?*; in another, we might say *Wanna go?* In one situation, we might call someone *inebriated*; in another, *stinking drunk*.

Level of formality is one factor connected to register. Formal situations tend to have clearer conventions about what is appropriate discourse and what is not. They call for certain rules of linguistic interaction: interruptions are frowned upon, one person speaks at a time, each person has a specific role that dictates who speaks when, titles are often used. In a courtroom, for example, certain terms of address are required of certain participants: the judge is addressed as *Your honor*; in many college classrooms, the instructor is addressed as *Professor* or *Doctor*. Other less formal settings, hanging out with good friends perhaps, call for different ways of interacting; jokes are common, overlaps occur easily, and nicknames and references to shared past interactions are common. Our discourse not only reflects what we see as the formality level of a setting; it can also construct a particular setting as more or less formal or informal. Formality and informality, then, apply both to settings themselves and to the discourse used in any situation. *Hello* is more formal than *howdy* or *hey*, no matter the setting, and the use of the latter helps construct a setting as informal.

Identity work

It seems obvious that an analysis of language in social interaction must include the participants, their social identities, and the roles they play. (The term *participants* is added here to includes more than interlocutors, for participants may not speak or sign but are still part of the context.) Participants' status or closeness vis-à-vis each other, for example, is important. If a good friend asked you for the time when a clock was on the wall right in front of her, you might make a snide remark about her powers of observation. Can you imagine a scenario in which you as a student would respond in a similarly snide fashion to a professor? The relationship, especially the power differential in the relationship, makes the latter scenario less likely. Not impossible, but certainly less likely.

When we interact with others through language, we are always to some extent doing **identity work**, indicating something about who we are and constructing a certain kind of relationship with others. A somewhat drawn-out example might help us examine the factors involved in this construction. Imagine two people talking in a coffee shop near a college campus. We might ask: Is this a conversation between friends or a conference between teacher and student? The interaction may well have elements of both; it may be a hybrid; one participant may see it as one thing, the other as something different. For now, our question is not what the context and relationship are, but *how do the interlocutors in this interaction signal their social identities and their relationship?* What linguistic forms are used by the professor, for example, to present herself as the professor, not the friend? What forms are used by the student to signal that she accepts that representation, a sort of metaphorical, *OK, I'll be the student now*?

As I was writing that paragraph at a coffee shop near a college campus, I noticed two people at the next table, one a male traditional-aged college student, the other female, a bit older. I wondered if they were friends or a professor and her student. Within a few moments of (inadvertently) overhearing their conversation, I knew. She was clearly a professor; he clearly a student. So how did I know? She established her identity as the professor through her discourse, by asking questions and offering evaluative comments; he established his identity as a student by reporting on his experience studying abroad, not his excursions to exotic parts, but what he learned and how he fared in classes. She listened attentively. She gave advice: *You need to send an email to the people you met there.* As the conversation moved on to other topics, she continued to give advice and offer judgments: *You need to read X* (not *you gotta* [with elongated vowel sound] *read X*, as a fellow student might phrase it); *I approve of that.* There were no hedges or fillers. His utterances included *I'll do that*; *I'm hoping to find a position at X. Do you have any advice for going about that?* And she was the one who indicated the conversation was about to end, saying *Well, it sounds like things are going well for you.* Both contributed smoothly to the construction of their roles as professor and student.

Clearly, the fact that the participants' roles outside of this conversation differ so clearly in power and status is important. There are words and deeds allowed a professor that are not allowed a student; the professor can make evaluations and demands (*Good point* or *Get this to me by tomorrow*) that the student cannot reciprocate. The professor can ask to be called by her title; the student cannot easily do so. As the person with more power in this situation, the professor can more easily frame the event; her interpretation will most likely hold sway. Indeed, the ability to have one's representation of the context and the relationship accepted by the other is one mark of power.

Sometimes, differences in status and power may be negotiated. For example, if a professor and her student meet by accident at a movie theater, each must come to an understanding of what their relationship is in *this* context. Each must decide (though probably not consciously) whether this is a chance meeting of acquaintances (in which case neither is owed deference by the other), or a chance meeting of teacher and student (in which case some deference may be owed to one). Each will signal how she sees the situation. The professor might signal that she sees this situation as the chance encounter of acquaintances by saying *hey* instead of *hello*; using contractions (*wanna, gonna* instead of *want to* or *going to*); and using colloquial forms such as *D'ya like it?* instead of *Did you enjoy the movie?* The decision to use the former forms may not be conscious, but it carries meaning. A different meaning would be expressed by other forms. Linguistic choices we make about words, topics, and pronunciation all signal how we see our social identities and the nature of the relationship in a particular context.

POLITENESS

Expectations of politeness or appropriateness are also important parts of any context. Politeness, in fact, is one reason we have many ways of saying the same thing. We probably all think we know what politeness and impoliteness are: we know it when we see it, at least. If we're going to examine politeness from a theoretical perspective, we'll need a bit more than that, however.

Perhaps the most influential theory of politeness is that of Brown and Levinson (1987), who define politeness as behavior, including linguistic behavior, used to express positive concern for others and/or not to impose on others. According to this theory, all people have two important needs: the need to be valued and the need for autonomy. That is, we all want our self-worth and our autonomy to be respected by others. Politeness is one way people accomplish that. In Brown's and Levinson's terms, politeness helps to mitigate possible threats to the listener's face that might be caused by the speaker's words or actions.

Face, a key concept related to those two needs, refers to the self-image a person wants to maintain in social situations. For example, if you are reluctant to answer a question in class for fear of appearing dumb, you are attending to your own face. If you are reluctant to speak up for fear of making another look dumb, you are attending to that other person's face. Politeness is about attending to others' face by enhancing it or not threatening it. An insult would threaten it; a compliment enhances it. Face can be saved, threatened, lost, maintained, or enhanced; it needs to be attended to for things to go smoothly in any social interaction.

Face has two related but distinct aspects: positive face and negative face. Despite their names, it is not that positive face is good and negative face is bad; both are normal parts of social interactions, neither good nor bad. We use different politeness strategies depending upon whether we are attending to others' positive face or their negative face.

Positive face and positive politeness

Positive face refers to our desire to be well thought of in whatever way is relevant in a particular context. It includes our need to be appreciated and approved of and generally to be thought of in a positive manner. **Positive politeness strategies** are efforts to enhance or avoid threatening another's positive face. They attend to others' positive face needs by, for example, overtly showing appreciation or making others feel good or included. Welcoming someone is a positive politeness strategy. Such strategies also avoid threatening another's positive face by avoiding overt disagreement or disapproval. *Thank you* is a prime example of positive politeness.

Negative face and negative politeness

Negative face refers to our desire to have our autonomy respected, that is, not to be imposed upon. **Negative politeness strategies** are used when an utterance might impose upon the other. Requests of someone to do something for us are good examples of utterances that threaten others' negative face by imposing upon their freedom of action; such requests, therefore, often include some negative politeness markers: *please, if it's not too much trouble, sorry to bother you*, etc. Suggestions and advice also have the potential to threaten a person's negative face, so they too are often expressed indirectly or with disclaimers that mitigate the threat: *I'm no expert, but you might want to try X*, for example. *Please* is a prime example of negative politeness.

In negative politeness, it is not that we necessarily want to avoid imposing on someone else. What we want to do is avoid appearing to threaten their face by imposing, and it is politeness strategies that allow us to do that. If we want the salt passed, and we must impose on the person at the end of the table to get that done, we do impose on them. We just do so politely by using strategies that give the appearance of choice: *Could you pass the salt*, for example. We know and they know that we are not really offering choice; we want the salt.

Politeness strategies are needed when what we are about to say may threaten someone's face, but not all expressions of politeness are equally polite. There are, in fact, levels of politeness. In deciding the degree of politeness we need to use in any one situation, we take into account three factors (two of which were mentioned earlier under indirectness): **power differential** between interlocutors, **social distance** between interlocutors, and **amount of imposition**. The larger any factor is, the higher the possibility that the other's face will be threatened, and thus the more polite we have to be. When we make requests, we are more polite to those of higher status or those with more power; we are more polite to those we are less close to, acquaintances or strangers; and we are more polite when the imposition is larger. Asking to borrow someone's notes from class requires more politeness than asking to borrow their pen.

The concept of face, and Brown's and Levinson's (1987) theory in general, can help to explain some instances of politeness, but certainly not all. Their theory focuses on utterances that are clearly and overtly polite: *Thank you; Do you mind if I close the window; Please, you go first*, things like that. Even with those that are clearly polite, however, politeness is not always just a matter of face. For one thing, politeness can be and often is seen as empty talk, as insincere, or as something used to manipulate others. For another, such phrases as *please* or *thank you*, it can be argued, are mere social conventions rather than politeness: in saying *thank you* to a server at a restaurant, for example, we are doing what is expected as appropriate rather than trying to enhance the server's positive face.

Appropriateness

According to recent theories of politeness, in addition to attending to face, politeness is a matter of judgments we make of others' behavior, especially judgments of the appropriateness of their behavior in a particular context. Appropriateness can be a tricky concept to pin down. For one thing, different social groups and individuals in different situations may have different ideas of what constitutes appropriate behavior, including, of course, linguistic behavior. Asking a stranger or a colleague at work to do something by saying, *Would it be too much trouble to ask you to move a bit?* might be deemed appropriate and thus polite; using the same phrase with your best friend might evoke a different interpretation: *Why is she mad at me?* It's not that we're impolite to our friends when we say, *move your ass*. It's that the rules of appropriate behavior are different in that context with that set of people than they would be in a different setting with different people.

Thus, politeness is not intrinsic to any utterance. We might think of *Thank you* as intrinsically polite, but that's not necessarily so. Several years ago, I taught at a Polish university for a semester. When I first got there, I tried to practice what little Polish I knew whenever I could, so in a restaurant, whenever a server filled my water glass or took a used plate away, I said *Dziękuję*, Polish for *Thank you*. I noticed that the servers often seemed a little put out by me, a fact I put down to my atrocious Polish accent. Later I found out that in Poland, unlike in the United States, to thank a server for such mundane tasks is not considered appropriate or polite but almost rude. From the servers' perspective, it is their job to deliver food and take plates away; they do not need to be thanked for doing their job.

As that anecdote and many studies have shown, what is considered polite varies greatly across cultures, across subcultures, across speech communities, even across situations within one culture. Different ethnic groups can have very different perspectives on what is appropriate. Most of us probably think finishing another's sentence is inherently rude. That's not always the case, however. I come from an Italian family, for example, in which interrupting was not impolite but a normal, appropriate part of conversations. And finishing another's sentence was not so much rude as an indirect way of saying: *I'm listening so closely to what you are saying that I can even finish your sentence!*

Since politeness is a matter of judgments of appropriateness in a particular context or group, it comes with all sorts of gender, racial, and class constraints. What is considered appropriate linguistic behavior for a man, for example, can be considered rude or totally inappropriate for a woman. Take swearing, for instance. In many situations, swearing is considered rude for both genders; in others, it's appropriate for men but not women. I remember as a college student using a swear word in front of my mother, who, of course, immediately told me never to use that word again. My brother came in a few minutes later, used the same word, and she totally ignored it. I was livid but was told it was okay for him because he's a boy! You can imagine how well that went down with me.

As noted in the discussion of indirectness, Moroccans, unlike most English speakers, often find indirectness less polite than directness. Asking a member of one's family for help by saying the Arabic equivalent of *Could you . . .* would be impolite, not polite. In Israel, directness rather than indirectness is similarly valued; what we would consider polite, appropriate behavior might be seen as potentially irrelevant or manipulative in Israel. In Deaf culture too, directness is considered appropriate, not impolite. The same linguistic behavior, then, can have different, even opposite, meanings in different contexts and cultures.

It is important to remember that just as judgments of polite, appropriate behavior vary, so do judgments of inappropriate behavior, what is called impoliteness. It is well known, so much so that it is almost a cliché, that Midwesterners who visit New York City often find New Yorkers rude and pushy, asking personal questions, and being too direct. What is less well known is that New Yorkers often find Midwesterners rude too, not because they are too direct but because they are too indirect, not asking questions, and not saying directly what they mean.

CHAPTER SUMMARY

- Conversations have a patterned organization which includes opening sequences, turn-taking, and closing sequences.
- Pragmatics is the field of linguistics that investigates how we use language in context, especially in everyday interactions. It focuses on discourse, any unit of language beyond the sentence.
- A key concept in pragmatics is that we do things with words. Speech acts are those things we do through language; each speech act consists of a locution, an illocution, or pragmatic intent, and a perlocution.
- To explain how interlocutors make sense of another's utterance, linguists posit the cooperative principle and its four maxims: quantity, relevance, manner, and quality.
- Indirectness, though more difficult for a listener to interpret, is very common. Utterances can be indirect, conventionally indirect, or very indirect. The functions of indirectness include being polite, avoiding overt markers of power, and creating solidarity.
- Contextual factors such as the social setting, the relationship among interlocutors, the purpose of the interaction, and the social identities are important to any understanding of language use.
- We use discourse to do identity work, indicating who we are and how we see our relationship with our interlocutors.
- Expectations of politeness and appropriateness are an important part of understanding language use. Politeness consists of attending to another's positive or negative face. It is also related to what is deemed to be appropriate behavior in a context and thus varies across cultures, subcultures, and speech communities.

KEY TERMS

discourse

conversational patterns: opening sequences, closing sequences, turn-taking, floor

silence

pragmatics; pragmatic intent

interlocutors

speech acts: locution, illocution, perlocution

cooperative principle: Maxim of Quantity, Maxim of Quality, Maxim of Relevance, Maxim of Manner

indirectness; indirect speech acts, conventional indirectness

register

politeness and impoliteness

face; negative face; positive face

power differential

social distance

appropriateness

EXPLORATIONS

Exploration 1: Class rules

Observe either a lecture class and a discussion class at your institution. Identify the unspoken rules of interaction common to that class so that someone who isn't familiar with higher education settings might be able to fit in. Comment on the interlocutors and their roles, the level of formality, meanings of silence, turn-taking patterns (who holds the floor the longest, for example), topics discussed and who gets to decide which topics are discussed. You might note the conversations that take place before and after class as well as interactions during class.

   Discussion Prompt: Share your observations with your group, noting which interactional patterns the two types of class share and what patterns differentiate them.

   Writing prompt: Summarize your observations, noting which patterns the two types of class share and which differentiate them.

Exploration 2: Locutions and illocutions

- *It's a snake?* Imagine the phrase, *There's a snake in there!* spoken by someone with outstretched arm pointing to the next room. (Take *snake* to mean the reptile, not a reprehensible person.) List as many speech acts (pragmatic intents) as you can to describe what that utterance might mean.

- *I kid not.* Imagine the phrase, *Are you kidding?* Like *It's a snake*, its speaker can have various pragmatic intents in uttering it. What are those pragmatic intents and what contexts might they be used in and with whom?

Exploration 3: Giving advice (group project)

There are many ways to make suggestions or offer advice. Imagine a friend coming to you for suggestions about a problem. In your small group, decide on a specific problem to offer suggestions about. Then list as many ways as you can for doing so, writing down exactly what you would say. Rank your locutions (what you'd say) from very indirect to conventionally indirect to direct. What factors might influence your choice of which form to use?

   Discussion prompt: Compare your findings with your small group; discuss any similarities or differences you see, using concepts from the chapter to guide you.

Writing prompt: Write a one-page description of what you found, using concepts from the chapter to guide you.

Exploration 4: Politeness

Choose a club or organization or group of friends you are part of. Describe how politeness and impoliteness work in this group. What is considered polite? Impolite? What type of politeness strategies, positive or negative, are most prevalent? What might be considered impolite or rude by an outsider but would be normal for this group? How do theories of politeness illuminate (or not) what is going on?

Discussion prompt: Share your findings with your small group and compare similarities and differences.

Writing prompt: Write a one-page description of how politeness works here.

Exploration 5: What'cha sayin'?

Using [ɪn] or [ɪŋ] for -*ing* at the end of verbs is related to both social identity and register. Notice your own use of these variants and their use by speakers around you. Imagine you are explaining them to a new student who is learning English and trying to fit in. What would you tell them about when to use which variant?

Exploration 6: What's so funny?

Figure 8.2 and Figure 8.3 show two cartoons. Which concepts from this chapter can be used to explain what's going on in each?

FIGURE 8.2 What's so funny here?

FIGURE 8.3 What's so funny here?

FURTHER READING

Austin, J. (1962). *How to do things with words.* Oxford University Press.

Gumperz, J., Jupp, T., & Roberts, C. (1979). *Crosstalk: A study of cross-cultural communication.* National Centre for Industrial Language Training and BBC. A video showing miscommunication between native and non-native speakers of English due to differing conversational norms.

Levinson, S. (1983). *Pragmatics.* Cambridge University Press. A classic in the field.

Wardhaugh, R. (1985). *How conversation works.* Blackwell. An accessible classic in the field.

REFERENCES

Brown, P., & Levinson, S. (1987). *Politeness: Some universals in language usage.* Cambridge University Press.

Mesthrie, R., Swann, J., Deumert, A., & Leap, W. (2000). *Introducing sociolinguistics.* John Benjamins Publishing Company.

CHAPTER 9

Language variation and society

....

INTRODUCTION

In Chapter 1, I mentioned how, when I lived in London many years ago, I took exception to the pressures on me to drop my American accent. I couldn't have explained then why that pressure made me uncomfortable, though I realized I didn't want to sound like something I was not. Now I understand those feelings a bit more. Language is a resource for expressing our social identities, who we are and how we want others to see us. Asking me to change my accent, then, was asking me to change who I was.

We all use language to express our social identities, but we can only do so because of the inherent variation in all languages. If we all sounded exactly alike, we'd have no way to mark who we are through our language use. Because of variation, we use certain lexical, phonological, and grammatical variants as resources to mark and construct ourselves as certain kinds of people in particular social contexts. The field of linguistics that looks most closely at this variation and its social meanings is sociolinguistics, a field we'll examine here. Sociolinguistics in its broadest form investigates how linguistic behaviors reflect and construct social distinctions and how language relates to various social phenomena, including social inequalities.

DOI: 10.4324/9780429269059-9

First, we'll look at variationist linguistics, those studies that examine different varieties and the social meanings ascribed to them. Then we'll turn to standardization, the process whereby certain varieties in modern nation states came to be valued and other varieties devalued. Finally, we'll look at critical sociolinguistics, a subfield that studies the ideologies that underlie and resist the pattern of valuing and devaluing that supports social inequalities. Throughout, we'll address the consequences of common attitudes about linguistic diversity and specific varieties, locating our discussion within larger systems of difference and inequality. And we'll revisit some of the myths about correctness we first touched on in Chapter 2.

A note about terminology

We noted in Chapter 2 that the very concept of a language is in some ways problematic. When we label a system of communication as English or Swahili or Tagalog, we imply an unchanging, monolithic entity and thus hide the staggering amount of variation found within most languages. Those labels are often convenient, if we keep in mind that they are imprecise terms for constellations of different varieties of what we call English or Swahili or Tagalog.

This constellation brings up an important question any discussion of variation must address: what term to use for those varieties? As we noted in Chapter 2, many people think of dialects as substandard or old-fashioned, as something others speak, or as slang. We know, however, that everyone speaks a dialect, no matter our educational level; that no dialect is substandard; and that slang is present in all dialects. Those negative connotations of the term *dialect* remain present for most people, so what term can we use instead?

Variety is one candidate, but as we saw in Chapter 8, there are many kinds of variation: variation based on the situation of use (register) and individual variation (idiolects), to name two. The variation we examine in this chapter differs from register and idiolect. For one thing, all dialects have different registers and idiolects. For another, dialect refers to a variety shared by a group that also shares some regional or social identity. In our discussion, we will use the term variety as a cover term for various types of dialects: regional dialects, sociolects, and ethnolects, each of which is examined in the following sections.

Of equal importance is the question of what label to use for any one variety. As with labeling a language, giving a variety a name carries implications: that this variety is somehow monolithic, that all speak it the same, that all who share a particular social identity speak it. Such a label essentializes both the variety and the group that speaks it. This is especially important when those groups are marginalized or stigmatized by mainstream society. The variety spoken by many, but not all, African Americans is often called African American English or African American Language. That label subtly equates ethnicity or race with speaking a particular variety, as though it is somehow part of one's genes. It is not. Just as we can talk about Minnesota English and acknowledge that not everyone in Minnesota speaks that variety or speaks it the same way, we need to recognize there are differences among speakers of African American English and all varieties. We discuss more of this variety in Chapter 10. For now, keep in mind that although we need labels to discuss difference, labels are always potentially problematic.

One more note about terminology: **sociolinguistic variants**, or just **variants**, here refer to the alternate forms of a linguistic feature that are associated with specific social groups or social identities. To give a simple example, the use of *G'day, mate!* as a greeting is a variant associated with Australians. For non-Australians, its use evokes that identity. For Australians, it is just the way they talk.

STRUCTURED VARIATION

Early sociolinguist research focused on the ways that variation within any one language is not random but structured; that is, it reflects social identities: our region of origin, our ethnicity, our gender, our social class, our age, among other identities. The pronunciation of /r/ can serve as an example of what is meant by **structured variation**. That feature varies greatly across varieties of English. To be precise, the pronunciation of /r/ in word-final position or before a consonant, what is known as post-vocalic /r/, varies greatly. Some varieties are what is known as **rhotic**: /r/ is pronounced. Some are **non-rhotic**: unless it is before a vowel, /r/ is not pronounced.

A classic study by William Labov (1966) investigated the presence of that post-vocalic /r/ in the speech of different socioeconomic classes of New Yorkers using a very clever technique: asking sales personnel in different department stores (Saks, an upper-middle-class store; Macy's, middle-class; and Klein's, working-class store) for a department located on the fourth floor. Labov then noted how often the /r/ was pronounced in the answer, *fourth floor*. What he found was a structured pattern: those from the upper-middle-class store pronounced it most often, those from the middle-class one less often, and those from the working-class store pronounced it least often. This and subsequent studies in various parts of the English-speaking world have shown that pronunciation of that sound and others reflects speakers' social identities in a structured way.

That post-vocalic /r/ brings into focus another key concept: value judgments of linguistic features are arbitrary, based on judgments of people rather than judgments of the language itself. In the United States, rhotic dialects, those that pronounce /r/, are generally more prestigious; in Britain, the opposite is true. The upper class tends not to pronounce that /r/, but the working class does.

Regional variation

Regional variation is the kind of variation most commented on by people, who often find accent and vocabulary differences fascinating. When I teach this in my classes, students readily come up with differences between the neighboring states of Minnesota and Wisconsin: *bubbler* vs *drinking fountain* or *duck, duck, grey duck* vs *duck, duck, goose*. These examples may create the impression that the line between varieties is clear cut. Not so. For one thing, varieties tend to blend into one another. For another, each regional variety has variation within it based on age, gender, class, or ethnicity.

The regional dialect divisions in Britain are quite old, reflecting conquest and settlement patterns from centuries ago. In the mid-5th century, the Angles, Saxons, and Jutes brought slightly different varieties of their Germanic language when they invaded and settled in different areas of Britain. The general dividing line for those areas remains a general dividing line among varieties today. When the Norse invaded a few centuries later, they tended to settle mostly in the northeastern part of England; the varieties spoken there still reflect the influence of the Norse language. English spread throughout the British Isles, coming into contact with the Celtic languages spoken by the Welsh, Scots, and Irish, all of whom gave their own color to the English varieties that developed in those areas.

In the United States the origins of regional varieties reflect regional varieties in Britain. In the 17th and 18th centuries, settlers from certain areas in Britain tended to settle in certain areas of what is now the United States, bringing their varieties with them. The result was the creation of three major dialect regions by the time of the American Revolution: Northern, settled mostly by people from Anglia; Midland, settled mostly by people from the Midlands of England; and Southern, settled mostly by people from Northern England, Northern Ireland, and Scotland. Later, people from all three areas took their varieties with them as they moved west. As they did so, they interacted with people from other areas speaking other dialects, resulting in a mingling of varieties and a leveling of some distinct features in each. Part of that intermingling also involved the languages of the peoples conquered in that western expansion, Native American languages and Spanish most notably.

Leveling is a process whereby differences among dialects decrease, usually the result of social or geographic mobility. This leveling partly accounts for the fact that there is less regional variation in the western United States than in the East. People from Los Angeles and people from Portland sound more like one another than do people from New York and those from Savannah.

English spread not just to the United States, of course, but to many regions of the world. It is spoken as the dominant language in Ireland, Canada, Australia, New Zealand, and South Africa, among other nations. Each of these nations has what is known as a **national variety**: Australian English, South African English, Canadian English, etc. The same is true for languages of other colonial powers who spread their languages across the globe; we have Senegal French and Colombian Spanish, for example. The Spanish of Colombia is different from that of Spain; the French of Senegal is different from that of France. Like those of English, the national varieties of Spanish and French spoken both inside and outside Spain and France have their own regional dialects, which reflect settlement patterns and interaction with indigenous groups and their languages and with immigrants from other countries. All of these varieties are rule governed and valid varieties of those languages, not broken Spanish or fractured French.

British English and North American English

The national varieties of those languages and of English are generally mutually intelligible; they share many features but differ in others. Those differences appear not only in vocabulary but in pronunciation, spelling, and syntax as well, so much so that there are books, for example, to help North Americans understand Australian English or Scottish English.

The British use of *lift* for U.S. *elevator* is among the most well-known differences in vocabulary; others include British *bonnet* and *boot* for North American *hood* and *trunk* of a car, *rubbish* for *garbage*, *chips* for *French fries*, *tin* for *can* of food, and *braces* for *suspenders*. Some of these differences can get you in trouble. In Britain, *knock up* does not mean to get someone pregnant but to wake someone up or cook something up; *mad* means *crazy* in Britain, not angry as in the United States; and if you *get pissed* in Britain, you've gotten drunk, not mad. Many pronunciation differences between British and North American English are well known: *dance* [a] or [æ]; *data* [dætə] or [detə], *luxury* [ləgʒəri] or [ləkʃəri], for example.

There are fewer differences in syntax or grammar among English varieties than in vocabulary or pronunciation, but there are some notable ones. The British say *in hospital*; North Americans say *in the hospital*; speakers in North America tend to prefer simple past as in *Did you eat yet?* The British prefer present perfect, *Have you eaten yet?* The British sometimes use a plural verb for some group nouns: *the committee are meeting tomorrow*, while North Americans normally use a singular verb: *the committee is meeting tomorrow*. Variation appears even in writing, where efforts to eliminate it are intense: in spelling (*honor* or *honour*, *tire* or *tyre*) and in punctuation (is a comma required after an introductory subordinate clause or not?). Canada, Australia, New Zealand, India, and many other countries that were once colonized by the British have generally adopted the British standard of spelling.

Regional variation in the United States

Like all varieties, regional varieties of U.S. English differ in phonology, vocabulary, and sometimes in syntax. One of the most well-known vocabulary differences is *pop* (in the North), *coke* (South), or *soda* (Midland and West). Others include *pail* (the North) or *bucket* (elsewhere); *skillet* (Midland) or *frying pan* (elsewhere); *quarter till* the hour (Midland) or *quarter to* (elsewhere). Some vocabulary differences are quite localized: what I call a *rubber band* is called a *gum band* in Pittsburgh and a *rubber binder* in Minnesota. In Colorado, certain mountain peaks, those above 14,000 feet, are called *fourteeners*. In the Pacific Northwest, an expensive item may be described as *spendy*, and in Southern California, numbers for freeways take a definite article: *the 580*, though that's not the case in Northern California.

Pronunciation differences abound in regional varieties. The Boston dialect tends to be non-rhotic: that non-postvocalic /r/ is not pronounced, though it is in most other parts of the country; in the Bronx and some other areas of the East coast, you can hear [dIs] for *this* and [tɪŋk] for *think*. In most parts of the United States, the vowel sound in *buy* is [ay], but it's [a] in the South. In the North and South, the second vowel in *pajamas* is pronounced [a]; in the Midland, it is [æ]. One phonological variant I still retain from my childhood in Baltimore is what is called **intrusive /r/**, adding an [r] sound where others don't. I still pronounce *wash* as [warʃ] even though I haven't lived in the East coast since I was a teenager. And I still get teased about it!

Based on differences in pronunciation and vocabulary, U.S. English is often divided into four major regional dialect areas: the North, the South, the Midland, and the West. There is a great deal of variation within each of these, of course, and many linguists divide U.S. English into many more smaller dialect areas, some as small as one city, New York City or Philadelphia, for example. Although speakers in the West share many features and are thus seen as speaking the same major regional dialect, they do not all speak the same, so much so that some linguists divide the Pacific Northwest dialect from the Pacific Southwest dialect and both from the Southwestern one and the Rocky Mountain one. There is even more variation in the eastern part of the U.S. The South often gets lumped together into one dialect areas, but there are many different dialects within that major one: Gulf Southern, Coastal Southern, Floridian, and Texas South, to name a few. The Northeast has perhaps the most variety: Inland North, East New England, West New England, Hudson Valley, and others. And the Midland dialect region, which stretches from Delaware to Kansas, contains Mid-Atlantic (that's where my intrusive /r/ comes from), Western Pennsylvania, and others.

Social variation: Sociolects

Sociolects is the term used for varieties related to social class and other aspects of social status. Social class variation was clearly shown in Labov's (1966) study examining the use of post-vocalic /r/ in Saks, Macy's, and Klein's mentioned earlier. Other studies have found similar results for class. Trudgill (1974), for example, found a connection between social class and the use of certain variants of the pronunciation of -ing: [ɪn] or [ɪŋ]. Members of the middle class generally used [ɪŋ] more than [ɪn], and members of the working class did the opposite. Use of [ɪn] is often believed to be sloppy pronunciation or just plain bad English, an erroneous belief but one that is still widespread. There is nothing in any feature or variety or language that determines its worth; it is the connection of that feature with certain social groups that determines its value, as we'll discuss further.

Rickford's (1987) study on the use of creole in Guyana can shed light on how social class interacts with language use. (Creoles, which are discussed in more detail in Chapter 12, are language systems created from two languages, usually in situations of colonization, such as in Guyana, which was colonized by the British.) Rickford found that class differences are more important than ethnicity in explaining linguistic differences: the speech of the working class, who do the lowest status jobs, contains more creole features, while that of the "estate class," shopkeepers, clerks, and skilled trade workers, contains more standard features.

The differences found in those studies, and in most studies examining social class, are not absolute. No one has found that all members of a particular social group use a particular variant and that no members of other social groups do. Rather, those differences are a matter of tendencies, of percentages rather than all or nothing. In fact, it is often the case that certain variants generally seen as part of working-class speech are used by all classes at times. Nearly all of us, for example, use [ɪn] for -ing in very casual speech, though we might not in formal settings.

Social classes are not monolithic, of course, and other aspects of our social identities are connected to sociolects. Those aspects can be quite local, as Eckert showed in her classic study of high school students. Eckert (1989) studied the speech of jocks and burnouts at a high school in Detroit, Michigan. The distinction between these two groups is a familiar one in many U.S. high schools, though they may have different names: jocks see school as part of their identity, participate in extra-curricular activities, and aspire to higher education; burnouts identify more with the local community, do not participate as much in extra-curricular activities, and do not aspire to higher education. Eckert found that jocks and burnouts pronounced the vowel sound [ay] very differently, as noted in Chapter 4. She also found that their speech varied in other ways: burnouts used variants connected to the local community and jocks used variants that carried mainstream social prestige. Each group saw itself as different from the other; their sociolects reflected that belief.

Social variation: Ethnolects

Recent work in sociolinguistics has focused a lot on ethnic dialects or **ethnolects**, especially those spoken by African Americans and Hispanic Americans in the United States, by Maori in New Zealand, by Aboriginals in Australia, and those of Caribbean ancestry in the United Kingdom. Chapter 10 discusses AAE in some detail; here I describe some other ethnic varieties and the social meanings those varieties can carry. It is important to remember that they are as rule governed and correct as Standard English and that each contains a range of registers and variation; Hispanic English is not spoken the same way in all situations.

What makes a variety a variety is not one or even a few lexical, phonological, or syntactic variants, but a cluster of them. Many of those can overlap with variants of other varieties. Double negatives, for example, are a rule-governed feature of many varieties of English, both in the United States and other countries. When we focus on differences that make varieties distinct, we can forget the deep similarities that make them all English. It is also important to remember that just because an ethnolect is called Hispanic English, for example, it does not mean that all who identify as Hispanic speak that ethnolect, nor that there is only one way to speak it.

Hispanic English

Hispanic English is the name used to identify the many varieties of English spoken by Americans of Hispanic descent. In the United States that descent may be from Puerto Rico, Cuba, Spain, Mexico, Dominican Republic, or other Central or South American nations. That's a lot of different places. These groups vary not just by their place of origin, but by how long they have been in the United States, both as individuals and as communities. Some Hispanic communities in parts of the Southwest have been in what is now the United States for centuries. Among the different varieties of Hispanic English, the most well-known and well-studied are Chicanx English, Puerto Rican English, and Cuban English. (That first variety is sometimes called Chicano English, a name that connects its use to males, for that -o is a masculine ending in Spanish. To avoid that implication, I use Chicanx.)

Many think Hispanic English is just English spoken with a Spanish accent or is what is sometimes called Spanglish, a mixture of English and Spanish. It is neither. Although recent immigrants may speak English with an accent influenced by their native Spanish, the accent of their children who grow up speaking English (or both English and Spanish) is not a "foreign" accent but merely a phonological variation of English, like that of New Yorkers or Southerners or any of us. They do not speak funny English; they speak a normal, valid variety of English, with a range of registers just like any other variety.

Chicanx English or **CE**, the variety examined here, is the variety spoken by people of Mexican descent in the United States. Spoken across the United States, in major cities and in rural communities, especially those in the Southwest, it is a distinct, stable variety of U.S. English spoken by a large percentage of the population.

Some phonological features of CE are most likely the result of influences from Spanish that have now become part of this variety. Since Spanish has no [I] vowel sound, the sound [i] takes on its role; thus, *leap* and *lip* are both pronounced the same [lip]. The [ʃ] sound in SAE is pronounced [tʃ] at the beginning of a word in CE, so *shame* becomes [tʃem] rather than [ʃem]. At the end of a word, the opposite occurs: [tʃ] in SAE is pronounced [ʃ] in CE, so *such* is pronounced [səʃ]. Word-final consonant clusters tend to be reduced in CE more so than in SAE, especially when the last consonant is a [d]: *kind* is pronounced [kayn] and *herd* can sound just like *her*. Like French, Italian, Spanish, and many varieties of English, CE allows for negative concord (aka double negatives), as in *I don't want nothing*. Perhaps because of consonant cluster reduction, CE often omits the past-tense morpheme {ed} when the verb ends with [t],

[d], or [n]. Although these features are highly stigmatized as uneducated or incorrect English, they are rule governed.

Code switching/translanguaging

Here might be a good place to discuss **code switching**, the phenomenon in which a speaker uses two or more languages or varieties of a language within one utterance or conversation. It seems to be a universal phenomenon when interlocutors share two or more languages or varieties. Many people have the mistaken impression that code switching indicates the interlocutors do not have mastery of either language. Far from it. Code switching occurs when someone has enough fluency in both languages to switch easily—a sign of mastery, not its opposite. Indeed, code switching is often used to signal membership in multilingual communities.

In code switching, interlocutors keep the phonological and grammatical properties of each language as they speak. A person bilingual in Spanish and English might use a noun phrase in Spanish within an otherwise English sentence, keeping the adjective after the noun, as it is done in Spanish, rather than shifting the adjective before the noun as in English. Phonological features from each language are kept too. In this way, code switching is different from borrowing in which the pronunciation of the borrowed term changes to fit the phonological patterns of the new language. An example from my own life might help here. In an Italian restaurant a few years ago I ordered a meal, saying *I'd like the manicotti*. Because I speak Italian, I pronounced the last word as it is pronounced in Italian [manikoti] rather than the way it is pronounced as a word borrowed into English, [manikaDi]. Unfortunately, the server did not understand me as I had broken a cardinal rule for code switching: both interlocutors must understand both languages.

An alternate perspective on what is called code switching is **translanguaging**, which offers a different way of looking at multilingual speakers. The term code switching implies the existence of more than one language within an individual in a way that emphasizes the separate nature of those languages. Individuals are seen as switching back and forth between them. Theories of translanguaging instead posit that individuals make use of all of their languages as part of an integrated communication system. That is, multilingual speakers utilize their entire language repertoire, whichever of their available linguistic resources seems most appropriate to the situation at hand, without worrying about what language they are using. What is often seen as code switching is not so much switching between languages, but rather choosing words or phrases from one's linguistic repertoire regardless of the language. Theories of translanguaging thus recognize that bilinguals are not two monolinguals in one body.

Sociolinguistics in your world: Mock Spanish

Mock Spanish is, as the name implies, a way of making fun of Spanish and Spanish speakers. It is not an actual variety of Spanish or English; instead, it consists of a limited number of terms that are generally used by monolingual speakers of English to impart a humorous or light touch, terms such as *Hasta la vista, baby* or *manana*. It "borrows Spanish-language words and suffixes, assimilates their pronunciation to English, . . . [and] changes their meaning" (Hill, 2008, p. 134). According to Hill, those who use Mock Spanish often see themselves as showing an openness and respect for the Spanish language and culture. She points out, however, that Mock Spanish is often seen as offensive by those of Hispanic ancestry. So why should such phrases as *Hasta la vista, baby* or *manana* be offensive?

To explore that, we should first remember that Spanish has been spoken in what is now the United States for centuries, not only in those areas that used to be part of Mexico but elsewhere as well. As such, English speakers and Spanish speakers have come into contact often. It would only make sense that such contact might lead to lexical borrowing. Mock Spanish is fundamentally different from such borrowing, however.

Hill points out that one way it is different is that it evokes racist stereotypes. For example, though it simply means *tomorrow* in Spanish, *manana* in English takes on a connotation of laziness or procrastination and suggests a stereotype of a lazy Mexican. *Hasta la vista* means *see you later*; *adios* means *good-bye*. In Spanish neither carries hints of a threat or a brush off. Yet they do when used in English and evoke an offensive stereotype of Hispanic treachery or duplicity. Does this mean that every time we use Mock Spanish, we are being racist? That's a tricky question. Most people who do use it do not, I'd guess, mean to be offensive and would be shocked to think they are insulting anyone. The problem is that through its use, negative stereotypes such as those we've discussed are continually circulated and normalized in ways we don't generally recognize.

Native American Englishes

Native American Englishes are not one thing but a range of diverse varieties of English spoken by those of Native American ancestry across the United States and Canada. These varieties differ linguistically, historically, and socially. For some speakers, this variety is their first or native language; for others, it is a second, learned language. Some Native American varieties are strongly influenced by the Native American language still spoken in the community; for others, only some features of the ancestral language remain. Thus, they are quite diverse.

It is important to remember the history of Native Americans and their languages as we discuss Native American varieties of English. At the time of first contact with Europeans, there were more than 500 separate languages spoken by indigenous groups in what is now the United States and Canada. These 500 languages were quite diverse. That linguistic landscape changed dramatically with the coming of Europeans in the 16th century, an invasion which had devastating effects on Native American cultures and languages. Today, of the 500 languages spoken before the 16th century, only approximately 200 are still being used and many of them are in danger of dying.

One important contributor to that devastation was the development of what were called boarding schools in the United States and residential schools in Canada. Starting in the mid to late 19th century, Native American children were taken from their families and communities, often forcibly, and sent to boarding schools where they were severely punished for speaking their native languages. The stated aim of the schools and of government policy in general was to eradicate their indigenous languages and cultures to force assimilation to English and White culture. These schools had catastrophic effects, disrupting families and communities, and leading to the loss of many Native American languages.

As Leap (1993) points out, the English these young Native American students learned was not necessarily the English the schools were trying to teach. Students learned much of their

English from other students—not from the teacher or in the classroom—on the sports fields or work shifts, in dormitories or dining halls. In those settings, they learned "varieties of English which are heavily influenced by . . . ancestral language grammars, rules of discourse and text making practices" (quoted in Mesthrie et al., 2000, p. 270). Leap calls the new varieties that developed *Indian-affirming English codes* and concludes that they allow speakers "to maintain ancestral language fluencies by incorporating the linguistic traditions of others into their own language resources" (quoted in Meshrie et al., p. 271).

One Indian-affirming English code used today is **Rez English** and its accompanying **rez accen**t, spoken in many indigenous communities. Although it is a variety of English, not of their ancestral language, Rez English has become emblematic of American Indian identity for many. It is well known that ancestral languages are often important to ethnic identity for indigenous peoples. Newmark et al. (2017) note, however, that Native American varieties of English can play an equally important role, especially given that many indigenous people have little or no access to their ancestral language. In a study in different locations in the United States and Canada, they found that through use of the rez accent, indigenous peoples create and maintain a Native ethnic identity. Echoing Leap (1993), they suggest that such use is a way to reconcile one's identity with not being able to speak the indigenous language of one's ancestors.

Variation in sign languages

Variation is inherent in sign languages, as it is in all natural languages. In fact, sign languages tend to be highly variable, partly because of their history and the ways that children learn them. Unless hard-of-hearing children are born to Deaf parents, they tend not to learn a sign language at home. Instead, they often learn it at school, often at a school for Deaf children.

As Mesthrie et al. (2000) note, this variation is related to the same factors as it is for spoken languages: region, gender, sexual orientation, ethnicity, and social class. The Black Deaf community in the United States has its own variety of ASL, a variety that was unfortunately seen as nonstandard for many years. The gay Deaf community likewise has its own variety, which includes its own set of signs, especially those that are integral to gay Deaf culture. The most noticeable differences are those in the lexicon, with different groups having different signs for the same thing, rather like *lift* and *elevator*, but there are also differences in morphology and phonology.

Factors specific to Deaf communities also play a part in this variation. Children of Deaf parents whose native language is a sign language tend to use certain variants more than those who learn it as a second language. Learning it before the age of six or being deaf oneself also plays a role in sign language variation.

STANDARDS AND STANDARDIZATION

So far, we've been discussing different varieties of English without naming the one that most people see as *the* language itself, what we've called Standard English. It's also called Proper or Broadcast English and sometimes BBC English in the United Kingdom. The standard varies across different nations, so Standard American English is slightly different from Standard Australian English or Standard British English, as anyone who has traveled from one nation to the other knows.

We've noted several times that all varieties of all languages are equally correct, valid and rule governed. And each variety of English has as much right to be called English as any other. We often subtly imply the opposite, however, through our labels. Calling a variety Hispanic English or Scottish English or working-class English implies that there is an English without a preceding adjective. There is not. The same holds true for other languages. Sicilian Italian is just as much Italian as what is called the standard. What most people consider the standard language is but one variety among many, granted one that is accorded prestige and respect. That term itself, standard language, is a misnomer, in fact. To be precise, it should be called a standard variety.

The standard is sometimes defined as the variety used by those who have status and power. And its use confers status and power on those who use it. It is also said that those who use the standard are considered well-spoken and that the standard is defined as the variety used by those who are considered well spoken. If those definitions seem a bit circular to you, they are. The point here is that what we mean by a standard variety is hard to pin down. There is even disagreement among linguists as to whether or not it really exists. Some say it is an idealized variety that no one actually speaks; others say that speaking a standard is mostly about avoiding stigmatized features like double negatives or *ain't*; still others that it is the native variety of the middle or upper-middle class. Still others term it a "mythical beast" (Lippi-Green, 2012).

Standard varieties are generally defined as codified forms of a language that come to be accepted as the dominant variety and the only correct way of speaking. They are the varieties generally expected to be used by political leaders, mainstream media, and educated professionals—in other words, those with high levels of education, status, or authority. A standard variety fulfills certain functions outside those of everyday language: it is the variety used in formal writing, education, mass media, government, and most professional endeavors. It can serve as an emblem of nationhood and make communication across diverse languages easier. It can also, however, contribute to social inequality.

The process of standardization converts one variety, or an amalgam of several varieties, into a standard by regulating its spelling, grammar, and pronunciation and by creating the expectation that it is the only acceptable variety. A central part of that regulation involves creating dictionaries and grammar handbooks to serve as authorities on the language, especially in education. That is what is meant by codified: dictionaries, grammar handbooks, and educators explicitly dictate what is correct and what is not.

Standardization is a recent phenomenon in the history of languages. It occurred earliest in Europe where the process went hand in hand with the growth of nation states and capitalism, with the newly emerging standards becoming prominent symbols of the new nations. In some cases, as in France, the central government played a direct role in the process. Standardization in France began in the early 17th century under King Louis XIV when the *Academie Francaise* was established with the express purpose of identifying explicit rules for the French language. Before that, various languages and dialects were spoken throughout France. After the Revolution of 1789, the new government decreed that to be French, one had to speak French, despite the fact that only about 10% of the population actually spoke it (May, 2017). None of the multitude of other languages spoken in what is now France was acceptable if one were to be a *citoyen*, a citizen of the new Republic. Nor were all varieties acceptable. It was the variety of French spoken in Paris, the economic, political, and cultural center of the new nation, that became the standard. This standardization took place over the next two centuries as the central government instituted educational policies to promote a uniform national language.

In England, the process was similar, but with less direct government control. The variety spoken in the Midlands, specifically the triangle formed by London, Oxford University, and Cambridge University, the area whose speakers had the greatest economic, social, and political power and prestige, became the standard variety. The process took place gradually through the 14th to 16th centuries. As in France, there was great variety in the dialects spoken and written throughout the land before this time. Variety in spoken language remains widespread to this day, but written language has been standardized.

The development and spread of printing and literacy helped enable this process, for literacy and standardization reinforce one another. When a language is written, it can be regulated and codified in a way not easily done when it exists only in spoken or signed form. Written language requires some codified standards so that people can understand it across space and time. The written language carries a great deal of prestige, a prestige shared with the standard. In fact, the written language is often seen as the purest, most correct form of a language. Despite this valorization, it is most definitely not the original form of a language, nor is it the purest or most precise or elegant form, whatever those terms might mean. Even more importantly, other varieties are not derivations or aberrations of that supposedly pure form.

Standardization is the result of both historical accident and deliberate planning. Historical accident only in that there is nothing inherent in the variety that develops into a standard that makes it more qualified to be one. Rather it is the connection of a variety with centers of power and influence that helps it become a standard. Still today, the rise of standards is essentially a social, economic, and political matter, not a linguistic one. It is a deliberate process, just as the development of standards for measurements was deliberate. That standardization arose because trade and commerce required it—an inch needed to be standardized as a certain length, an hour a certain duration, a pound a certain weight—a no variation, one-size-fits-all system, which as we know from trying on clothes, rarely works.

The development of Standard American English differed in some major respects from the process in England, France, and other European nations. There, the standard variety emerged from the variety spoken in centers of economic, political, and cultural power. Given that, one would expect the speech of New York City to emerge as the new U.S. standard because it was the center of commerce and culture. It did not, however. Instead, that of the Midwest became the basis, at least for pronunciation, of standard U.S. English. Bonfiglio (2002), in his study of the rise of Standard American, notes that it is unusual for a standard to develop from the speech of rural areas, which the Midwest was. It did so here for specific reasons having to do with demographics and stereotypes about those demographics. New York and its speech were associated with immigrants, especially those from southern and eastern Europe, immigrants who were seen as undesirable. The Southern Italians and Eastern European Jews came in for special vilification during this time. In contrast to them, the Midwest was seen as White (Southern Italians were not considered White) and Christian (which Jews were not), a purer America whose speech was not debased by outside influence (Bonfiglio, 2002). Thus, when radio arose as a mass medium in the early 20th century and broadcasters had to decide which accent should be the standard for radio announcers, and later for television and other media, the speech chosen was that of the Midwest, and it quickly became the standard accent.

Policing standards

Because it is an imposed characteristic of language communities, that is, not a necessary occurrence in the evolution of any language, the standard must be continually maintained, even policed. Some countries have institutions specifically designed to do so; the *Academie Francaise* in France is probably the most famous and *Accademia della Crusca* in Italy is the oldest linguistic academy in the world. In English-speaking countries, dictionaries often serve a similar role, deciding what is acceptable. Such decisions can be a source of fierce debate, especially about new terms entering the language. Should *ghosting* be included as a real word, for example? How about *google* as a verb? Those decisions change over the years. Certain variants that used to be considered standard can become nonstandard. In the North American standard variety, for example, the past tense of *sneak* remained the old form *snuck*, a word that became nonstandard in Britain, where they now use *sneaked* instead.

Despite its conceptual vagueness, the process of standardization remains a main agent of inequality today. That is partly because what nearly always comes along with the rise of a standard is a subsequent devaluing of other varieties. Varieties other than the standard come to be seen as a threat to the nation state. As such, they are banished from public and civic spheres. I remember being at a community meeting a few years ago when a Hispanic woman got up to speak. As soon as she began, people around me began to mutter, asking why we should have to listen to her since she couldn't even speak proper English. The points she was making were insightful and important, but many could not seem to hear them. Such incidents happen often, effectively barring certain groups from having a voice in civic discourse.

Our linguistic behaviors have not just social but market value. One generally needs some mastery of whatever is considered the standard to succeed in professional, educational, or power settings. When we speak a certain way (using the standard, for example), it connotes certain personal characteristics (a certain level of education and intelligence) that are valued by society in general. Indeed, the standard carries social prestige and benefits that are then accorded the speaker in many important settings: job interviews, educational settings, political discourse. In other words, the standard variety has substantial market value in a way other varieties do not. Since access to the standard is unevenly distributed across society, such connections to power effectively disempower those groups who do not speak it.

Standard language ideology

If the standard is no more logical or correct, then why do we so strongly believe it is? And more importantly, why do we so strongly believe that other varieties are incorrect and illogical? Both beliefs are part of what is called the **standard language ideology**. Ideology here can be defined as a "constellation of fundamental or commonsensical, and often normative, ideas and attitudes related to some aspect(s) of social 'reality'" (Bloommaert & Verschueren, 1998, p. 25). Language ideologies are those ideas, norms, and values that inform how we think about languages. The standard language ideology has several components. First, if there are two or more variant forms, only one can be correct. Second, varieties can be ranked according to their correctness and some varieties or languages are deservedly more prestigious and accepted because they are more correct. Third, the optimal society is one that is culturally and linguistically uniform. Fourth, linguistic and cultural heterogeneity is a threat; differences are dangerous.

This ideology, though based on misapprehensions about language, is widely believed and has important social consequences. One is that the social and economic benefits that accompany speaking the standard are seen as rightfully deserved, as are the stigmas that come with not speaking it. Not to acquire it is seen as a sign of moral failure, lack of ambition, or lack of ability, and those who do not acquire it are seen as willfully ignorant or recalcitrant. None of these conclusions is based in fact, of course, even if the standard language ideology seems to justify them.

Related to those conclusions are the illusory promise and threat of the standard: if you speak the standard, you'll get economic and social rewards; if you don't or won't, you'll never succeed, a threat aimed at those who speak what is seen as a nonstandard variety. That puts a big burden on those speakers. It asks them to change their way of speaking to succeed in school, to get a good job, or to be seen as credible in public settings. Two things to notice about that burden: One, since how we speak is part of who we are, asking people to change it is asking them to change who they are. Two, it is important to note who we ask to change: not someone from Australia in the United States, whose accent will be noticed but not condemned, but someone with a Hispanic accent who may be told they need to change their accent in order to get a job or succeed in school. The former need not hide part of who they are to succeed; the latter are asked to.

Competing ideologies about language

People, especially those who speak some version of the standard, often ask why those who speak a stigmatized variety don't just learn to use the standard so that they are no longer stigmatized? That's a complicated question. As noted earlier, the suggestion that they should change their way of speaking ignores the fact that our way of speaking is a potent symbol of who we are. We might more productively ask, why should they have to give up part of who they are to get a good job?

We should also note that the original question entails another question: stigmatized to who? Not all speech communities share the standard language ideology discussed previously. That is, they don't necessarily see the standard as better than the local variety they speak. In fact, a local variety, even if it is stigmatized by mainstream society, can carry a different kind of prestige, what is called **covert prestige**, a sort of hidden positive connotation.

Sociolinguists use the terms overt and covert prestige to distinguish the different values that language varieties may have. In mainstream, dominant society, the use of Standard English carries with it an overt prestige; people generally think you're smarter and more capable. And nonstandard variants, like double negatives or *ain't*, carry stigma. In some communities, that's not so. Working-class communities, for example, may consider those nonstandard variants as markers of group loyalty. Thus, they carry prestige, rather than stigma, in the local community. To return to our original question, if the use of a stigmatized feature brings prestige to a speaker in their local community, the impetus is to continue using it, since street cred is an important aspect of language choice, whether it be Wall Street or the street we hang out on.

All of this underscores the fact that there are often competing ideologies about language. Concepts of status, stigma, and prestige vary across communities, ethnicities, and social classes. What is seen as prestigious in one can be seen as stuck up or disloyal in another, so that the same linguistic feature can carry stigma in one community but prestige in another. Some communities may value solidarity above status, so adherence to local norms, including linguistic norms, is valued above accepting non-local or standard norms to gain status and get ahead.

CRITICAL SOCIOLINGUISTICS

As the discussion about standard language ideology indicates, social inequalities often have a linguistic component; those who speak what are considered nonstandard varieties or non-dominant languages experience discrimination often justified by the standard language ideology. Critical sociolinguistics examines the role language plays in creating and maintaining social inequalities and discrimination. It seeks to enlarge our understanding of the relationship of language, society, and power, especially how power can be hidden in discourse. Critical linguists examine how societies and individuals come to accept or resist that standard language ideology; how individuals construct their identities in diverse social contexts; how educational institutions promote language standardization and the subsequent devaluing of other varieties; and how language and society are related both locally and in our globalized world that communicates increasingly through cyberspace. Thus, critical sociolinguistics, in locating linguistic choices within larger social systems of inequality, advocate for a more just and equitable world. We will be touching on these issues in the following chapters, but first let's focus on a few key concepts.

Critical discourse analysis, a part of critical sociolinguistics, analyzes discourse—oral, signed, and written texts—to make visible the ways language creates and maintains social inequalities. Discourse here has a slightly different meaning from our examination of it in Chapter 8. Here, **discourses** are common ways that groups use language or images: their characteristic ways of speaking, writing, signing. All discourses contain within them underlying values and beliefs about how the world is and how it should be, values and beliefs generally shared by a group. These values and beliefs are not necessarily stated overtly; they are usually embedded in such a way as to appear natural and as just plain common sense. If we critically analyze discourse, we seek to bring to light the ways that language helps reproduce and create social relations, especially social relations of power and domination. This entails examining those aspects of life we take for granted in order to learn to see them as historically and socially constructed.

Take a simple phrase like *mankind's greatest asset is his imagination*. Such a phrase represents humanity as male; the simple use of *man* does so without having to state it overtly. A phrase like *humans and animals* represents humans as something other than animals, when of course we are not.

I'll borrow an example from Fairclough (2014) to illustrate how discourse can hide power. Saying *Thousands are out of work* represents the situation as a fact, something that just happens, with no indication that there were people behind it. Saying *Company directors have sacked thousands of workers* represents the situation as the direct result of specific actions by certain people. The first sentence hides the decision by those in power who have caused the layoffs; the second describes the action and names those responsible for it. Use of the first subtly presents a world in which no one is to blame for layoffs and renders invisible those who make decisions about those layoffs. The point is that repeated use of such phrases, or any ideology embedded in discourse across multiple texts, forms patterns that shape how we see the world. Such patterns can be destructive, as they misrepresent human social and economic relations. We return to this type of analysis in Chapters 11 and 14.

Language and local identity

Identity construction, from a critical perspective, moves beyond broad social categories to a view of identity as multifaceted. None of us is simply one thing. Our social identity includes many factors: our gender, social class, ethnicity, race, sexual orientation, ableness, educational level, and others, including factors important in the local context. Since, from a critical perspective, languages are not separate, distinct entities but social practices that always occur within particular local and social contexts, we need to look beyond those broad categories to understand their underlying meanings.

Two recent studies illuminate how those intersecting identities and local contexts play important roles in language choices. Slomanson and Newman (2004) found that among young male Latino New Yorkers, differing variants of particular consonant sounds were connected to the subgroups they were part of. Thus, although all shared a male Latino identity, their language use differed noticeably in ways connected to the local environment they lived in. Mendoza-Denton (2008) found the same overall pattern for young Latinas in Los Angeles: they used differing pronunciations of certain vowels to construct identities as part of different Latina gangs. Mendoza-Denton also notes another important point: these girls, like all of us, signal their identities not only through linguistic choices, but also through choices in other areas. For these girls, their choice of color of lipstick, type of music, and hair style are also semiotic resources that can be used to convey social meanings like *I'm part of this group, not that one*. Together with their linguistic choices, these girls use all their semiotic resources to construct distinct identities as part of different local groups. And the identity they thereby construct is complex and local, not just based on their gender or their ethnicity but on iterations of those identities important to a particular place and time. In this sense, identity construction is an act of languaging rather than a passive reflection of already existing social categories.

Looking back at the concept of covert prestige mentioned earlier, we can illuminate an added perspective. Variationist sociolinguists focus on language variants and what they mean. Do they impart prestige or stigma? How do different groups view their social meanings differently? Those are still important questions to examine. A languaging perspective enlarges that focus by asking how individuals use those variants for their own purposes. The Latina girls mentioned earlier choose their vowel variants, though not consciously, to gain prestige within their particular social context, regardless of whether the variants have prestige or stigma in the wider society. They are thus agents of their own identity.

CHAPTER SUMMARY

- Variation, which is inherent in all languages, allows us to construct our social identities through use of different sociolinguistic variants.
- Variation includes regional varieties (those tied to region), sociolects (those tied to social class or other aspects of social status), or ethnolects (those tied to ethno-racial groups).
- Hispanic Englishes, varieties of English spoken primarily by those of Hispanic ancestry, are not English spoken with a Spanish accent but fully formed, rule-governed varieties of English.
- Code switching is the process of using two or more languages or varieties in a conversation that occurs when both interlocutors know both languages or varieties.
- Translanguaging describes that process not in terms of languages being spoken but in terms of individuals using their entire linguistic repertoires for communicative purposes, no matter the language.

- Native American Englishes are diverse varieties of English spoken primarily by those of Native American ancestry. Rez English, an Indian-affirming English variety, allows its speakers to construct and maintain their Native American identity even if they do not speak their ancestral language.
- Standardization is the process whereby a variety becomes codified and accepted as the correct form of a language. Standard varieties, which emerged with the growth of nation states, often become potent symbols of nations.
- Ideology can be defined as a pattern of ideas and attitudes about social reality that appear commonsensical. Language ideologies are those ideas, norms, and values that inform how we think about language.
- The standard language ideology posits that if there are two or more variant forms, only one can be correct; that varieties can be ranked according to their correctness; that some varieties are deservedly more prestigious and acceptable than others; and that the optimal society is one that is culturally and linguistically uniform.
- In some communities, forms that would be considered nonstandard, and thus incorrect, can have covert prestige as symbols of community solidarity.
- Critical sociolinguistics examines the role language plays in creating and maintaining social inequalities and discrimination; it seeks to deepen our understanding of the relationship of language, society, and power.
- Within critical theories of language, languages are not separate, clearly distinct entities but social practices that always occur in particular social contexts.

KEY TERMS

sociolinguistic variant

structured variation

rhotic and non-rhotic varieties

regional dialect

leveling

national variety

sociolects

ethnolects

Mock Spanish

Hispanic Englishes

Chicanx Englishes

code switching

translanguaging

Mock Spanish

Native American Englishes

rez English and rez accents

standardization

standard language ideology

covert prestige

languaging

critical sociolinguistics

critical discourse analysis

EXPLORATIONS

Exploration 1: What do you call that?

If you've traveled to other areas or countries that speak English, what unfamiliar terms or pronunciations did you notice? What did you think of them and the people who used them? Did they evoke any stereotypes? Did your way of speaking seem unfamiliar to them? Were you teased about it? Share your responses in small groups.

Exploration 2: Group talk

We use certain variants, words, or pronunciations to identify ourselves as members of a particular community or group. Can you identify any variants used by you or people you know that signal such membership? These might be abbreviations, clipped forms, particular pronunciations, or other features. Groups may relate to academic major, occupation, neighborhood, ethnicity, region of origin, sexual orientation, religion, or any number of other social identities. Share these in small groups. Did any of you come up with the same terms or groups? Were there any disagreements?

Exploration 3: Movie stereotypes

Movie directors and advertising professionals are aware of the stereotypes evoked by certain accents, both regional and social. As you watch TV or movies or other media, notice any characters whose accents or varieties differ from the standard or from other characters. Do you see any language stereotypes at play?

Discussion prompt: Compare your conclusions with your classmates. What conclusions can you draw?

Writing prompt: Write a two-page essay describing your observations and what conclusions you draw from them.

Exploration 4: Animated accents

Animated characters are often revealing about accent-based stereotypes since writers can give them any accent they want. Choose an animated feature (*Aladdin*, *The Lion King, South Park, The Simpsons)*. What do you notice about who speaks which accents? What conclusions can you draw from your observations? Compare notes with your classmates.

Exploration 5: Spanglish

Investigate the use of the term Spanglish by googling it or entering it in Urban Dictionary or another such site. Ask others what it means. How would you characterize the definitions—complimentary or demeaning?

Discussion prompt: Share your conclusions with your group. How would you define Spanglish now?

Writing prompt: Write a two-page essay describing what you found and what conclusions you draw from your findings. Define Spanglish as you see it now.

Exploration 6: Dissing a variety

We've talked about how some languages or varieties are treated as less valuable than others in many circumstances. Have you seen this devaluing in any social settings or interactions you have been part of? Have you ever had it directed at your speech?

Discussion prompt: Share your stories in small groups. Are there any similarities, differences, or surprises among them?

Writing prompt: Write a two-page essay describing what your experiences and what conclusions you draw from them.

> **Exploration 7: Covert prestige**
>
> Are you part of or do you know of any communities in which certain variants carry covert prestige? What local social meaning do they carry?
>
> **Discussion prompt**: Share your responses in small groups. Are there any similarities, differences, or surprises among them?
>
> **Writing prompt**: Write a two-page essay describing the community, the variants, and their social meanings.

FURTHER READING

American Tongues: This video, though a bit dated, is an engaging presentation of regional accents in the U.S.

Fought, C. (2003). *Chicano English in context*. Palgrave Macmillan.

Lippi-Green, R. (2011). *English with an accent* (2nd ed.). Routledge.

Mesthrie, R., Swann, J., Deumert, A., & Leap, W. (2000). A case study: Language contact, maintenance, and shift among Native Americans, Section 8.5. In *Introducing sociolinguistics*. John Benjamins Publishing.

Trudgill, P. (2000). *Sociolinguistics: An introduction to language and society*. Penguin. A brief coverage of basic concepts in sociolinguistics.

REFERENCES

Bloommaert, J., & Verschueren, J. (1998). *Debating diversity*. Routledge.

Bonfiglio, T. (2002). *Race and the rise of standard American*. Mouton de Gruyter.

Eckert, P. (1989). *Jocks & burnouts: Social categories and identity in the high school*. Teachers College Press.

Fairclough, N. (2014). *Language and power*. Longman.

Hill, J. (2008). *The everyday language of white racism*. Wiley-Blackwell.

Labov, W. (1966). *The social stratification of English in New York City*. Center for Applied Linguistics.

Leap, W. (1993). *American Indian English*. University of Utah Press.

Lippi-Green, R. (2012). *English with an accent*. Routledge.

May, S. (2017). Language, imperialism and the modern nation-state system. In O. Garcia, N. Flores, & M. Spotti (Eds.), *The Oxford handbook of language in society*. Oxford University Press.

Mendoza-Denton, N. (2008). *Homegirls: Language and cultural practice among Latina youth gangs*. Blackwell.

Mesthrie, S., Swann, J., Deumert, A., & Leap, W. (2000) *Introducing sociolinguistics*. John Benjamins Publishing Co.

Newmark, K., Walker, N., & Stanford, J. (2017). The rez accent knows no borders: Native American identity expressed through prosody. *Language in Society, 45*(5), 633–664.

Rickford, J. (1987). *Dimensions of a Creole continuum*. Stanford University Press.

Slomanson, P., & Newman, M. (2004). Peer group identification and variation in New York Latino English Laterals. *English World-Wide, 25*(2), 199–216.

Trudgill, P. (1974). *The social differentiation of English in Norwich*. Cambridge University Press.

CHAPTER 10

African American Language

....

INTRODUCTION

Imagine elementary school students learning to read. As part of the drill, each student is asked to read aloud a passage. One African American girl reads her passage, clearly understanding what she's reading. She pronounces the word *passed* as [pæs] instead of the way her teacher does, [pæst]. The teacher asks her to read it again, and again she says [pæs]. The teacher tells her she's wrong, corrects her pronunciation, and then concludes that she has problems reading and doesn't understand the past tense. Not true, of course. Our student has no problem reading; she just has a different pronunciation of *passed*, one based on the rules of her variety of English, African American English.

This fictional scene is, unfortunately, not all that fictional. Every day African American students have their language mistakenly disparaged, corrected, and scorned in school. That scorn and constant correction have consequences: as Lanehart (2015) points out, "diminishing a child's language diminishes and ultimately silences the child" (p. 869).

DOI: 10.4324/9780429269059-10

It is those consequences that make it important for us to examine African American English in some detail. In this chapter, we examine African American English and the mistaken judgments about it that often have dire consequences for those who speak it. I begin with an overview of ideas about this variety, go on to discuss its history and describe salient parts of its structure, including variation. I then discuss some connections among language, race, and identity, especially in the educational system of the United States.

OVERVIEW

By now, if you've worked your way through the first six chapters, you know quite a bit about the morphology, phonetics, phonology, and syntax of English—of what we call Standard American English (SAE), that is. Most of our examples have been from that variety of English because it's the one typically used in educational settings. We could just as easily, however, have taken examples from any variety of English—British English, Australian English, Indian English, Appalachian English, Latinx English, or African American English. It's easy to see the rule-governed nature of SAE; most of us were forced to study some form of those rules in school. For many, it's a bit more difficult to see how other varieties of English, especially heavily stigmatized varieties, are equally rule governed, equally correct, and equally valid. In this chapter, we will examine one of the most stigmatized varieties of English in the United States, what linguists call African American Language, to identify its rule-governed nature and to interrogate its place within educational settings and U.S. society.

One of the first questions to arise in any discussion of this vibrant variety spoken by millions of people in the United States is what to call it. It has gone by various names, some used in scholarly discourse, others not. In one of the first scholarly treatises from 1884, it was referred to as *Negro English*. When linguists first began studying this variety, they referred to it as *Nonstandard Negro English*. In the 1960s that gradually changed, and the terms *Black Vernacular English* or *Black English* became prevalent. (Vernacular refers to the everyday language used by people as opposed to written or formal language.) Those terms soon changed to reflect changes in how Americans of African descent often preferred to be called, and linguists began using *African American English*.

Spoken Soul, coined by the writer Claude Brown to connect the spoken variety and the soulful attitudes and qualities necessary for it, is the term used by Rickford and Rickford (2000) in their book of that name. *Ebonics*, a term coined by Dr. Robert Williams in 1973 (cited in Rickford and Rickford) combining ebony (black) and phonics (sound), was used by the Oakland School Board in a resolution recommending its use in the classroom (see further for a summary of the debate over that resolution). Recently, the term *African American Language* or *AAL* has come to be used as a mark of respect for the many ways it functions as a language. I use that term here.

Some people wrongly insist that there is no such thing as African American Language, claiming it is merely slang or lazy, ignorant English. AAL is no such thing; it is a valid and expressive variety of English that has long been recognized as such by linguists who study its structure, history, uses, and meanings. It is, as Rickford and Rickford (2000) note, "an inescapable vessel of American history, literature, society and popular culture" that "lives on authentically . . . in homes, schools, and churches, on streets, stages, and the airwaves" (p. 3).

African American writers have long been aware of the importance of AAL to its speakers' lives. James Baldwin (1979) called AAL "this passion, this skill, . . . this incredible music," echoing a passage from Shakespeare. June Jordan notes that its speakers "depend on this language for our discovery of the world" (1985, p. 124). Toni Morrison describes AAL as "a love, a passion." She goes on to add, "The worst of all possible things that could happen would be to lose that language. There are certain things I cannot say without recourse to my language" (cited in Lippi-Green, 2012, p. 185). Its place in U.S. history is complex, long-standing, and intimately related to issues of race and class within American society.

Many non-speakers of AAL have a somewhat skewed idea of what it is. They tend to focus on one or two features—the use of *be* and the pronunciation of *ask*. Studies have shown that non-speakers will throw in a random *be* to try to sound as if they are speaking AAL or to mock its speakers as ignorant. As we will see later, these features are not random but part of its grammatical system; similarly, they are not the result of laziness or ignorance or stubbornness but of the rules of this variety of English.

Non-speakers also often have a skewed idea of who speaks AAL, perhaps because of the way it is portrayed in the media—as spoken by poor people living in inner cities, by drug dealers and other criminals, and by street-savvy youth who've dropped out of school. Although this perception might be understandable given the media portrayal, it is quite simply a misperception. AAL is spoken not just by the poor, but by the middle class; not just in the inner city, but in suburbs and rural communities; not primarily by drug dealers, but by working women and men and families across the country. Exact numbers are hard to determine, but it has been estimated that 80%–90% of African Americans can speak some variety of AAL, making it the second most spoken variety in the United States (Smitherman, 1977).

HISTORY OF AAL

The history of AAL is, like that of all languages, closely connected to the history of those who speak it—that is, the history of those Africans forcibly brought to work as slaves in the United States and their descendants. Although there is debate about the exact nature of its development, linguists generally agree that AAL developed out of three main sources: the African languages that enslaved peoples brought with them from Africa; the varieties of English they were exposed to; and creoles that developed among enslaved peoples in the Caribbean, many of whom were later brought to the United States. Linguists agree that there are elements of all three sources in the AAL spoken today but debate their relative importance.

As Smitherman (1977) points out, AAL developed in a time of enslavement as a vehicle of solidarity among oppressed people. The harsh circumstances suffered by enslaved Africans probably contributed to the development of AAL in that it may have become quite early on a marker of oppositional identity (Rickford & Rickford, 2000). After the Civil War and emancipation, most African Americans continued to live in Southern states until the early 20th century. The migrations of African Americans to the North, especially the Great Migration that took place from 1916 to 1930, and the urbanization of African-America populations that resulted from that migration, helped create the AAL we see today. The speech of those from various parts of the South converged in Northern cities to produce an urban variety that then spread across the country. Its status as a marker of oppositional identity continued, fueled by segregation in housing and education and by the discrimination that many African Americans faced and continue to face.

Part of the history of AAL includes the stigmatization that has too often accompanied it: the refusal of many people to recognize it as a valid variety of English and the persistent disparaging of it as "lazy, ignorant, uneducated slang." As we saw in Chapter 2, language is an integral part of people's life, culture, and identity. What does it mean if the dominant culture mocks and disparages one variety while upholding another as proper? The consequences of this inequality echo through the education system, affect employment opportunities, and foster other social injustices. The long history of stigmatization of AAL illustrates the effects of this linguistic inequality even as its continued survival demonstrates how strongly language and identity are intertwined. That AAL is alive today is testament to its remarkable vitality, surviving and thriving despite several hundred years of extreme stigmatization and attempts to eradicate it.

STRUCTURE OF AAL

Here we will examine some of the structure of AAL, just as we examined the structure of SAE in previous chapters.

There are several morphological and phonological features of AAL that set it apart from SAE; some of these features are noticed and highly stigmatized while others are often unnoticed by non-AAL speakers. In the following section, we offer but a brief glimpse of the structure of AAL as we examine some of the most noticed and stigmatized features. To cover the phonological, morphological, and syntactic rules in detail would require an entire textbook; there are several excellent ones listed at the end of the chapter.

Morphological structure

While AAL shares most of the structural and grammatical features of SAE, it has many distinctive rules of its own, including distinctive rules for certain morphemes.

{s} morphemes

You will remember that in SAE there are three morphemes with the same phonological representation: the plural morpheme {s}; the possessive morpheme {s}; and the third-person singular, present tense morpheme {s}. AAL has the same three {s} morphemes, and it treats each slightly differently in terms of use. Despite the misconception that AAL speakers drop the {s} everywhere, they rarely drop the {s} morpheme when it means plural. Use of the third-person singular, present tense {s} is in some ways optional; it is sometimes applied and sometimes not: both *I always listen to what she say* and *I always listen to what she says* are possible. The possessive {s} is also optional. The context of the sentence and the positioning of the two nouns, the possessor immediately followed by the thing possessed, make the meaning clear without adding the morpheme {s}; for example, *The President speech was long and rambling.*

Be verb

The use of the verb *be* is one of the most distinctive and misunderstood features of AAL. Because of this distinctiveness, it serves as a marker often used when non-AAL speakers mimic or mock the language. And because the rules for its use are often misunderstood, those trying to imitate AAL often get it wrong. AAL uses *be* differently from SAE in several ways.

Invariant be

As the name suggests, **invariant be** does not vary; it does not become *am*, *are*, or *is*. Invariant *be* occurs in SAE, for example, after modal verbs such as *can* or *must* (*They must be quick*), in infinitives with *to* (*They tried to be quick*), or as an imperative (*Be quick!*). AAL uses invariant *be* in these structures too. AAL also uses invariant *be* in other situations where it might not be used in SAE.

The most distinctive usage of invariant *be* in AAL is the **habitual invariant be**. Because the meaning of habitual invariant *be* is misunderstood by outsiders, many think African Americans are just replacing *is* and *are* with *be*. Not so. Its use is rule governed and carries meaning: that the action is habitual, happening on a regular basis. In the sentence *She be runnin' with her team*, the invariant *be* indicates that she *regularly* goes running with her team. If the speaker were describing an event happening right now, she would say, *She runnin' with her team*. These sentences are not interchangeable as they have different meanings.

An examination of how to form the negative of a sentence further illustrates how habitual invariant *be* is part of the grammatical system of AAL. Usually, one would use the word *ain't* to form a negative sentence in AAL: *She ain't runnin' with her team*. But in a sentence using the habitual invariant *be*, *ain't* is not used; instead, *don't* is: *She don't be runnin' with her team everyday*. The sentence *She aint' be runnin' with her team everyday* is simply not a well-formed utterance in AAL.

Zero copula

Another distinctive grammar rule in AAL related to the verb *be* is the absence of a copula in certain situations—what is called **zero copula**. A **copula** is a be verb used as a connecting verb such as *is* or *are*. The rules of SAE demand that we use *is* or *are* in such sentences, as in *She is a student* or *They are tired*. That is not the case in many other languages, including Russian. To say *She is a student* in Russian, for example, one would say *ona studentka*, literally *she student*, with no copula (and no article *a*, but that's another story). Similarly, the copula is not required in AAL: *She ready now* and *They tired* are perfectly well-formed utterances. Interestingly, only *is* and *are* can be deleted when used as copulas; *am*, *was*, or *were* are generally not deleted, at least not if you are trying to create well-formed AAL utterances.

The rules for zero copula are a bit more complicated than that, however. Those two forms of *be* (*is* and *are*) cannot be dropped in every situation. Generally speaking, if you can contract the form in SAE, you can delete it in AAL. Where you cannot contract the form in SAE, you generally cannot delete the copula in AAL. In the sentence, *I'm not a runner, but she is*, the *she is* cannot be contracted in SAE and the copula cannot be dropped in AAL. In addition, the copula cannot be deleted when it is in the past tense; *was* and *were* are not left out.

Existential it is

Instead of the *there is* or *there are* used in SAE, an AAL speaker may use the alternatives *it's* or *i's* (reductions of *it is*) to express the same meaning. The **existential it is**, **it's**, or **i's**, like the existential *there is/are*, signals the existence of something. If we say in SAE, *There is (or* *there's) a problem with his logic*, we are positing the existence of a problem. The *there* does not indicate a particular place as it might in the sentence, *Put it over there*. Instead, the construction *there is* or *there are* in SAE merely indicates that something exists. The constructions *it's* or *i's* similarly mean that something exists: *i's a problem with his logic*. Unlike SAE, where a distinction is made between singular and plural (*there is a snake in that room* or *there are a lot of snakes in that room*), AAL uses *it's* or *i's* for both singular and plural nouns: *it's a lot of people here*, for example.

Phonological structure

The phonological rules of AAL are in most ways similar to those of SAE, but there are some interesting and important differences in terms of both the articulatory processes and the phonological rules that produce distinctive AAL pronunciations.

Consonant cluster reduction

As we saw in Chapter 4, we all use articulatory processes for ease of pronunciation. Consonant cluster reduction, a common articulatory process in many languages of the world, including English, occurs more frequently in African American Language than in many other varieties. Consonants are not deleted randomly, however; their deletion is dependent on the phonetic environment. Two aspects of the phonetic environment are important here: whether the consonant to be deleted is surrounded by other consonants or by vowels and whether the consonants in the cluster are voiced or unvoiced.

For example, the consonants [l] and [r] can be deleted only if they follow a vowel, not if they follow a consonant: *help* can be pronounced [hɛp] and *cold* as [kod]. These two consonants can also be deleted if they are at the end of a word and are preceded by a vowel sound, even if they are not part of a consonant cluster: *car* is pronounced [ka] and *ball* pronounced [ba] unless the following word begins with a vowel.

The rule governing the deletion of consonants in a cluster appearing at the end of a word is dependent on the voicedness of those sounds: to delete the final consonants in a cluster, all of the consonants must be either voiced or all unvoiced. If they are a mixture, you can't do it. In the word *band* [bænd], the final sound [d] can be deleted and the pronunciation becomes [bæn] because [n] and [d] are both voiced. Our previous rule still applies too; this only occurs if the word is not followed by a vowel sound. This attention to voice means the word *link*, for example, cannot become *lin* in AAL because [n] is voiced and [k] is unvoiced. There is an exception to this rule. The negatives *won't*, *can't*, and *shouldn't* can lose their final unvoiced [t] sound despite the voiced [n] immediately preceding it. That's the rule. It may seem a bit complicated to those who do not speak AAL, but for those who do, it's just the way the language works.

There is a pattern of pronunciation in AAL that may seem at first glance to be another example of deleting a final consonant: dropping the final 'g' in words like *thinkin'* or *walkin'*. This so-called dropping is not the result of deletion. Instead, the velar nasal [ŋ] in *walking* is replaced with the alveolar nasal [n], as it is in the casual speech of most American English speakers.

Other features

One feature often noted about AAL is its use of [d], [t], [f], or [v] where SAE would use [θ] or [ð]. As with consonant cluster reduction, this phenomenon is not random. Just as *dance* is pronounced with an [a] in British English but with a [æ] in American English, certain words are pronounced with [t] or [d] or [f] or [v] in AAL but with [θ] or [ð] in SAE. The correspondence depends on voice again. Unvoiced [θ] corresponds to unvoiced [t] or [f]; voiced [ð] corresponds to voiced [d] or [v]. *Mother*, for example, pronounced with a voiced [ð] in SAE, is pronounced with a voiced [v] in AAL, not with an unvoiced [f]. Similarly, *bath*, pronounced with an unvoiced [θ] in SAE, is pronounced with an unvoiced [f] in AAL, not a voiced [v]. Thus, unvoiced [t] or [f] is used in AAL where the unvoiced [θ] is used in SAE, and voiced [d] or [v] are used in AAL where the voiced [ð] is used in SAE.

Several features of AAL are regularly stigmatized as nonstandard or illogical. We discussed negative concord, also known as double negatives, in Chapter 2, noting that many languages require that all elements in a sentence that can be made negative must be made so for the sentence to be negative; AAL is one of those languages. As also noted there, double negatives are not illogical, nor are they difficult to comprehend. Other AAL phrases are also stigmatized. *I'm going to find you* in SAE would be said, *I'ma find you* in many varieties of AAL. That phrase is not a mispronunciation nor a slurring of words; it is simply the way it is said in AAL.

We discussed the pronunciation of *ask* in Chapter 5, noting its long history and the articulatory process that led to two different pronunciations: [æks] and [æsk]. Despite its long history, the stigmatization of the pronunciation of [æks] has, alongside other judgments, had damaging consequences for African Americans. In school, students are often sent to remedial speech classes partly because they say [æks]; in the courtroom, witnesses' testimony has been dismissed as unreliable by jurors who mention [æks] specifically; in the business world, applicants for jobs may not even be considered; in public settings, speakers have been reprimanded and dissed specifically for their use of [æks].

A short anecdote may help illuminate the issue here. The former mayor of New York City, Edward Koch, once chastised a young African American student who read an essay she had written to an audience which included Koch. In responding to her, he noted not the quality of her essay but her pronunciation of that one word, claiming it detracted from, indeed almost ruined, what would otherwise have been a good performance (Lippi-Green, 2012). To return to the comparison between pronunciation differences in *schedule* and in *ask* made in Chapter 2, it is hard to imagine him doing anything similar if she had been the daughter of British parents and had used [ʃɛdyul] instead of [skɛdyul]. Most likely, such a pronunciation would have gone unnoticed or at least unremarked upon. Yet the girl's similar minor pronunciation difference was noticed and used to discredit her. Seems a bit unfair, yes?

VARIATION WITHIN AAL

Not all speakers of AAL speak it in the same way, as is true of all languages. There are differences related to region, class, and gender, among other factors. Early studies of AAL tended to focus on young inner city males, seeing them and their language as the core of AAL. Subsequent research, and everyday experience, shows that AAL is spoken by diverse groups: by families, preachers, comedians, women, old and young, by "poets, disc-jockeys, and rappers . . . politicians, academicians, and preachers," by members of the middle class as well as members of the Hip Hop Nation (Rickford & Rickford, 2000). Britt and Weldon (2015) describe the use of AAL among the African American middle class, noting that their grammar is usually that of SAE, but they employ AAL rhetorical strategies such as signifying, which is "highly stylized lying, joking and carrying on as part of ritualized wordplay" (Rickford & Rickford, p. 81) and tonal semantics, the "use of voice rhythm and vocal inflection to convey meaning" (Smitherman, 1977 p. 134). For these speakers, AAL "is valued as a tool that keeps them connected to their African American heritage" (Britt and Weldon, p. 810).

AAL use can also vary by gender. Both women and men use AAL to construct their identities as African Americans but do so differently. Black Masculine Language, which is discussed in more detail in Chapter 11, conforms closely to what is usually seen as AAL, including those grammatical and phonological features described earlier, perhaps because research in AAL has focused mainly on males. As a result, African American women's speech is often absent from linguistic studies of AAL. It is similarly often absent from linguistic studies of women's language because research on women's language has too often focused on White women (Morgan, 2015). Recently, more research has focused on **African American Women's Language (AAWL)** and how certain features are used to express solidarity among women, indirectness, for example. Spears (2009) describes the use of *girl* by women and girls (spoken with long rising intonation) as a way to express solidarity and identity with other African American women: "In using GIRL, they . . . mark their discourse as AAWL, i.e., as African American women talking in AAWL" (Spears, p. 86).

AAL IN THE COURTROOM

In 2013, an African American boy, Trayvon Martin, was shot and killed as he was walking back to his father's house in a suburban subdivision in Florida. The man who shot him, George Zimmerman, was tried and found innocent. The use of AAL by a key witness for the prosecution, Rachel Jeantel, whose evidence supported Zimmerman's guilt, played an important part in the jury's deliberations. Morgan describes reactions to Jeantel's testimony by both the defense and the media. Both disparaged it as hostile, aggressive, and unintelligible. Her use of AAWL was seen as hostile and aggressive when compared to what is considered proper women's language, yet "had she been a vernacular-speaking Black male, her speech . . . might have been viewed as the norm for [an African American] teenager" rather than unintelligible and hostile (Morgan, 2015, p. 829). Such characterizations were doubly unfair to Jeantel.

MICRO-AGGRESSIONS

Recently social media has been paying a lot of attention to micro-aggressions. Instead of making overt statements stigmatizing a particular group, micro-aggressions express that stigmatization subtly and indirectly. They may not be intentionally offensive, but to the recipients, they often feel that way. I recently saw micro-aggressions in action when a Latina student dropped off a book at my house. As I was walking her out to her car, a neighbor walked by and stopped to chat. Without even being introduced, he asked her, *Where are you from?* She answered, *St. Paul.* His response was, *No, where are you really from?* because he assumed because she looked Latina she could not really be from here. The student handled it much more graciously than I would have; she just smiled and said, *No, I'm from St. Paul* and then got in her car.

African Americans, like members of all marginalized groups, complain about these sorts of encounters because they happen a lot. Another student, who is African American, told me people are often visibly surprised when she speaks Standard English. Even presidents are not exempt. When Barack Obama was running for president, several newscasters commented on how articulate he was, as though being articulate was odd for an African American male. No one commented on the articulateness of his opponent, who, of course, was White.

LANGUAGE, RACE, AND IDENTITY

In Chapter 9, we began an examination of the many connections between language and racial or ethnic identity. Here I'd like to take that discussion a step further. When sociolinguists speak of the connection between language and identity, they sometimes frame it in ways that essentialize groups; that is, people tend to speak a certain way because they are members of a certain group: African American or Latinx or Minnesotan or working class. This perspective assumes the existence of predetermined social categories such as race, class, ethnicity, and gender. Certain ways of speaking, then, are seen to be indicative of a speaker's race, and because of this, listeners can use these ways to assign racial categories to speakers. In some ways this is true. Studies have shown that listeners can often accurately label a speaker's race by speech alone, even when they cannot identify specific features that led them to their conclusion.

Those labels can and do lead to discrimination. One study found that landlords responded differently to prospective tenants requesting to see a rental unit based on whether their speech on the telephone contained AAL features or not. Even if they did not consciously assign a racial category to the speakers, they invited those whose speech contained those features to visit the rental unit less often. Since the interactions took place on the telephone, landlords did not know the race of the caller; they did, however, react in race-based discriminatory ways based on the perceived race evoked by the speech on the telephone.

Recent studies challenge the assumption that there is a one-to-one correspondence between language and race or ethnicity, the idea that AAL is used only by African Americans, for example. Paris' (2016) study of students at a Southern California high school found that not to be the case, for Latinx and Pacific Islander immigrants used AAL in many contexts, both social and academic. They effectively became "proficient in AAL as part of their linguistic socialization into American Englishes" (p. 248). That did not mean they gave up the heritage languages of their parents. Essentially, the linguistic landscape of these students included heritage languages such as Spanish or Samoan, the AAL learned in the school community outside the classroom, and the standard being taught in the classroom, demonstrating both traditional notions of language as being tied to race or ethnicity and contemporary notions of language use as being dynamic and varied.

Other recent scholarship complicates the relationship between language and race even more, noting that people do not just use language a certain way based on their social identities. Instead, they perform those identities through their use of language. In other words, it's not so much a matter of speaking a certain way because of one's particular social identities, but a matter of people unconsciously using the linguistic resources available to them to create and recreate those identities. Thus, language plays a central role in constructing and shaping racial and ethnic identities across diverse ethno-racial contexts.

Local context is important to how speakers use their linguistic resources to position themselves and construct identities. In their study of the use of AAL among different groups, Blake and Shousterman (2010) note that the use of *Black* and *African American* as interchangeable terms glosses over the differences among the many groups in the United States that see themselves as Black: not just African Americans but also immigrants from the West Indies, for example. They studied the speech of second-generation Caribbean Americans and African Americans in New York City, two groups who were often seen as speaking AAL. Their study showed that the second-generation Caribbean Americans used subtle differences, the pronunciation of post-vocalic /r/, for example, to differentiate themselves from native African Americans. Their use of this feature had specific meaning in the local context of New York City as it was not present in their parents' speech nor common in that of African American New Yorkers. Its increased use by this group, then, was a way of shaping a distinct identity, saying "I'm a Black New Yorker, who is somewhere between African-American and West Indian" (Blake, 2016, p. 164). In other words, the speech of two groups who might be seen as identical in an essentialist understanding of identity and language (both African Americans speaking AAL) showed important differences tied to distinct local context and identities.

AAL AND EDUCATION

In the United States the achievement gap in education is correlated with race in uncomfortable ways, with African American students scoring consistently lower on standardized tests than White students. Often the blame for this gap is erroneously put on the language of African Americans. African American Language has long been labeled as deficient in educational settings: "a non-logical mode of expressive behavior . . . lacking the formal properties necessary for formulating cognitive concepts" to quote a report by Bereiter and Engelman, education psychologists of the late 20th century (Smitherman, 2015, p. 549). Students were seen as needing to be "cured of their dialects" before they could succeed. Such sentiments might not be stated as overtly today, but they still exist.

Rickford and Rickford (2000), however, point out it is not the students who have been failing, but "schools [who] nationwide have been failing African American students" (p. 163). In 1996 the School Board of Oakland, California, decided to do something about that situation. They had a large number of children in their schools, most of whom were African Americans, who were failing. With input from linguists, the Oakland School Board recommended that the students' home language, AAL or what they called Ebonics, be used in the classroom to help students learn Standard English, the language of wider communication—a perfectly reasonable recommendation. Unfortunately, the media picked up on this story and misrepresented it as the School Board wanting to teach Ebonics instead of Standard English. A media storm erupted, with many decrying the Board's recommendation without fully understanding it or its purpose.

Among those who didn't understand were many experts, including the U.S. Secretary of Education, who refused to see AAL as a valid form of English. Newspapers and pundits regularly referred to it as gibberish, vulgar slang. Cartoonists made fun of it, often in offensive, racist ways. AAL was regularly disparaged as "disgusting English," "nothing more than igno-rance," "lazy English," "bastard English," "ridiculous," a "made up language," and more. Although these descriptions were inaccurate, much damage was done with their use. Even today, over 20 years later, the term Ebonics denotes the speech of African Americans but connotes disparagement and ridicule. What was lost in all the media storm was the reason the Oakland School Board was doing this in the first place: to change their way of teaching so as to help their students succeed in school and beyond.

One part of the Oakland School Board resolution called for the recognition of Ebonics as a legitimate, rule-governed language system, something linguists have demonstrated over and over. The Linguistics Society of America publicly supported the Board's resolution and noted substantial research showing that using students' home language to teach the standard is an effective pedagogy. Rickford and Rickford (2000), in their discussion of that extensive research, also advocate using AAL as a resource in the classroom to help students learn Standard English.

Recently studies of AAL in the classroom have echoed that idea. As Baker-Bell (2020) points out, there is a connection between linguistic hierarchies and racial hierarchies; people's language experiences are not isolated from their ethno-racial experiences. As noted at the beginning of this chapter, diminishing a student's language has consequences, for it can and does diminish and silence the student. Such diminishment need not be overt. Students who speak a variety other than the standard are often told that their language is fine, but it is not appropriate for school. The implicit message here is that their language is not good enough, for it cannot be used in schools, in writing, or in any formal or official setting. So not good enough, period. Advocates for linguistic justice in the classroom see this implicit messaging as **linguistic discrimination** and have called for recognizing AAL, and all students' languages, as rich resources to be used in the classroom for learning about and understanding the world.

Paris (2016), in the study mentioned previously, adds that given its use not just by African Americans but by other students of color, the use of AAL in the classroom can also help stu-dents learn to navigate the multilingual, multicultural future that demographics show is here, repositioning not just AAL but the "languages, literacies, and cultures of youth of color" as an asset rather than a hindrance to classroom learning (Paris, p. 251). Given that more than half of public-school students nationally are now students of color, compared to only 20% in 1970, it seems timely that changes are made. We return to some of these ideas in Chapter 12 in the discussion of multilingual education.

CHAPTER SUMMARY

- African American Language, which has been called by various names over the years, is a variety of American English widely spoken across the United States. It has been a part of American history and culture from the beginning. It is estimated that 80%–90% of African Americans speak some variety of AAL.
- Linguists generally agree that its origins lie in the languages of Africa brought over by those who were enslaved, in the English varieties those enslaved peoples were exposed to, and in the creoles of enslaved peoples brought here from the Caribbean.
- Its history is closely connected to the history of those who speak it, including their expe-riences as enslaved peoples and as victims of discrimination.

- As with all varieties of all languages, AAL is rule governed; those who view those rules as instances of bad grammar are mistaken.
- Although the pronunciation of ask as [æks] is unjustly stigmatized, that pronunciation has a history that goes back to Old English.
- Language is connected to race in multiple and complex ways; it is both tied to our ethno-racial identity and used as a way of constructing or shaping our identities.
- Variation within AAL is related to gender, socioeconomic class, and local contexts.
- Micro-aggressions are a form of covert linguistic discrimination. Such covert discrimination can also take place in the classroom when AAL is presented as not appropriate for school or other important settings.

KEY TERMS

invariant *be*

zero copula

existential *it is*

African American Women's Language

Ebonics

micro-aggressions

linguistic discrimination

variation within AAL

EXPLORATIONS

Exploration 1: Short writing assignment

This is a fictional letter written to the Linguistics Society of America, based on a real letter written as an editorial.

Dear Sirs and Madams,

I write to you today in frustration and confusion. I was taught that there is a right way and wrong way to speak English. Yet around me I hear utterances that seem to break all the rules of English, especially from inner city Black youth. And I hear experts such as you say, "This is their dialect. It is rule-governed just like every other language variety." I simply do not believe it. If you listen to how they speak, I'm sure you'll agree with me; there are no rules.

How can a dialect of English include such utterances as "She pass the test yesterday," or "They code" (meaning "They're cold"). I've even heard such craziness as "Can ya hep me?" for "Can you help me?" and "They went over to that girl house." Surely this is not English.

Even worse, these speakers seem to have no understanding of English grammar. What does "It's a lot of food here" even mean? Or "he seem kinda crazy"? And why can't they conjugate the verb *be* like the rest of us? "She be talkin' with her man every day"—what is that? Or "She ready now." HUH? I can figure out what some of it means—"I done had enuf" is certainly clear, but why not say it like it is *supposed* to be said?

Can you enlighten me about all of this? Isn't this just jibberish?

Sincerely,

A concerned American

The Society, of which you are a well-known and well-respected member, has asked you to formulate a reply.

Discussion prompt: Discuss in your small group how you would reply to this letter, if you have heard others voice ideas similar to those in the letter, and what you would say to such comments now.

Writing prompt: Write a letter answering this writer, explaining what is really going on, using your knowledge as a linguist. The Society asks that you cover both the big picture and the details the writer mentions. Feel free to use IPA if that helps you explain your ideas.

Exploration 2: Well-formed utterances in AAL

Which of the utterances are *not* well-formed utterances in AAVE? Why or why not?

1. She be here right now, watchin' the game.
2. Us wented home yesterday.
3. We young kids when that happened.

Exploration 3: AAL in the courtroom

First read the blog about testimony at the Trayvon Martin case by John Rickford at https://languagelog.ldc.upenn.edu/nll/?p=5161. You might also want to find out more about the case in general. Then see what more you can find about people's reactions to the witness' language. What was your response to the comments?

Discussion prompt: Compare notes with your small group. Share what you found out and your reactions.

Writing prompt: Write a short essay explaining your reactions to the comments about Rachel Jeantel and where you think such comments come from.

Exploration 4: Micro-aggressions

There are many videos about micro-aggressions on YouTube and other social media. Track some down to see what you can find; then discuss your findings in your small group. Have you ever been the victim of micro-aggressions? Have you ever perpetrated such aggressions, even if not intentionally?

FURTHER READING

Ebonics Information Page: www.cal.org/topics/dialects/aae.html Useful discussion of issues related to Ebonics.
Green, L. (2002). *African American English*. Cambridge University Press.
Linguist List Topic page on Ebonics: http://linguistlist.org/topic/ebonics/

REFERENCES

Baker-Bell, A. (2020). *Linguistic justice: Black, language, literacy, identity, and pedagogy*. Routledge & National Council of Teachers of English.
Baldwin, J. (1979, July 29). If Black English isn't a language, then tell me what is? *The New York Times*, A28.

Blake, R. (2016). Toward heterogeneity: A sociolinguistic perspective on the classification of Black people in the 21st century. In H. S. Alim, J. R. Rickford, & A. F. Ball, (Eds.), *Raciolinguistics: How language shapes our ideas about race* (pp. 153–169). Oxford University Press.

Blake, R., & Shousterman, C. (2010). Second generation West Indian Americans and English in New York City. *English Today*, 26(3), 35–43.

Britt, E., & Weldon, T. (2015). African American English in the middle class. In S. Lanehart (Ed.), *The Oxford handbook of African American Language* (pp. 800–816). Oxford University Press.

Jordan, J. (1985). Nobody mean more to me than you and the future life of Willie Jordan. In J. Jordan (Ed.), *On call: Political essays* (pp. 123–139). South End Press.

Lanehart, S. (2015). African American Language and identity: Contradictions and conundrums. In S. Lanehart (Ed.), *The Oxford handbook of African American Language* (pp. 800–816). Oxford University Press.

Lippi-Green, R. (2012). *English with an accent*. Routledge.

Morgan, M. (2015) African American Women's Language: Mother tongues untied. In S. Lanehart (Ed.), *African American Language* (pp. 817–833). Oxford University Press.

Paris, D. (2016). It was a Black city: African American Language in California's changing urban schools and communities. In H. S. Alim, J. R. Rickford, & A. F. Ball (Eds.), *Raciolinguistics: How language shapes our ideas about race* (pp. 241–253). Oxford University Press.

Rickford, J., & Rickford, R. (2000). *Spoken soul*. John Wiley & sons, Inc.

Smitherman, G. (1977). *Talkin and testifyin: The language of Black America*. Wayne State University Press.

Smitherman, G. (2015). African American Language and education: History and controversy in the twentieth century. In S. Lanehart (Ed.), *African American Language* (pp. 547–565). Oxford University Press.

Spears, A. (2009). Theorizing African American Women's Language: Girl as a discourse marker. In S. Lanehart (Ed.), *African American Women's Language: Discourse, education and identity* (pp. 76–90). Cambridge Scholars.

CHAPTER 11

Genders, identities, and linguistic performance

··

First glance

Do women and men speak different languages?

Early studies: Report style, rapport style

Deficit, dominance, or difference?

How do languages encode gender?

Multiple identities: Black Masculine Language

Gender as performance

Gender binary revisited

INTRODUCTION

The belief that women's and men's speech styles are so different that they cause a great deal of miscommunication in everyday interactions is so widespread it is almost a cliché. Books based on that belief (*Men are from Mars, Women are from Venus* and *You Just Don't Understand* to name just two) continue to be published and widely quoted. But is it true? Do women and men really use language so differently? That's part of what we'll investigate in this chapter.

If I were writing this chapter 60 years ago, I would most likely have called it *Women's Language*, if I addressed the issue of gender at all. If it were 30 years ago, I would probably have titled it *Language and Sex*, examining how women and men speak differently and how language is sexist. And I'd probably have assumed that terms like *woman*, *man*, and *sex* were not problematic. It's a bit harder to do that today. For one thing, we always need to ask: Which women? Which men? In what circumstances? Much of the early research was done on white, middle-class English speakers in industrialized societies. It's not that their findings are

DOI: 10.4324/9780429269059-11

necessarily wrong; it's just that they are more narrowly applicable than we thought. Different identities, based on both broad social categories (race, ethnicity, social class, age, ability) and smaller local categories (a member of a motorcycle gang, a farmer in rural Canada, a high school nerd, a community organizer in the inner city) will express their gender differently.

For another thing, although gender has become a substitute for the term sex in linguistic studies, it too is not unproblematic: how many genders are there, anyway? Can we choose our own? Can we be more than one? There are increasing challenges to the idea that gender, with a few minor exceptions, is a binary thing. Those so-called exceptions have entered the main event as intersex, trans, queer, asexual, and more. And gender has come to be seen as fluid, mutable—something performed, not given. All of this has implications for how we discuss and investigate the role of genders in language use, as we will see.

EARLY STUDIES OF LANGUAGE AND GENDER

Robin Lakoff's 1975 *Language and Women's Place* is often credited, along with the women's movement, with inspiring the huge upsurge in research on language and gender that has taken place since then. Lakoff claimed that certain features used predominantly by women make them appear indecisive, hesitant, and weak: features such as uptalk (rising intonation at the end of a statement that makes it sound like a question); empty adjectives like *nice*; tag questions (*it's hot, isn't it?*); hedges (*sort of*); and avoiding interruptions and swear words. Two questions immediately arose here: do women really use these features more often than men, and do those features cause speakers to appear indecisive and weak? Linguists eagerly began investigating those questions, with sometimes contradictory results. And they began examining ways a language itself, in this case English, can be sexist. We'll discuss the findings and limitations of these investigations before going on to problematize some basic assumptions they are based on.

Do women and men speak differently?

Studies inspired by Lakoff often examined her claim that men and women speak differently by measuring the frequency of specific features for women and men: the number of occurrences of interruptions, hedges, silence, tag questions, and other features. Based on these studies, much early work on language and gender concluded that women and men do indeed speak differently. Men, at least in cross-gender interactions, tend to be the ones who talk more, despite the stereotype of the talkative woman. When men raise topics, they tend to be picked up on more by women than women's topics do by men. According to Fishman (1978), cross-gender interactions function despite the difference in style because women do most of what she calls the "interactional shitwork" required to keep them going: asking questions; showing they are paying attention through minimal responses like *um, yeah*; picking up on others' topics. Two broad generalizations arose from these findings: women tend to be cooperative, and men tend to be competitive in their speech styles. Women's **rapport style** is meant to open up space for others to contribute and men's **report style** is meant to get and maintain the floor.

When we look in detail at some of these results, however, we see things are a bit more complicated than those two styles suggest. Women, for example, both do and don't interrupt more than men. One study found that women, even those in positions of power, were interrupted by men at a higher rate than were men by women (Zimmerman & West, 1996). James and Clarke (1993), however, noted that in the 54 studies about interruptions they examined, there was basically no difference in use, except perhaps in some circumstances where women used a certain type of interruption more often: one that served a rapport-building function. Not exactly a ringing endorsement of difference.

Although the public seems to believe that men speak quite differently from women, there is nearly always at least as much variation within each group as there is between them. Hyde's 2005 meta-analysis of numerous studies showed that nearly all the differences reported were very small or close to zero, "statistically negligible" in analysis-speak. In other words, there were few differences in language use directly attributable to gender, even when we just count occurrences.

It seems clear, then, that simple totals do not tell the whole story. One also needs to look at function and context: who is speaking to whom, and what are they using a particular linguistic feature to do? Any utterance can potentially carry different meanings in different contexts and be used for very different functions. Cameron (2008) elaborates on the importance of function with what she calls the missing link, the function of the feature in question and the roles of speakers. An examination of tag questions can illuminate that missing link. One common generalization is that women use more tag questions than men. **Tag questions** are those little questions that we add to the ends of statements: *The meeting starts at 11, doesn't it? Those flowers are lovely, aren't they?* Much early research assumed that their use makes the speaker seem insecure, needing confirmation about what she is saying. Some tag questions do function this way. In our first example, the speaker seems to be asking for confirmation that she's correct about the starting time. Others, however, function quite differently. Our second example is not asking if the flowers are indeed lovely. That tag question seems more like a conversation facilitator, an invitation for the interlocutor to add a comment on the flowers. We can see from these examples that tag questions can serve different functions, and these functions are the missing link that needs to be taken into account when examining any potential gender differences in their use.

Still other tag questions are not seeking confirmation or inviting a comment. *You are going to clean your room, aren't you?* is more like a command. The thing is, only certain roles in certain relationships use that type of tag question: a parent, perhaps, but not a roommate. Thus, it's also important to examine roles and relationships among the interlocutors. Expectations about the roles and behaviors appropriate for each gender are especially important when examining language use. If societal expectations are that women should play a facilitative role in cross-gender conversations, then we'd expect to find women using more tag questions, especially those facilitative ones.

The point is this: "Speaking like a woman, or a man, is not just the automatic consequence of being one" (Cameron, 2008, p. 152). That is, gender doesn't directly lead to differences; rather, it is the expected gendered roles that do. As Cameron puts it, "just because the frequency of a linguistic feature is higher in one gender's speech than in the other's, we cannot assume that it is 'about' masculinity or femininity" (p. 152). It may be about the function that a particular feature fulfills, or about the local context in which we interact. The Latina girls in Mendoza-Denton's (2008) study (described in Chapter 9) used slight linguistic differences not to differentiate themselves from Latino boys but from other Latina girls in the context in which they lived.

A look at high school groups illustrates another important factor in understanding language and gender: we use the resources available to us to construct our identities. In her study of burnouts and jocks in a California high school described in Chapter 9, Eckert (1989) found that boys gain status within their groups through sports (for the jocks) or fighting (for the burnouts). Those opportunities are generally not open to girls. Instead, girls are restricted to symbolic ways—language, for example—to gain status. The girls Eckert studied tended to use more of the features that characterized their group than did the boys because that was the only way available to them to say, *I'm a jock* or *I'm a burnout*. In other words, these girls used those features to construct an identity not so much as a girl rather than as a boy, but as a jock or a burnout, using the resources available to them in that context.

Deficit, dominance, or difference?

Interpretations of gender differences in language use have generally fallen into one of three models: deficit, dominance, or difference. A **deficit** model echoes Lakoff's (1975) claim that women's ways of speaking make them appear hesitant and indecisive. It is not that these ways of speaking necessarily and always indicate weakness, but they are seen that way because the criteria used to judge speech is men's language. Since women's language does not meet those criteria, it is deemed inferior.

In a **dominance** model, interactional patterns that differ by gender are seen as evidence of the dominance men have in most areas of life, conversations included. It is not necessarily the case that any one man is intentionally dominating a conversation, but the social practices and patterns of interaction are such that he does so, even if he is not conscious of it. Terms such as *mansplaining* allude to this domination. There is obviously some truth to this perspective. We must be careful, however, not to overgeneralize or essentialize; not all men have power over all women, nor are all women victims of male domination.

In a **difference** or two-cultures model, these differences stem from the fact that men and women have different cultural styles of speaking. Thus, cross-gender interactions are prone to the same types of misunderstandings as cross-cultural ones. This model in some ways seeks to value women's ways of speaking, seeing their style not as abnormal but equal, if not superior to, men's. One problem is that this model is based on the false premise that boys and girls, women and men, live in separate subcultures. They may indeed be socialized differently, but to claim they live in separate cultures is, at the least, an overstatement. Boys and girls, women and men, interact on a daily basis. More importantly, this model ignores the very real power differentials between many women and many men. Also, the characteristics attributed to women's speech style closely echo traditional ideas about what is appropriate for each gender. Ideas about women's communication style (women are cooperative, build rapport, talk about their feelings more easily, prefer verbal interaction to action) reflect stereotypes similar to claims that women make good nurses, primary school teachers, counselors, and social workers but not scientists, engineers, computer programmers, or architects. Not surprisingly, jobs in the first list are generally less prestigious and well-paid than those in the second, which are male dominated. Ideas about gendered communication styles can thus reinforce stereotypes about appropriate gender roles.

Sugar and spice or puppy dog tails?

Stereotypes such as those mentioned earlier assume an innate, natural connection between one's gender and one's language use. Differences between women and men are seen as the result of biology, often attributed to differences in brain structure. Pitch can serve as an illustrative example of the limitations of this type of generalization. There is a noticeable difference in the pitch of adult men and adult women. Men's vocal cords tend to be thicker and longer, thus producing a lower pitch. Women's pitch is generally higher as their vocal cords tend to be thinner and shorter. This natural difference is only part of the explanation, however. Holding size constant, Polish men have a higher pitch than American men. And the average pitch for women in Japan is substantially higher than that for American women, again holding size constant. If pitch in speaking were the natural result only of physical size, we would not find such discrepancies. Thus, any gender differences in pitch result not solely from innate differences in vocal cords but from learning to conform to social norms. As with most things in life, there may be a natural element, but social norms play an equal, if not more important, role.

We can see society's norms playing out in how differences in pitch are talked and thought about. Women's voices are often called shrill; they are seen as too high because the norm is taken to be men's voices. Men's voices are seen as commanding, unless of course they are high-pitched and sound like a women's voices. Women's pitch range, which is usually wider than that of men, is seen as indicative of being over-emotional, again because the norm is taken to be men's more limited range. These differences are often cited as evidence that women are more emotional by nature, a conclusion certainly not true.

How do languages encode gender?

Do languages, not just speakers, treat women and men differently? If so, how? Does the fact that some languages have masculine and feminine nouns mean they are sexist? To begin to answer that second question, we first need to discuss a concept introduced in Chapter 3: grammatical gender. **Grammatical gender** refers to different classes of nouns that occur in many languages. We noted in Chapter 3 that most Indo-European languages have a system that classifies nouns as masculine or feminine (Spanish, French, Italian, for example) or as masculine, feminine, or neuter (German). That classification determines which morphological endings are used in articles, adjectives, and sometimes verbs. In French, for example, to say *the dog left*, one would say, *le chien est parti* but to say *the car left*, it would be *la voiture est partie*. That extra *e* is necessary because *car, la voiture*, is feminine, and feminine nouns require it. But the noun *dog*, *le chien*, is masculine, no matter whether we are referring to a female or male dog, so no final *e*. This concept of grammatical gender does not necessarily correspond to what we have been calling gender.

Languages like English that do not have grammatical gender, and even those that do, encode gender in other ways. Linguists have long been interested in the ways that women and men are represented in language itself. Much of the early work grew out of the women's movement and sought to identify the many ways women were rendered invisible or subtly dissed in everyday discourse. An early focus was on **androcentric generics**. These are terms like *man* or *mankind* when used for all humans, the pronoun *he* when used for everyone (*everybody should bring his own book*), and male-centric terms for groups of people who could be either male or female (*mailman, fisherman*, etc.). There are, of course, certain terms that are used only for women: *stewardess, waitress, actress*, even *poetess* (yes, that used to be a word and people actually used it). The two sets of terms work in different ways, as we shall see.

Androcentric generics imply that the norm for humanity is male, as several studies have shown. Although some claim that terms like *mankind* or *man* do not exclude women, if we look at analogous terms for other species, we can gain some insight into that claim. *Dog* is used for both sexes, but there is a separate term only for a female dog, *bitch*. In this way, it is analogous to the system for humans: *man* as supposedly inclusive of both genders, with a separate term for female humans, *woman. Dog*, however, clearly does contain the idea of female because we can talk about a dog giving birth. Try that with the term *man: The man gave birth*? Hmm, doesn't quite work. Thus, it is subtly gendered male, no matter what people say. Despite efforts to get people to understand that such androcentric expressions render women invisible, *man* is still routinely used to mean humans. As an example: On a box for a new type of coffee maker I was thinking of buying just last week, I found the following state-ment: *I own every brewing device known to man*. I added to myself, *and a few known only to women*. Of course, I did not buy it.

Recognition of the sexist nature of terms like *mailman* has been more widespread than for *mankind* and has led to efforts to reform the language to eliminate those overtly sexist terms, in some ways a quite successful effort. *Mailman* has now regularly become *mail carrier; stewardess* is now *flight attendant, waitresses and waiters* are now *servers*, and both males and females are *actors*, except at the Academy Awards. Whether such reforms have changed social expectations and stereotypes is a question still up in the air, however.

The example of *actor* and *actress* brings up another aspect of the English language often seen as sexist: terms differentiated by gender that are supposedly equivalent: *governor, gov-erness; master, mistress; bachelor, spinster*. Most of these now seem outdated; who talks about spinsters or governesses anymore? We do, however, still use *master* and *mistress*, and their different connotations can tell us something about sexism in our language. The phrase *a master of his trade* could refer to any of a number of professions; the phrase *a mistress of her trade* sounds odd and has a definite sexual connotation. And we still have *bachelors*, though not *spinsters, bachelorette* being used instead, at least on television. That's not much of an improvement to me. In fact, that term takes us to another problem: adding that feminizing ending (*-ette* or *-ess*) to a term that is unmarked as male implies that males are the norm, and women need to be marked somehow as an abnorm.

Viewing male terms and designations as unmarked and female ones as marked runs through a lot of our discourse. *Astronaut* is unmarked for male but marked for female, as recent headlines about the space walk by several astronauts who happened to be women clearly showed. No headlines mentioned men astronauts; it is assumed astronauts are male, just as it is assumed that architects, presidents, and basketball players are. We have the NBA, National Basketball Association (men's teams, no initial adjective needed), and the WNBA, the Women's National Basketball Association, with the required initial adjective to mark it. Although terms for many professions, especially high status ones, are generally unmarked as male, that's not the case for some other professions. *Prostitute* is unmarked female; it goes without saying that when we say prostitute, we mean women. We have to add an adjective to mark a prostitute as male, *male prostitute*. Similarly, for *nurse*; we mark it when the nurse is a man by saying *male nurse*. It's the opposite for *doctor*, of course. Despite the fact that more and more doctors are women, they are still marked as abnormal in that profession; the term *woman doctor* is common, *man doctor* is non-existent.

MULTIPLE IDENTITIES: BLACK MASCULINE LANGUAGE

As we saw in Chapter 9, our socioeconomic class, ethnicity, nationality, age, education, occupation, and sexuality affect how we talk, as do our political or religious allegiances and the subgroups we belong to or want to belong to. Gender is but one aspect of this multifaceted identity. How we experience gender and what roles and activities are seen as appropriate for our gender are affected by those other aspects. Not all women talk the same, nor do all men. Thus, although gender as an important part of our identity will be expressed through our language use, its expression will not be the same for all.

As we discussed in Chapter 10, African American Women's Language (AAWL) was often left out of studies of African American Language (AAL), which focused on men's language and out of studies of language and gender which focused on White, middle-class English-speaking women. Here I'd like to examine a variety of English rarely investigated in studies of language and gender, what is called **Black Masculine Language (BML)**. After all, men have gender too.

BML is an especially stigmatized variety in American society, often associated with street talk, at least by those who do not speak it or know much about it. It is, however, as all language is, a rule governed, valid variety that is spoken in daily life to accomplish all those actions we want to get done. BML, as described by Kirkland (2015), conforms closely to what is usually seen as AAL, including use of those grammatical and phonological features described in Chapter 10. Kirkland defines it as the "communicative practice associated more or less with Black male identity" (p. 835). Although it is demonized in the wider society, it is, according to Kirkland, used by many African American males to define themselves and express solidarity with their community.

For many of its speakers, especially young Black males, BML serves as a language of resistance, a way to define themselves rather than be defined by a White society that systematically devalues and oppresses them, a way of "languaging Black masculine being" (Kirkland, 2015, p. 842). We can see a glimpse of this use with an example from Hip Hop language: a new use of the invariant be discussed in Chapter 10. Instead of only indicating a habitual action, it is used by rappers to construct and brag about a self-identity: *I be the king supreme* (p. 841). Such uses go beyond just bragging; they allow the speakers to have agency over their own self-definition and resist images of them and their language as deficient.

GENDER AS PERFORMANCE

Earlier we noted that recent theory sees gender as something we do, not something we are. What does that mean? Aren't we born girls or boys, as those birth announcements proclaim? Yes, we are born with certain chromosomes and genitalia, though not all who are proclaimed girls or boys have identical chromosomes or genitalia. In recent years we have become more aware that there are intersex individuals who have some of both and trans people whose gender identity doesn't match the sex assigned to them at birth. It's complicated, even on the physical level.

It's even more complicated when we turn to the social level. What does it mean to say we perform femininity or masculinity? We do so through our choices in such areas as dress, hairstyle, way of walking or sitting or talking, to name but a few. Here's where language comes in. Linguistic resources are important resources to perform gender and perhaps the ones used with the least conscious attention. We have seen that certain linguistic forms **index** a feminine identity and others a male one. The term *index* has a specific meaning of evoking specific identities without explicitly stating them. That indexing, that evoking by some linguistic features of masculine or feminine identities, is necessary in order to create those gendered performances. What any one linguistic feature indexes varies across cultures, of course. In Madagascar, for example, directness and swearing are seen as women's ways of talking (Keenan, 1983). To perform femininity there, or to undermine it, requires a different set of linguistic resources than it would in the United States.

Ideas of gender as a social construct mapped onto a biological designation are common. These ideas assume that biological designations somehow exist outside of and before any socialization. In her ground-breaking book *Gender Trouble*, the philosopher Judith Butler (2006) challenges that idea. She suggests that the gender binary has its existence mainly in the performance and the interpretations of that performance. It's not that, for example, as men we act a certain way because of an innate nature or brain structure or hormones or whatever we are born with. Our performance does not reflect the fact that we are born men or women; it creates the whole idea of man or woman.

From this perspective, the idea of male and masculinity, or female and femininity, is a largely social construct. We learn to be men or women by performing masculinity or femininity, and that performance comes out of what we see as masculine or feminine and what society tells us is masculine or feminine. This is true whether we are conforming to society's vision or challenging it. And we learn what it means to be a man or a woman from reactions to our performance. We do not, of course, exist in a vacuum in which we can create any ideas of gender we want. We interact within what Butler calls a *rigid regulatory frame* about binary gender, one that presupposes what masculinity and femininity already are. It is within and against this frame that we perform gender. One small example of that frame: when Sally Ride became the first American woman in space, one headline noted the momentousness of the moment by remarking that she had no lipstick out there. That headline frames women, even those working professionally in outer space, as mere users of make-up, thus trivializing their considerable achievements.

Focusing on the local context allows us to see ways that individuals' performances, although always constrained by those rigid frames, can be and are creative and agentive not only for heterosexual individuals, but also for those regarded as marginal or non-normative. That is, those frames do not totally determine how we speak, partly because the norms contained in them vary greatly in their local articulation. Dominant ideologies of gender and gendered language are played with, undermined, manipulated, or challenged when they interact with local norms, as we saw with the jocks and burnouts.

Linguistics in your world: The heterosexual marketplace

In her study of pre-adolescent boys and girls, Eckert (1989) examined some of the linguistic changes they go through upon reaching adolescence and entering the heterosexual marketplace, becoming interested in and interesting to the so-called opposite sex. Both boys and girls are expected to do so, but they have different sets of resources with which to gain status in that marketplace. Boys can continue being boys; playing sports and being rambunctious still bring them status. Girls, however, must find different ways to gain status, unless they want to be called tomboys, a label not designed to enhance one's status in the heterosexual marketplace. They must become spectators rather than participants, cheerleaders not quarterbacks. And they must pay attention in a new way to their bodies and their speech: new ways of walking; using nail polish, lipstick, and make-up; shaving their legs; and talking like a girl. These gender performances are often policed, sometimes overtly, sometimes not so overtly. Girls are told not to yell or swear, but they are also tacitly told not to interrupt, especially not to interrupt boys. Teen girl magazines are full of advice about how to talk to a boy so he'll like you: agree a lot, don't contradict him, compliment him on his abilities, and most of all, smile a lot. Now obviously this sort of advice is not relevant to all girls; many reject it and rebel against its strictures. Nevertheless, those magazines help reinforce heterosexual gender performances as normal, what is known as **heteronormativity**, a view in which the natural state of affairs is a world where girls and boys, men and women, are distinct, binary and heterosexual.

The gender binary revisited

The early work we previously examined focused on the differences between men's and women's use of language and assumed that all humans are either one or the other and that basically all individuals of one gender are pretty much alike. Today, linguists challenge those assumptions. Instead of a gender binary (males and females are all there is), they have begun to focus on how language is used to construct the diverse forms of femininity and masculinity we see around us, including identities that embrace one, both, or neither of those binaries. Thus, we see more interest in the ways a person may not be what society calls a woman or a man but rather may be **gender nonconforming**: **transgender** or **queer** or **intersex** or any number of other nonbinary identities. Each of these identities, of course, is also multiple.

What's all this got to do with language? For one thing, as we saw in Chapter 3, the pronoun *they* is increasingly used to avoid having to assign a binary gender. For another, those challenges have led to a host of new words in English, and at least one new and fluid abbreviation: LGBTQIA (lesbian, gay, bisexual, trans, queer, intersex, asexual). Increasingly, one sees that abbreviation in newspapers and other media, often with no explanation of its meaning, a sign that it is becoming part of the lexicon of the language. *Trans* and *queer* are also used increasingly outside of LGBTQIA circles, though they often are accompanied by some explanation. *Trans* can be taken to mean either transsexual or transgender, though it seems to have come to refer to those who identify with a gender not assigned to them at birth, whether they have sexual reconstruction or not. *Cisgender* refers to those who live the gender assigned to them at birth. *Queer* today is often used as a form of gender subversion, undermining the binaries encoded in our language that categorize people as male or female and as heterosexual or homosexual. This subversion is often reflected in the language use of trans and queer communities, where these terms are used as markers of positive in-group identity, thereby undermining the use of *queer* as an insult.

CHAPTER SUMMARY

- Early studies concentrated on assumed differences between the ways men and women use language, especially in conversational interaction. They sought to determine if women and men did indeed use language differently and, if so, whether women's ways of speaking caused them to be seen as hesitant and insecure.
- These studies often focused on interruptions, tag questions, silence, and hedges; many studies found that women and men do indeed differ in their use of these features. Various models seek to explain these results: deficit, dominance, and difference.
- Subsequent studies did not support a claim of significant difference. Instead, the local context and the function of any one feature may influence the use of language more directly than gender. These studies note that there are nearly always more differences within each group than between groups.
- Other studies have examined the ways that languages encode gender in general and the ways that women are rendered invisible in specific. Androcentric generics and marked and unmarked terms for sports teams and professions are among the most noticeable ways.
- More recent theory has questioned the idea that gender is an innate characteristic of any individual. Instead, it is seen as a social construct, created through our acts, our linguistic acts among them. These gender performances vary across other social identities.
- This theory also challenges the idea of a binary view of gender. That binary perspective ignores the various ways that gender is lived and performed by trans, queer, or other gender-nonconforming individuals.

KEY TERMS

rapport style	cisgender
report style	gender binary
deficit model	androcentric generics
dominance model	heteronormativity
difference model	gender nonconformity
grammatical gender	trans
Black masculine language	queer

EXPLORATIONS

Exploration 1: Greeting cards

On your own, examine 10 to 15 greeting cards that are explicitly or implicitly aimed at women or men or boys or girls, such as those expressing appreciation for friendship or birthday cards for little girls and little boys or other family members. What stereotypes about gender can you glean from those cards? How is gender constructed in them: in the discourse, the images, the colors, etc.

Discussion prompt: Bring your notes to class and compare them with several of your classmates. In your group, create a summary of how these cards construct gender.

Writing prompt: Write a two-page essay describing what you found.

Exploration 2: She's a cow; he's a pig

Derogatory words and insults tend to be very gendered. We use some for men, some for women, and some for those who don't fit gender norms. Make a list of such words referring specifically to women, then to men, then to nonconforming genders.

In small groups, compile a comprehensive list with everyone's input. Which list is longer—derogatory words for women or for men or gender nonconformists? What do they tell you about society's ideas about gender? What a woman should and shouldn't be, what a man should and shouldn't be, what nonbinary genders should and shouldn't be?

Exploration 3: Food and animal terms

Terms for food are often similarly applied to people: calling someone a cupcake or a sweetie pie, for example. Make a list of as many of these terms as you can, both positive and negative; then determine who each term might be applied to, whether men, women, or gender nonconformist? In other words, who gets called a cupcake?

Exploration 4: She's a *they*

In Chapter 3, we discussed the use of *they* as a non-gendered, third-person pronoun for an individual. One of the explorations asked what you thought of that use. Given what you've learned in this chapter, has your perspective changed? Why or why not?

Exploration 5: Bossy women, independent men

As we noted, some terms tend to index women and some index men. Since people sometimes are not aware that these terms do so, to investigate their use, it is best to ask indirectly, as we will do. Ask several people to write a sentence about a person who epitomizes each term from the list that follows, using a separate sentence for each word. Do not tell them why you are asking, and don't mention gender at all.

In small groups, compare your results. What do your data tell you about how these words are marked for gender? What do they tell you about how women and men are viewed? Note: not all of the words index gender.

calm	strong	frumpy	creative	feisty	mechanical
musical	shrill	blonde	smart	ditsy	emotional

Exploration 6: Reclaiming slurs

Recently, people in some marginalized groups have tried to reclaim the slurs used against them, turning them into positive markers of group identity rather than insults. Some LGBTQIA individuals have reclaimed *queer*, as mentioned earlier, and some women have reclaimed *bitch* and *slut* as positive terms. There were even slut marches a few years ago.

What do you think of these efforts? Can one reclaim a derogatory term used for a group and get rid of its toxicity?

Discussion prompt: Share your reactions to these questions in small groups. If you know of any other efforts, add those to the discussion.

Writing prompt: Write one to two pages explaining your response to those questions.

FURTHER READING

Cameron, D. (2008). *The myth of Mars and Venus: Do men and women really speak different languages?* Oxford University Press.

Holmes, J., & Meyerhoff, M. (Eds.). (2005). *The handbook of language and gender.* Blackwell.

Zimman, L., Davis, J., & Raclaw, J. (2014). *Queer excursions: Retheorizing binaries in language, gender, and sexuality.* Oxford University Press.

REFERENCES

Butler, J. (2006). *Gender trouble: Feminism and the subversion of identity.* Routledge.

Cameron, D. (2008). *The myth of Mars and Venus: Do men and women really speak different languages?* Oxford University Press.

Eckert, P. (1989). *Jocks and burnouts: Social categories and identity in the high school.* Teachers College Press.

Fishman, P. (1978). Interaction: The work women do. *Social Problems, 25*(4), 397–406.

Hyde, J. (2005). The gender similarities hypothesis. *American Psychologist, 60*(6), 581–592.

James, D., & Clarke, S. (1993). Women, men, and interruptions: A critical review. In D. Tannen (Ed.), *Oxford studies in sociolinguistics: Gender and conversational interaction* (pp. 231–280). Oxford University Press.

Keenan, E. O. (1983). Norm-makers, norm-breakers: Uses of speech by men and women in a Malagasy community. In R. Bauman & J. Sherzer (Eds.), *Explorations in the ethnography of speaking* (pp. 125–143). Cambridge University Press.

Kirkland, D. (2015). Black Masculine Language. In S. Lanehart (Ed.), *The Oxford handbook of African American Language* (pp. 834–849). Oxford University Press.

Lakoff, R. (1975). *Language and woman's place.* Harper & Row.

Mendoza-Denton, N. (2008). *Homegirls: Language and cultural practice among Latina youth gangs.* Blackwell.

Zimmerman, D., & West, C. (1996). Sex roles, interruptions and silences in conversation. *Amsterdam Studies in the Theory and History of Linguistic Science, 4*(1), 211–236.

CHAPTER 12

Multilingualism

....

INTRODUCTION

When I graduated from college (I won't tell you how many years ago), I set off on a trip around the world. As part of that trip, I hitch-hiked my way through Africa, ending up out of money as I entered South Africa. So I stayed there a while to earn enough money to continue on. While there, I met Sophia, the maid employed by the family of a friend of mine. They were White; she was Black, and this was before the end of apartheid, the legal segregation and oppression of the majority population (Blacks) by a small minority (Whites). What I remember vividly about her was her fluency in so many languages. She spoke English well. I was surprised to discover that she also spoke Xhosa, her first language; isiZulu, her husband's first language; Afrikaans, South Africa's other official language along with English; and Greek, which she learned when she worked for a Greek family. Five languages, and none of them learned in school. I was in awe, even more so when I discovered that this situation was far from unusual, at least among the majority native population. They were forced to learn the

DOI: 10.4324/9780429269059-12

languages of their White colonizers to survive; the latter had no need to learn any native languages, though Whites were generally bilingual in the languages of the two White dominant groups: English and Afrikaans. Under apartheid, South Africa was an officially bilingual nation; after apartheid, it is now officially a multilingual nation with 11 official languages and many non-official ones.

In this chapter we will examine multilingualism in some detail. Why an entire chapter on multilingualism, you might ask? Isn't multilingualism unusual? Well, no. It turns out that, despite the ideology of one-nation-equals-one-language we discussed in Chapter 9, nearly all nations, even those that see themselves as monolingual, are in fact multilingual, as are the majority of the world's population. Grosjean (1982) estimated that at least half the world's population was multilingual. That number has likely increased by now with increased global migration. Worldwide, monolingualism is the exception rather than the rule.

We'll start our examination by asking what multilingualism is and how it functions in societies, touching on common beliefs and myths about it. Then we'll turn to what happens when speakers of different languages come into contact, how people learn a second language, how ideologies affect how we perceive multilingualism, and how multilingualism is handled in educational settings.

WHAT IS MULTILINGUALISM?

We can define **multilingualism** as the use of two or more languages or varieties either by a single individual or by a society. For our purposes, that definition includes bilingualism, so a person who speaks two languages is multilingual, just as is someone who speaks three or four languages, even if the speaker is not equally fluent in all of them.

Linguists differentiate between individual and societal multilingualism. **Individual multilingualism** refers to one individual's use of more than one language. **Societal multilingualism** refers to a community's regular use of multiple languages. There are different ways that societies come to be multilingual. Migration, the movements of large numbers of people from one area to another, is perhaps the most common. The causes of migration are many: wars, famines, or any number of social, political, or economic upheavals.

The redrawing of political boundaries is another common way that nations become multilingual. After World War I, for example, the victorious European nations unilaterally drew the national boundaries of several countries in the Middle East. As a result, various ethnic groups suddenly found themselves part of a newly created nation, one that was perforce multilingual, or found they were split up as populations within several different nations. The Kurds, for example, became part of Syria, Iraq, Iran, and Türkiye, with the Kurdish language contributing to the multilingual makeup of those countries.

In some countries that are officially multilingual, multilingualism is based on region, with some regions speaking one language and others a different language. Switzerland, for instance, has French-speaking, German-speaking, and Italian-speaking regions. In Switzerland, most people can speak more than one of those languages, even if most of their daily interactions take place in only one. In Canada the situation is different. Quebec is mostly French speaking, though most individuals also know some English. In the other Canadian provinces, though, people speak mostly English, with bilingualism in French much less common. Among Canada's First Nations, speakers may use their heritage languages and English.

In major cities in many countries, the regionality is even more local, with certain neighborhoods being multilingual. You can find neighborhoods across the United States where speakers regularly use, for example, Somali and English, Spanish and English, Farsi and English, or combinations of many other languages. In many countries, we find what is known as **asymmetrical multilingualism**, a situation like that in South Africa mentioned previously, where groups with less power are expected to learn the language of the dominant group, but the dominant group does not generally learn the languages of those less powerful groups. Thus, groups of lower status tend to be more multilingual than those of higher status.

People who speak more than one language often use those languages in different domains for different purposes, a situation known as **diglossia**. **Domain** here refers to the context in which a language is used, that is, a sphere of activity with particular roles in a particular setting. These domains can be formal—such as religious rituals, government settings, courtrooms, or some types of employment—or they can be informal, such as family or neighborhood activities, particular types of employment, or informal gatherings.

Not all multilingual societies are diglossic in this strict sense. With increasing mobility, especially across borders and into large metropolitan centers, we often find speakers of many languages interacting on many levels with more fluid rules and boundaries among those languages (a point we will return to later in the chapter).

Social meaning

In any multilingual setting, speakers' choice of language or variety is not neutral; it always carries social meaning. In diglossic situations, that meaning is related to the situation of use. As we've seen already, however, languages and varieties also index social identities. They send messages about who we are and who we are not.

Traditional studies of code switching generally assume languages have clear boundaries that separate them, what are called bounded languages. This is French; that is German. This assumption of clear linguistic boundaries is challenged, however, not only by language theorists, but by multilingual speakers themselves. For some multilingual speakers, the languages do feel compartmentalized, with one language linked to one part of their identity and another to a different part (Koven, 2007). For others, their multilingual practices are fluid and dynamic, making use of multiple linguistic resources with little regard for which language those resources are part of. Speakers may translanguage, as we discussed in Chapter 9, and index social identities that are not separate, but mixed. In fact, for some speakers, that mixing of languages itself indexes a new sort of identity, one that is blended and multiple.

Deciding which language to use

Obviously, in deciding which language to use, people use the language they have in common with their interlocutors if the interlocutors speak only one language. If both interlocutors speak the same two or more languages, code switching or translanguaging often takes place. In other situations, communities have conventions about which language to use. Leap (1993) describes how Native Americans, before the arrival of Europeans, managed that decision for trade among groups speaking different languages. If the languages were closely related, speakers used their own language, adjusting expectations as to correctness and learning to figure things out as they went along. If they were not closely related, basic rules about which language should be used in any given situation were developed by each community: in some cases, the host was expected to use the language of the guest; in others, the guests were expected to use the language of the host. Alternatively, a lingua franca developed. A **lingua franca** is a language learned as a second language and regularly used for interactions among speakers who do not speak each other's language. Ojibwe functioned this way for many years in the Great Lakes region of North America.

A similar decision must be made by individuals in many societies: if two multilingual speakers meet, what language do they use? Some communities consider it appropriate that speakers accommodate to the needs of the least fluent speaker. This is the expectation in some parts of South Africa. If we both speak isiZulu and Xhosa, but you speak only isiZulu well, I will use isiZulu with you to accommodate to your best language. Some other societies, such as the United States, expect the speaker of the less dominant language always to accommodate to speakers of the dominant language, in this case, English.

LANGUAGE PLANNING

Deciding what language to use is sometimes an individual decision. Sometimes, though, there are laws and policies that encourage the use or disuse of certain languages. Efforts by governments, educational institutions, the media, and the courts that seek to influence or change linguistic behavior are part of **language planning**. Language planning decisions can range from the selection of an official language to the choice of language to use in the classroom or on ballots, from mandating interpreter services in the courtroom or in health settings to obscenity laws and spelling reform. Some language policies seek to promote assimilation of linguistic minorities to the dominant language, while others seek to protect the rights of speakers of all languages and promote linguistic pluralism. For language communities that do not have a written form to their language, language planning may include the development of an orthography to represent their language.

Language planning can be official or de facto. In the United States, for example, Congress has never officially recognized English as the official language. It is, however, a de facto official language; all government interactions take place in English, all laws are published in English, schools are taught in English, and judicial proceedings take place in English, though there are laws requiring interpreters for those who do not speak it. Congress has passed a few laws to protect the rights of some non-English languages; the Native American Languages Act of 1990 sought to protect and support those languages. Support for other languages such as immigrant languages, however, is not part of U.S. law. In fact, the situation is one of de facto support for linguistic assimilation, encouraging immigrants to not only learn English but to give up their home language.

LANGUAGE CONTACT

Multilingualism is often the result of what is known as **language contact**, in which speakers of two or more languages come into prolonged contact with one another. Such contact comes about in different ways, mostly through trade, invasion, colonization, or migration. Language contact can lead to different outcomes: maintenance of separate languages; emergence of new languages; language shift; or linguistic diversity, even superdiversity, within a community. In Switzerland and Belgium, the languages in contact are maintained by each group. In Belgium, most people speak both French and Flemish. Although Belgium is officially bilingual, tensions around language issues often run very high. When I was in Brussels many years ago, one morning I woke up to see street signs in French (most signs are in both French and Flemish) having been blacked out by those who championed Flemish. The next morning, the opposite happened.

New languages: Pidgins and creoles

New languages sometimes emerge from language contact. **Pidgins** and **creoles** are two types of contact languages that developed in the 17th through 19th centuries; they emerged when people needed to communicate but did not know each other's language and there was no lingua franca available. Some of these new languages emerged in what we might now call global trade centers, where traders from around the world came to buy and sell wares. Most, however, developed out of language contact in colonial situations. Under colonization, especially of the Western Hemisphere by European nations, various subjugated peoples, often enslaved peoples brought from elsewhere, were forced to work side by side. They often spoke different languages and did not speak the language of the colonizers, a language contact situation that resulted in many new pidgins and creoles.

Pidgins are languages that developed when groups of people who did not speak each other's languages needed to communicate over a period of time, most often in colonial situations. Combining elements of two or more languages, they have simplified syntax and morphology, a limited range of use, and a small set of content words, generally taken from the colonizer's language, that allow just enough communication for getting work done. The definition of a pidgin, then, combines sociological, historical, and linguistic characteristics. Thus, we had various English, French, Portuguese, and Spanish pidgins in lands forced into a colonial relationship by speakers of those languages. These pidgins became the way the colonizer and the colonized communicated; they also often became the language of interaction among the colonized peoples themselves, especially when they were brought from overseas as workers or slaves.

Pidgins have no native speakers; they are always learned languages. Once they acquire native speakers, as linguists say, they become what are called **creoles**. **Creolization**, the process whereby pidgins become creoles, does not happen overnight. When the social situation is stable, pidgins begin to be used in more and more domains and serve more and more functions in a community. They then become a group's primary means of communication and are learned by children as their first language. Once this happens, the structures of creoles gradually become more complex, and their lexicon increases dramatically to meet the needs of their speakers. As with all languages, there is variation within creoles based on speaker and situation, and as with all languages, they develop to fulfill the needs of their speakers. Rather than simplified versions of a language, creoles are languages like any others, with their own lexicon, phonology, morphology, syntax, and all the other characteristics of language. Creoles have become the national language in many places in the world.

In Papua New Guinea, for example, Tok Pisin, an English-based creole, is used in government, the media, literature, and education. It is even used in road signs, such as the following provided by Romaine (2000):

Wok long rot: Ol kar mas stop.

If you say this aloud, you may be able to figure it out, especially if you remember the underlying source for words here is English: *Work along road; all cars must stop.*

It is estimated that 60 to 100 creoles are spoken around the world today. In Anglophone countries of the Caribbean such as Antigua, Barbados, Jamaica, and Belize, creoles based on English are spoken by most of the population: they include Jamaican Creole; Barbadian Creole; and Trinidadian Creole, also called Trini. Another creole based on English is Hawaiian Creole, which is often mistakenly call Hawaiian Pidgin. Those based on French include Haitian Creole, with nearly 10 million speakers, and Guadalupe Creole. Nubi and Juba Arabic are both creoles based on Arabic and are spoken in South Sudan, Kenya, and Uganda; and Andaman Creole, spoken on the Andaman Islands, is based on Hindi, Bengali, and Tamil.

Language shift

In many cases of language contact, it is not so much that new languages emerge but that speakers shift their language practices. **Language shift** refers to a situation where a community stops using its language and begins using another in more and more domains to such an extent that the first language is no longer passed on to the next generation. We see this shift with immigrant communities, with indigenous communities that were colonized, and with globalization. Reasons for such a shift include economic circumstances, trade, employment opportunities, and urbanization.

My family history illustrates the language shift that has taken place in most immigrant communities in the United States. My grandparents, who migrated to the United States as adults, were more or less monolingual in Italian. My father, the second generation, was equally bilingual in Italian and English. My siblings and I, the third generation, were raised as monolingual English speakers. (I learned Italian as a foreign language when I was in college.) Within three generations, Italian disappeared from not only my family but also from the community in which they lived. This pattern of language loss or shift in three generations has long been common among immigrant groups to the United States and many other nations. Recently, studies have shown that language shift among immigrant groups now happens even more quickly, often within two generations.

Deliberate, intentional efforts by a government to eradicate an indigenous language can also lead to language shift, as we saw in Chapter 9 with Native American languages. Unfortunately, such efforts are not just a thing of the past. To use a contemporary example, in 1959 the Chinese invaded and annexed Tibet. They then imposed the Chinese language on all governmental and educational domains, so that Tibetans are forced to learn Chinese to live in their own country. The Chinese government also encouraged its citizens to move to Tibet, where they set up schools taught in Chinese and where they eventually became the dominant population. In this way, Tibetans became second-class citizens in their own country, and their language became a minority language looked down upon as not modern or sophisticated enough for use in public.

We discuss language shift in more detail in Chapter 13.

SUPERDIVERSITY

In Chapter 1, we discussed the difficulty of defining a language or a variety, noting that common definitions often have more to do with political and social realities than linguistic ones. That difficulty becomes even more apparent when we turn to multilingualism. Questions of who speaks which language(s)—questions that seem simple on the surface—turn out to be quite complex, especially because many modern metropolitan centers are superdiverse in terms of languages and varieties.

Globalization is one factor that has led to this superdiversity. Globalization is often thought of as the increased flow of money, goods, culture, and media around the world. That flow also includes an increased movement of peoples. As Bloommaert (2013) puts it, since the end of the Cold War, "more people from more places [have] migrated into more and different places and for more and different reasons" (p. 5). And they have brought their cultures and languages with them. The result in many cities has been linguistic **superdiversity**, both an increase in the amount of linguistic diversity present and a difference in the functions of that diversity.

One aspect of modern communication plays an important part in these superdiverse communities: the increased ability to communicate across space enabled by technology. Cell phones and social media, to name just two technologies, allow people to keep in contact across vast distances easily and instantaneously. Individuals are now able to keep in touch with the people and languages of their home countries, even as they daily interact with speakers of other languages. Thus, they can more easily maintain their languages.

If we look at certain neighborhoods in large cities today, we can see how linguistically diverse they have become. Bloommaert (2013) describes the neighborhood of Brussels where he lives, one that has changed dramatically in the last 20 years through migration from Türkiye, Morocco, various parts of West Africa, and elsewhere. In this neighborhood, where before one heard mostly French or Dutch, one now also hears varieties of several West African languages, West African English, Turkish, Arabic, Urdu, and Punjabi. Residents use many languages or varieties daily. He describes how an Igbo-speaking Nigerian immigrant may use Dutch to interact with shopkeepers and then turn to Nigerian English to speak to her child's teachers, who would in turn speak to her in their Belgian-Flemish variety of English. A bewildering mix of languages, to say the least. As Bloomaert points out, it is hard to say what the dominant language in the community is, given this diversity on the street.

Nigerian English is one of what are called World Englishes, new varieties of English that have arisen in the last few centuries. I discuss these in more detail in Chapter 13.

Hip Hop as a multilingual phenomenon

Hip Hop is now a global phenomenon, performed around the world in multiple languages. It is both global and local, with young people forging local Hip Hop cultures by drawing on and reframing references to African American Hip Hop, including African American English, and to local conditions, including local languages and varieties. It seems the more established

Hip Hop becomes, the more it utilizes local references and languages. We see this clearly in Williams' 2016 study of how Hip Hop rappers in Cape Town, South Africa, use multiple languages and varieties: Colored South African English, African American English, Cape Afrikaans, and Sebela. Colored South African English is a variety of English spoken by what are known as Coloreds in South Africa, those with both African and White ancestors. Afrikaans is a variety of Dutch spoken by descendants of South Africa's Dutch settlers. Cape Afrikaans is a variety of Afrikaans spoken mostly by Coloreds, and Sebela is a local street variety that draws from Xhosa and isiZulu (local indigenous languages) as well as Cape Afrikaans and English. Both Sebela and Cape Afrikaans are highly stigmatized in education, politics, and the job market; their speakers are similarly stigmatized as "unintelligent, lazy, and criminal" (p. 114).

Hip Hop performers challenge those stereotypes and construct alternate identities by using those stigmatized varieties and what Williams calls "extreme locality," the use of references to local spaces, slang, sports teams, and values. In the performances described by Williams (2016), performers creatively use local languages and varieties to express their "marginalized and ethnic identities" (p. 132). As Williams points out, similar creativity in reclaiming stigmatized identities through an imaginative mixing and remixing of languages and varieties in Hip Hop can be seen in diverse places around the world: from Fresno, California to Tanzania, Brazil, and Nigeria.

LINGUISTIC RELATIVITY

In any discussion of language differences, the idea of linguistic relativism usually arises. **Linguistic relativism**, also known as the **Sapir-Whorf hypothesis**, is the theory that the structure of the language we speak determines, or greatly influences, the way we perceive the world. Language is seen to work like a filter on reality. Because languages differ, this filter, and thus our worldviews, will differ, and cultures that speak different languages will think and behave differently. There are two versions of this hypothesis: a strong one in which language is thought to determine how we see the world (**linguistic determinism**) and a weak one which claims instead that language influences it (**linguistic relativity**).

The reasoning goes something like this: as we learn our first language, its structure and lexicon provide systems for organizing our experiences in the world. These systems come to seem natural; we see the world the way those systems organize it without even realizing it. It's not a matter of imposition but of language predisposing us to perceive the world in certain ways. The examples often used come from Native American languages, which require certain elements that English and most Indo-European languages do not. Hopi, for example, has no morphological way of indicating that an event took place in the future or the past, no equivalent to our {ed} morpheme, for example. From this, Whorf concluded that the Hopi world view did not include concepts of past and future. Not true, as Malotki (1983) notes; her study among the Hopi showed that they have several ways of indicating both past and future tense; they just don't do it morphologically.

The strong version of this theory has been pretty much debunked. For one thing, if it were true, we would not be able to translate from language to language. For another, if one language does not have a word for a particular concept, does that mean its speakers can never understand that concept? That seems a bit far-fetched. We have the ability to be creative with language, and languages themselves change, for example, by borrowing a word for that new idea or creating a new word.

The weaker version is not so easily dismissed. Most would agree that different cultures perceive the world differently and those differences may well be related to their languages. Proposals to alter language to lessen sexism or racism, for example, rely on this reasoning. If we can change how people talk about a group, we may change the way they think about them. Propogandists also rely on this. To constantly refer to enemies or opponents as vermin or savages dehumanizes them and helps to legitimize their oppression.

LEARNING TO BE MULTILINGUAL

Some speakers learn more than one language in early childhood, having in effect two or more native or first languages. In fact, some estimates are that half of the world's population are native speakers of more than one language. Many others learn a second language after acquiring their first: in childhood, adolescence, or as adults. Some learn it at home; some in a community where it is used; some in the classroom; and some online. The circumstances in which people learn a second or third or fourth language vary greatly. The field of **second language acquisition (L2 acquisition)** examines how we learn a language beyond our first one, whether it be our second, third, or fifteenth language. There is no one clear answer to how we do so, but linguists agree that social, linguistic, cognitive, and affective factors play a role in this complex process.

Linguists tend to use the term acquisition rather than learning in talking about this process, partly to emphasize that much of the process is unconscious and unknown. We can learn grammar rules, for example, but being able to use them automatically requires more; acquisition refers to that more. Linguists also make a distinction between a second language and a foreign language. Second language acquisition refers to a language learned for communication in communities that are multilingual, not necessarily in international communication. Foreign language acquisition generally refers to languages learned for international communication or for study in school to meet a requirement. With the increased spread of English globally, and its use by many different peoples for many different purposes, that distinction may no longer be valid, as we will see in Chapter 13.

In terms of the process of L2 acquisition, we might start by asking how L2 acquisition is different from first language acquisition. The most obvious difference was mentioned earlier: everyone learns a first language fluently but not all who attempt it learn a second one equally well. The learning of that first one appears effortless; it just seems to happen. In acquiring our first language, we seem to move quickly and effortlessly from hearing or seeing it to producing it. Yet that movement from learning words and grammar rules to producing language is often difficult in acquiring a second language. When we are doing so, we are not a blank slate, for we already know our first language. And that knowledge can either interfere with or help our learning. The circumstances in which we learn and our motivations for learning also play a role in L2 acquisition, as we'll see further.

What does success in L2 acquisition look like? Do you have to be totally fluent in all aspects of a language to be considered successful? Obviously, how we define success in learning a second language, what is known as the **target language**, will vary. If we look around, it's easy to see that there is a range of mastery when it comes to learning a second language:

some become fluent, some can hold a simple conversation, some know enough phrases to get by in a tourist situation, some can speak it but not read, some can read it but not speak it. There's no clear-cut line here; we see rather a continuum of mastery. To my mind, all are examples of some success in SLA.

Linguistic factors in L2 acquisition

Age has something to do with success in L2 acquisition. There may be a **critical period** for acquiring a second language, a biologically determined point beyond which we find it difficult. The exact time of the critical period is debated: 8 years old? Puberty? Puberty seems to be a cutoff point after which native-like proficiency in phonology is rarely achieved. In other words, if we start learning after puberty, we're always going to have what is called a foreign accent. Aside from accent, however, it is possible to become fluent in another language at any age, although there is a general decline in our ability to do so as we age. It seems that the older we are, the harder it is, but whether that has to do with biology or other psycho-social factors is not clear.

One key question here is how our first language influences our learning and use of a second language. One way seems clear: **interference** from our first language can be a source of error in the target language. If our first language does not use articles such as *a* or *the*, for example, we are more likely to omit them when using a second language that requires them. If our first language does not make a sound distinction that is important in the target language, it will be harder to learn that distinction. In Arabic, for example, [b] and [p] are allophones of the same phoneme, so when Arabic speakers are learning English, they often mix up those two sounds. Some errors, however, do not seem to be the result of interference. Instead, they arise from specific aspects of the target language. In English, for example, we can say either *I like swimming* or *I like to swim*, but if we use the verb *enjoy*, we can only use the *-ing* form, *swimming*, not the infinitive *to swim*. Learners of English commonly say *I enjoy to swim*, at least until they've mastered this little complexity and *I enjoy swimming* has become automatic.

Affective factors in L2 acquisition

How we get to that automatic production remains somewhat of a mystery, but we do know two mechanisms that are related to it: the monitor and affective filter. The **monitor** is the part of us that watches what we say and tries to make sure it is correct. Our monitor is mediated by an **affective filter** that can facilitate or inhibit our efforts by making us more or less willing to use the target language. If we are afraid of making mistakes, for example, our affective filter is high, and we will be less willing to speak or to ask for clarification, hindering our efforts to learn. I remember my French teacher in high school saying that to learn any new language, you needed to be willing to make a fool of yourself, that is, lower that affective filter. The presence of this filter may be one key difference between L2 acquisition and L1 acquisition; young children learning their first language do not seem to worry about being wrong or making fools of themselves.

Motivation appears to play a key role in learning, especially the difference between instrumental and integrative motivation. **Instrumental motivation**, learning a language to achieve another goal, includes learning a language for a school requirement or business reasons with little desire for integration into a new community. **Integrative motivation** is more complex, but generally includes a desire to become part of a community or to learn more about, and be able to partake in, a different culture. Integrative motivation can include a willingness to take on a new identity. Our learning, both what we learn and how well we learn it, can be affected by these motivations. Instrumental motivation can lead to successful acquisition of a limited range of aspects needed for our purposes. Integrative motivation generally leads to more successful acquisition of a wider range of registers.

Social factors in L2 acquisition

Individual attitudes toward language learning often reflect attitudes prevalent in the local community and wider society. During and after World War I in the United States, for example, the number of students learning German decreased drastically as a result of intense and widespread anti-German sentiments. In many parts of the world, in addition to being necessary for a career or higher education, English carries social prestige, a situation that may well contribute to the motivation to learn it. In some communities, multilingualism is valued and expected. Such expectations undoubtedly contribute to learning. In other communities, multilingualism is neither valued nor expected. Or some types may be valued and other types not. In the United States, for instance, bilingualism in French/English or German/English is thought admirable; bilingualism in Hmong/English or Somali/English carries much less prestige.

Sociocultural theories of L2 acquisition note that second learning acquisition may not be a universal process, but rather one mediated by the social, historical, cultural, and political contexts in which it occurs. From this perspective, language is predominantly a social tool, one that we learn to use through interacting with others in various contexts. Since these contexts and our roles within them will vary greatly, our learning may do so as well. Similarly, our needs as learners will vary according to our goals in learning a language, which can range widely. Some learn for a specific job, some to be able to read scientific material, some to travel, some to move to a new country, some to be Hip Hop artists, some to fulfill an educational requirement, some to experience a new culture, and some because they've fallen in love with someone who speaks a different language. Each of these goals may affect how we interact with others using the target language and thus affect how we go about acquiring it.

MULTILINGUALISM IN EDUCATION

Given the amount of multiculturalism in the world, the role it plays in education is important to examine. Decisions about which language to use within a school system are faced by all communities but are especially complicated in multilingual communities. Should children be taught in their home language to begin and then transition to the dominant or school language? Or should they be taught to read and write in the school language from the beginning? In communities that see themselves as monolingual, that question is often not even asked, even though students bring various languages to school.

In the first few years of schooling, many children do not learn to read and write in their home language. Even if they do, most children worldwide must transition to a different language to continue learning. Globally, education beyond early primary school happens in only a small percentage of the world's languages. In fact, more and more secondary education takes place in one of a small number of other languages: English, Arabic, Spanish, French, Chinese, or Hindi. That means that for most children around the world, the school language they are expected to use does not match their home language or home variety. There is, in other words, a mismatch.

This mismatch is obviously different for different populations; for example, speakers of languages of immigrant groups, of indigenous heritage languages, of varieties different from the dominant one. In Minnesota, where I live, Anashinabemowin-speaking children, Somali-speaking children, Hmong-speaking children, and African American English-speaking children may all come to school with little knowledge of the Standard English they will be taught in. In other parts of the world, it may be Luo-speakers in Kenya or Sebela-speakers in South Africa. What do the experiences of these groups have in common?

First, all of these children bring rich linguistic resources to the classroom, even if those resources do not include the school language. Many bring more than one set of resources, speaking more than one language before they even enter a classroom. They also often face an educational system that shows little understanding of this richness, instead seeing their language as unsuitable for educational purposes, something to be corrected. Their languages are thought to stymie their success in school. It is no wonder, then, that for far too many children, going to school in a language not their home language leads to high failure and dropout rates.

The blame is often put on the fact that the children do not speak the school language, or that their parents do not speak it at home, or their parents do not engage in the child's education—in essence, blaming the victims. As Labov (1972) notes, however, nonstandard varieties or languages are not in themselves an obstacle to learning. It is the lack of understanding about language on the part of administrators and instructors that is the chief problem. In fact, it is not these children who fail, but the educational institutions that are failing to educate them.

Numerous studies have shown that children learn to read more easily in their home language. That seems like common sense. Learning to read is a difficult endeavor; doing it in a language that you do not speak well makes it even more difficult. Studies also show that literacy skills, once learned, can be and are transferred to another language. Yet too many schools still teach basic literacy in the school language rather than the child's home language. In one study of students in Papua New Guinea, Siegel (2012) describes what happened when schools began using Tok Pisin, an English-based creole that is the students' home language, as the medium of instruction in schools. Instead of falling behind in learning Standard English, students who first learned to read and write in Tok Pisin did better academically, not just in the early grades but in the higher grades as well. Similar educational results have been found in other studies as well.

In countries with large immigrant populations, people are often afraid that letting children learn in their own languages will lead to social disunity, with ethnic communities refusing to learn the dominant language. Most parents of immigrant or minority-language students, however, want their children to learn the dominant language, the language of opportunity. They also want to maintain their home language and culture (Romaine, 2000). Linguistically, there is no reason that cannot happen. Some people also believe that teaching students in their own language and in English will confuse children, so they discourage students from speaking their home language in favor of speaking only English. We know this is not so; students do not need to stop using their home language to learn the school language.

Monolingual mindset

The assumption that children need to give up their home language to learn the school language is part of the **monolingual mindset**, a concept closely related to the standard language ideology discussed in Chapter 9. A term coined by Michael Clyne (2004), monolingual mindset refers to the belief that monolingualism should be the norm for nation states and that multilingualism is strange and dangerous. This mindset underlies objections in the United States and other English-speaking nations to the use of languages other than English in public spaces. Thus, we hear about people being told, *This is America; speak English.* Just today I read of notices put up in an apartment block in Norwich, England, the day after Brexit took effect: *We've got our country back. Speak English.* (To their credit, the managers of the block quickly took those notices down.) Such sentiments exemplify this mindset: the devaluing and fear of languages other than English.

As part of this mindset, educational success is often equated with mastery of the standard language. Think of all the standardized tests students in the United States take, many of which focus on the grammar of Standard English. Other codes—any languages or varieties that do not match the school language—are considered not only nonstandard and inappropriate for school but illogical, and those who speak them are often seen as morally deficient. (Remember that double negative we discussed earlier?) Thus, speakers of languages or varieties that do not match the school language are seen as needing constant correction, both grammatically and morally.

We know that multilingual children bring remarkably complex linguistic skills to the classroom, skills that should be valued and rewarded, even if their language is highly stigmatized by society at large. Multilingual children code-switch and translate multiple languages regularly. Perez (2016) notes that Zapotec-speaking students in California often serve as trilingual interpreters for their families, moving between their indigenous language, Spanish, and English as the need demands. Instead of measuring success in terms of mastery of one standard language, as most schools do, what if we defined success as being able to use two or more languages in appropriate situations?

Bilingual education in the United States

Such a definition might lead to more support for bilingual education, a topic that has long been fiercely debated in the United States. It is helpful to look at a bit of the history, as it gets to the heart of much thinking about multilingualism in the United States. For much of U.S. history, bilingual programs were available in many schools: German/English bilingual schools were common in Ohio until World War I, during which anti-German sentiments led to their closure. In the latter part of the 20th century, bilingual educational programs became more common after the Supreme Court mandated programs for students who did not speak English. Since around 2000, however, with the passage of the No Child Left Behind legislation, those programs have been effectively eliminated.

To understand recent debates about bilingual education in the United States, it is important to know that even when they were available, these programs reached only a small portion of the students who could have benefited from them. And the types of programs varied greatly. Most were **transitional programs** whose purpose was to get students speaking English as soon as possible so they could transition into English-only classes. They used the student's home language merely as a tool to support learning English, not as a valuable skill worth developing. This attitude usually led to **subtractive bilingualism**, in which learning the dominant language leads to losing the home language. Very few programs were **maintenance programs** whose aim was to help students maintain and develop their first language while also learning English. Maintenance programs lead to **additive bilingualism**, where a second language is learned without leading to loss of the home language. How successful were bilingual programs? It depends on which type you are assessing. Cummins (1979) notes that nearly all studies that show a negative outcome for bilingual programs are assessing transitional programs. Studies assessing maintenance programs, however, show a high degree of success.

Proponents of bilingual programs point to those studies and argue that, as a 1953 UNESCO (United Nations Educational, Scientific and Cultural Organization) report noted, all children have a right to an education in their home language. They also point out that such an education leads to improved educational success. Critics of bilingual education often draw upon the monolingual mindset mentioned earlier. In addition, they see these programs as "special treatment" for Hispanic students since most of them were for Spanish-speaking children, the majority of non-English speaking students when the programs were developed. It is interesting to note, however, that the Supreme Court case that made bilingual programs mandatory, Lau vs Nichols, was brought by parents of Chinese-speaking children. Nevertheless, arguments against bilingual programs occur within the larger context of immigration and the place of Spanish in the United States.

Spanish in the United States

The United States was a multilingual nation at its beginning; it remains so today. According to recent U.S. census data, there are 14 languages other than English spoken by more than half a million speakers each: Chinese by over three million people and Spanish by over 37 million. Some people see these data as proof that immigrants today, unlike those of the past, are not learning English. Such claims are, however, untrue. Census data also show that over 80% of speakers of languages other than English also speak English well or very well.

The perception that newer immigrants are not learning English is often directed specifically at Spanish speakers. The second most spoken language in the United States, Spanish holds a unique place in the linguistic landscape of the United States not only because it is so widely spoken but also because it has such a long history here. It was the first European language spoken in what is now the United States with the Spanish settlement of St. Augustine, Florida, in 1565, long before Jamestown or the Pilgrims. It spread in the 16th to 19th centuries as the Spanish conquered and settled many parts of the southwestern North America. Many communities in that area became part of the United States through military annexation from Mexico, leading to a large number of Spanish speakers becoming part of what are now the states of Texas, New Mexico, Arizona, Colorado, and California. Thus, Spanish has been part of the U.S. landscape for centuries, well before the recent immigration from various Spanish-speaking countries in Latin America.

Many Americans today think of Spanish as an immigrant language, forgetting its long history here. Throughout that long history, Spanish has had a conflicted place. The original constitution of California, for example, ensured that governmental decrees would be issued in both Spanish and English; within a few years, however, that policy was abandoned as Anglos became the majority.

Both Hispanics and non-Hispanics hold a range of attitudes toward Spanish. For many non-Hispanics, Spanish is seen as a threat to the English language. Hispanic students have even been expelled for speaking Spanish in school, not in the classroom but outside of it with friends. Non-Hispanic students learning Spanish and using it outside the classroom would most likely not face such punishment. Despite these sentiments, statistics show that it is the Spanish language, not English, that faces a threat. In fact, Bills and Vigil (2008) conclude that Spanish-speaking immigrants are shifting to English and abandoning Spanish even more quickly than earlier immigrant groups.

For some Hispanics, English is the language of opportunity, education, and power, while Spanish is the language of the barrio, not a language that will help them succeed. For many others, it serves as a potent emblem of their heritage, one they are proud of. Indeed, there are some forces contributing to its maintenance today: the ease of travel to and communication with Spanish-speaking countries, now made easier by modern communication technologies, and a new respect for the Spanish language and Hispanic culture among many young people.

Spanish speakers are often seen as having an L2 accent, what is generally called a foreign accent. If they learned English as adults, that L2 accent is difficult if not impossible to lose. Despite this fact, Spanish accents are stigmatized. In the movies, Spanish accents are used to suggest a drug dealer or gang member, a *wetback* (an ethnic slur for Mexicans who enter the United States without legal permission), or as just plain lazy. My guess is that such stigmatizations would not occur with Swedish or French accents.

Sign language education

When we speak of multilingual education, most people probably don't think of the education of Deaf students, but that is indeed a type of multilingual education. How does one best teach Deaf students? That question was heatedly debated in the late 19th century, with some arguing for an oralist approach and others for the use of sign languages. The oralist approach included teaching lip reading and oral language, both extremely difficulty to learn for hard-of-hearing students, especially if deaf from birth. And this approach insisted that signed languages had no place in the classroom. By the end of the 19th century, the oralist approach was almost universally accepted in Europe and North America. Before that, in the mid-19th century in the United States, nearly every school for Deaf students used American Sign Language or a local sign language; by 1907, none did (Dolnick, 1993). In Britain, there were similar policies, with students reporting being hit if caught using their sign language (Harris, 1995).

By the 1960s, educators began to reconsider this approach in light of activism by the Deaf community and new research demonstrating that sign languages are fully functional languages like any other. Today, Deaf people are increasingly recognized as a linguistic and cultural minority and sign languages recognized as their first language. As a result, in some schools in Europe and North America, bilingual education programs have been developed for Deaf and hard-of-hearing children. In these programs, students are taught first in the sign language of their Deaf community and then taught the language of hearing society as a second, written language (Mesthrie et al., 2000). In Sweden, these programs align with the legal recognition of the Deaf as a linguistic and cultural minority. In the United States, such legal recognition does not exist; instead, Deaf students' educational rights fall under the Americans with Disabilities Act, which guarantees them equal rights based on that disability. Many Deaf people object to being seen as disabled and advocate for the right to be taught in their own language, not because they are disabled but because American Sign Language is their native language. That language is used in the only liberal arts university for the Deaf in the world, Gallaudet University in Washington, D.C.

Multilingualism on Martha's Vineyard

Martha's Vineyard, an island off the coast of Massachusetts, offers an interesting case of community bilingualism, in this case in English and a local sign language. During the 18th and 19th centuries, a relatively large proportion of the island's population was Deaf. As Groce (1985) notes, instead of being marginalized and discriminated against, as happened in many other places, Deaf people were fully integrated into society, with both hearing and Deaf people learning sign language and using it to converse with each other. There was a high degree of bilingualism throughout that time, especially in the towns with the highest number of Deaf inhabitants. Hearing inhabitants learned sign language casually from an early age, and English/sign language bilingualism became an emblem of island identity. However, as more and more people began moving to the island in the early 20th century and as the percentage of Deaf individuals decreased, this bilingualism began to disappear and today is almost gone.

CHAPTER SUMMARY

- Multilingualism refers to the use of two or more languages or varieties by individuals, societies, and/or nations. Multilingualism, which includes bilingualism, is more common than monolingualism around the world; most of the world's population is multilingual.
- Societies come to be multilingual through migration, trade, invasion, and colonization.
- The situation in many multilingual societies is diglossic, with different languages being used in different domains.
- Language contact occurs when speakers of different languages interact on a regular basis. It can lead to any of several different outcomes: diglossic multilingualism, super-diversity, language shift, and new languages (pidgins or creoles).
- Pidgins are simplified languages created for specific purposes among those who do not speak the same language. Many have arisen in colonial circumstances.
- When pidgins become the common language of communication and are learned by children as their first language, they develop into creoles.
- Language shift refers to a situation in which speakers of one language begin using another language in its place.
- Superdiversity refers to the increased linguistic and cultural diversity seen today in large metropolitan centers.
- Second language acquisition differs from first language acquisition in important ways, with linguistic, social, and affective factors all playing a role.

- Educational settings are important sites where multilingualism plays a role. Although children learn best in their home language, most children in the world are taught in a language not their own.
- Despite the fact that most of the world is multilingual, in many English-speaking countries a monolingual mindset prevails, one that sees multilingualism as odd and a threat to national unity.
- The United States has always been a multilingual nation, despite what many believe. Among the many who speak a language other than English, nearly 80% also speak English well.
- Among multilingual phenomena discussed are Hip Hop, Spanish in the United States, and multilingualism on Martha's Vineyard.

KEY TERMS

bilingualism/multilingualism
individual multilingualism
societal multilingualism
asymmetrical multilingualism
diglossia
domain
lingua franca
language planning
language contact
pidgins
creoles, creolization
language shift
superdiversity
linguistic relativity
linguistic determinism

Sapir-Whorf hypothesis
second language (L2) acquisition
target language
critical period
interference
affective filter
monitor
instrumental motivation
integrative motivation
interference
monolingual mindset
transitional bilingual programs
subtractive bilingualism
maintenance bilingual programs
additive bilingualism

EXPLORATIONS

Exploration 1

1. How many languages do you know? (Remember, you need not be totally fluent to claim some knowledge of a language.) How often do you use them? In what circumstances? How about if we enlarge the definition of multilingualism to include using more than one variety? What happens to your answers then? Revisit your language autobiography from Chapter 1. Would you change any of it now?

2. Do a survey of your classmates and friends to determine the extent of multilingualism in your community now and in the past. Start by asking people your age how many speak a language other than English; then how many of their parents do, then how many of

their grandparents or great-grandparents. What languages do they speak? What happened to knowledge of those languages over time? Compare your findings in your small groups. What do they tell you about multilingualism in your community? Discuss whether you think the results would be different if you had asked other groups or those living in other regions.

Exploration 2

1. To discover more about multilingualism in the United States, investigate census information online at the U.S. census (www.census.gov/data.html). Did any of the language-related statistics there surprise you? Why?
2. Investigate the linguistic situation in a country other than the one you live in. South Africa, Finland, Papua New Guinea, Belgium, India, China, and Israel all have complex linguistic histories. Share your finding with your small group.

Exploration 3

1. There are many English-based creoles around the world: Tok Pisin, Hawaiian Creole, Gullah, Cameroonian English Pidgin, and many more. Choose one and investigate its history, origins, and current status.
2. Using an online source such as YouTube, find a video of someone speaking an English-based creole. How much of it can you understand? If you listen longer, does it become more comprehensible?
3. Show that video to some friends not in this class and ask them what language they think is being spoken. What is their reaction when you tell them it is an English creole?

Exploration 4

1. Where do you see evidence of the monolingual mindset around you? Have you heard people say, "*This is America. Speak English*" or other similar comments? What would you say to someone who made such comments?
2. Have you spoken a language other than English in public? Have you had hurtful or dismissive comments aimed at you? What was your reaction?

Exploration 5

Currently, the United States does not have an official language, though English is clearly the dominant language. Over the last several decades, several organizations have pushed to make English the official language of the United States. Other organizations have fought against it and pushed for language rights for speakers of all language, a campaign called English Plus.

1. Investigate the main arguments of the first type of organization:
   • U.S. English (https://www.usenglish.org)
   • Pro-English (http://proenglish.org/).

2. Then examine the arguments of the second type:
   • Conference on College Composition and Communication, The National Language Policy https://web.archive.org/web/20080726173538/www.ncte.org/cccc/resources/positions/123796.htm

- Center for Applied Linguistics https://web.archive.org/web/20080724024953/www.cal.org/resources/archive/digest/1992englishplus.html
- League of United Latin American Citizens https://lulac.org/advocacy/issues/english_vs_spansih/index.html

3. Debate these arguments in your small group. Do concepts from this chapter shed any light?

FURTHER READING

Appel, R., & Muysken, P. (2005). *Language contact and bilingualism*. Academic Archive. A good introduction to language contact that focuses on bilingualism and language acquisition.

Gass, S., & Selinker, L. (2008). *Second language acquisition: An introductory course*. Routledge. Accessible and informative.

MacGregor-Mendoza, P. (2005). Bilingualism: Myths and realities. In K. Denham & A. Lobeck (Eds.), *Language in the schools: Integrating linguistic knowledge into K-12 teaching*. Lawrence Erlbaum.

Weinreich, U. (1953). *Languages in contact*. Linguistic Circle of New York. Classic work in the field.

Winford, D. (2003). *An introduction to contact linguistics*. Blackwell.

Yip, V., & Matthews, S. (2007). *The bilingual child: Early development and language contact*. Cambridge University Press. An interesting study of children learning two languages.

REFERENCES

Bills, G., & Vigil, N. (2008). *The Spanish language of New Mexico and southern Colorado: A linguistic atlas*. University of New Mexico Press.

Bloommaert, J. (2013). *Ethnography, superdivesity and linguistic landscapes*. Multilingual Matters.

Clyne, M. (2004). Trapped in a monolingual mindset. *Prime Focus, 37*, 40–42.

Cummins, J. (1979). Linguistic interdependence and the educational development of bilingual children. *Review of Educational Research, 49*, 221–251.

Dolnick, E. (1993). Deafness as culture. *Atlantic Monthly, 272*(3), 37–53.

Groce, N. (1985). *Everyone here spoke sign language*. Harvard University Press.

Grosjean, F. (1982). *Life with two languages: An introduction to bilingualism*. Harvard University Press.

Harris, J. (1995). *The cultural meaning of deafness: Language, identity, and power relations*. Avebury.

Koven, M. (2007). *Selves in two languages: Bilinguals' verbal enactments of identity in French and Portuguese*. Benjamins.

Labov, W. (1972). *Language in the inner city: Studies in the Black English Vernacular*. University of Pennsylvania Press.

Leap, W. (1993). *American Indian English*. University of Utah Press.

Malotki, E. (1983). *Hopi time: A linguistic analysis of temporal concepts in the Hopi Language*. Mouton.

Mesthrie, S., Swann, J., Deumert, A., & Leap, W. (2000). *Introducing sociolinguistics*. John Benjamins Publishing Co.

Perez, W. (2016). Zapotec, Mixtec, and Purepecha youth: Multilingualism and the marginalization of Indigenous immigrants in the United States. In H. Samy Alim, J. Rickford, & A. Ball (Eds.), *Racio-linguistics: How language shapes our ideas about race* (pp. 255–271). Oxford University Press.

Romaine, S. (2000). *Language in society: An introduction to sociolinguistics.* Oxford University Press.

Siegel, J. (2012). *Second dialect acquisition.* Cambridge University Press.

UNESCO. (1953). *The use of vernacular languages in education (Monographs of Fundamental Education No. 8).* UNESCO.

Williams, Q. (2016). Ethnicity and extreme locality in South Africa's multilingual Hip Hop ciphas. In H. Samy Alim, J. Rickford, & A. Ball (Eds.), *Racio-linguistics: How language shapes our ideas about race* (pp. 113–133). Oxford University Press.

CHAPTER 13

Language birth and death

···

INTRODUCTION

When I was traveling around the world in my early 20s, using local transportation and places to sleep, I was amazed that everywhere I went, from a small village in the Sudan to the back streets of Lahore, I could find someone who spoke English. That widespread use of English was certainly helpful for me as a traveler. I remember walking down the one street in a small village in the Sudan, looking for some food to buy, when I came upon a Coca-Cola machine outside a small shop. The owner came out and asked, "Can I help you?" in English. Though his accent was very different from mine, I could understand him and get the food I needed. I remember even at the time wondering how it was that he, and so many others around the world, spoke English. It wasn't that everyone did; far from it. But you could almost always find someone who did, even those many years ago.

How did that come about? That's one of the questions we'll be addressing in this chapter. We'll also look at how languages come into existence, how they spread, and how they die. We don't usually think about languages being born and dying; after all, for most of us, the

DOI: 10.4324/9780429269059-13

language we speak has always been around. Like any human artifact, however, they have not always been around. And like all human artifacts, they do not necessarily last forever.

ORIGINS OF LANGUAGE

Linguists estimate that there are approximately 7,000 languages used in the world today. That's a lot of languages, but not as many as the 10,000 that are estimated to have existed thousands of years ago. What did those early languages sound like? Where did they come from? Although most cultures have some sort of story or myth about the origins of human language, we don't really know much about how it evolved.

Linguists disagree about how and when humans first started using language; most agree, however, that language probably began with the emergence of *Homo sapiens* in sub-Saharan Africa around 150,000 to 200,000 years ago. Those early humans took language with them when they migrated to other parts of the world, spreading it around the globe.

There are two conflicting theories as to how language arose. **Discontinuity** theorists generally believe that language, being unique to humans, most likely appeared all at once, probably from a genetic mutation. It is, then, not related to other animals' ways of communicating. **Continuity** theorists, on the other hand, believe that human language evolved from communication systems of our primate ancestors, most likely growing out of the social interactions of our human ancestors at the same time as the emergence of human symbolic culture: ritual practices, art, song, and tool making, all of which are facilitated by language.

If language did not suddenly appear due to some genetic mutation, then how did it emerge? There are various theories, all still being debated. It may have evolved from the gestures used by our ancestors, from the vocal signals between mothers and babies, from song, from imitation of animal cries or natural sounds, or from grunts and other vocalizations when working. Or it may have evolved from a combination of any of these. One interesting theory posits that language evolved when social groups of early humans grew so large that the manual grooming of one another done in primate social groups became impossible. Primate groups use grooming to maintain cohesion and solidarity in the group. For early humans, vocal signals took the place of that grooming. In this theory, one of the earliest uses of language was gossip, which, according to Dunbar (1997), functions like manual grooming for these larger groups of humans, allowing them to maintain social cohesion.

When those early humans began leaving Africa, they not only spread the human species globally, they also spread human culture and language. We know very little about the language they spoke; after all, there are no written records from those migrations. Some linguists posit an original language, sometimes called Proto-world, with the many thousands of languages spoken today and in the past evolving out of that one proto-language. A **proto-language** is a hypothesized older language from which other languages have descended. Other linguists doubt this theory, believing that human language most likely has more than one origin. That debate and the ones about how language developed are likely to continue for some time, as there is little evidence to support a definitive answer. The time frame involved in trying to determine the origins of language, hundreds of thousands of years, means that we do not know much about any supposedly original language if one did exist.

LANGUAGE SPREAD AND LANGUAGE FAMILIES

We may not know much about possible languages from 100,000 years ago, but we do know something about languages spoken 5,000 years ago and how they spread. We talk about languages spreading, but of course it's not so much languages that spread as the people who speak them migrate and take them into new environments that may or may not have speakers of other languages there. As they spread, languages invariably change, partly as a result of natural language change and partly as a result of speakers adapting to new environments and interacting with speakers of other languages.

Linguists place languages into various language families. **Language family** here is used metaphorically to describe the relationship among certain languages: a parent language with daughter languages that have evolved from that parent language and that are, therefore, related. When linguists say that languages are **related**, often referred to as a **genetic relationship**, they mean that those languages share a common ancestor language. For example, French, Italian, Spanish, Portuguese, Romanian, Galician, Provencal, and Catalan, collectively known as Romance languages, are related in that they each evolved from Latin. Those relationships are fairly easy to trace as we have written records for hundreds, even thousands, of years. But what about when we have few or no written records, as is the case with languages spoken thousands of years ago? Can we reconstruct those familial relationships? Yes. In fact, linguists have done so for several language families.

Indo-European language family

The idea of a common ancestral language for languages of Europe had long been conceived of, but the work of Sir William Jones in 1786 provided evidence for it. As a judge in India for the British, Jones studied Sanskrit, an ancient language of India, after already having learned Latin and Ancient Greek. In the course of his study, he noticed many similarities between Sanskrit and Latin and Ancient Greek. Jones posited a common source for them and for many other languages of Europe, India, and parts of the Middle East. His theory sparked further scholarship, with the eventual conclusion by scholars that most of the languages of Europe, as well as several in Iran, Afghanistan, and India, are related, all part of the **Indo-European language family**, having descended from a common language, what we now call **Proto-Indo-European**.

So how did linguists come to this conclusion? Basically, they examined cognates from modern and past languages. **Cognates** are words that have a similar form (pronunciation or spelling) and meaning in two or more languages. Some cognates may result from borrowing or from historical accident. But when there are a lot of them, especially cognates for words that refer to common, everyday objects, linguists conclude that the languages have evolved from a common mother language. We can see this relatedness among several Indo-European languages by examining the cognates shown in Table 13.1.

Not all the similarities are immediately evident. The Greek word for *senile*, for example, does not begin with /s/ but /h/; that's because the [s] sound changed systematically to a [h] sound in Greek. You'll notice also that the English words differ from the others too; we'll discuss those differences later.

Once it was concluded that there must have been an original language from which these and other languages descended, the question became this: Where was it spoken and by whom?

TABLE 13.1 Cognates in various Indo-European languages

Sanskrit	Ancient Greek	Latin	English
pitar	pater	pater	father
bhrater	phrater	frater	brother
sanah	henee	senex	senile
padam	poda	pedem	foot

That question is still being debated, but the means used to answer it are interesting. Scholars examined the words that were common across most Indo-European languages as clues to its original speakers. Words denoting the physical landscape, such as those for plants and animals or the climate, give us some information about where they lived; words denoting relationships or cultural artifacts, such as words for tools or activities, give us information about how they lived. These scholars found cognates in many Indo-European languages for certain trees (birch, oak, and willow) but not others (palm trees); for certain animals (bear, wolf, horse, deer) but not others (camels or monkeys); for snow, winter, and cold (but not desert); and for certain artifacts and activities, such as wagons and wheels and sewing, weaving, and planting. From these language clues, scholars concluded that the speakers of Proto-Indo-European lived a settled agricultural life in either Eastern Ukraine or Türkiye around 5,000 to 7,000 years ago. From their original home, they spread in various waves of migration to Europe, Iran, Afghanistan, Pakistan, and India, taking their languages with them.

As they settled in different areas, they lost contact with the original group. Through this isolation, their languages changed, as all languages do. Some of this change arises from internal causes, changes in pronunciation for ease of articulation, for example. Others result from interaction with new environments that necessitate new ways of doing things and new words. Groups of speakers of those new languages may then migrate to new places themselves, beginning the process all over again. This is what happened with the parent language Proto-Indo-European, as waves of speakers left and lost contact with the original group. As they spread, new languages emerged, all related through the original parent language but grouping into different smaller language families as time passed, as illustrated in Figure 13.1.

You can see from this tree that many Indo-European languages are spoken outside of Europe. Most people are surprised to learn that Farsi and Pashto, spoken in Iran and Afghanistan, are Indo-European languages related to English and Italian and Polish. The same for Hindi and Urdu, spoken in India and Pakistan. The chart also shows that most modern Indo-European languages are not direct descendants of Proto-Indo-European. Instead, over thousands of years and many migrations, Proto-Indo-European branched into other language families: Germanic, Italic, Hellenic, Balto-Slavic, Indo-Iranian, Celtic, Albanian, and Armenian. Each of these families consists of several languages, with the exceptions of Albanian and Armenian, which are the sole survivors of their respective language families.

How do we determine the members of a language family? One way is to look for **regular sound correspondences**, regular sound differences between languages. For example, if almost everywhere Language A uses /p/, Language B uses /f/, that would be a regular sound correspondence. These correspondences result not from changes to the pronunciation of one word but from changes that affect the pronunciation of sounds across the board. Through analyzing these correspondences, we can see that languages such as English and German, though

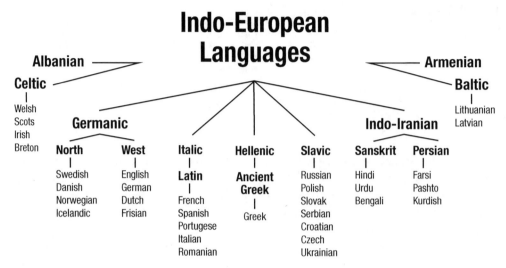

FIGURE 13.1 Family tree for Indo-European languages

Indo-European, differ in systematic ways from languages such as Italian or Portuguese, which are also Indo-European.

As mentioned earlier, the Romance languages are descendants of Latin and thus part of the Italic language family. The Germanic languages (English, Dutch, Swedish, German, Danish, Norwegian, Icelandic, Yiddish) are not. Instead, they are descendants of **Proto-Germanic**, an Indo-European language whose speakers separated from the main group around 1500 BCE and gradually spread across much of Northern Europe. Over many years, Proto-Germanic consonant sounds diverged in systematic ways from those of other Indo-European languages such as Greek and Latin. Thus, we see that where Latin has certain consonant sounds, Germanic languages regularly use different sounds. Table 13.2 shows a few examples of this regular sound correspondence:

The Germanic languages are not identical, of course. Each went through changes of its own, creating the different languages we hear today.

Language families around the world

Not all European languages are part of the Indo-European language family. Hungarian, Sami (spoken in northern parts of Finland and Sweden), and Estonian, for example, all belong to

TABLE 13.2 Sound correspondence in Latin and English

Latin	English
/k/ canis, cornu	/h/ hound, horn
/t/ (initial) tre	/θ/ three,
/t/ (medial) pater	/ð/ father
/d/ duo, decem	/t/ two, ten
/p/ piscis, pater	/f/ fish, father

a different language family, the Finno-Ugric family. And Basque, spoken in the Pyrenees mountains of southern France and Northern Spain, is not related to any other language in the world as far as linguists can tell. It is a **language isolate**, with no known linguistic relatives.

And, of course, Indo-European is not the only language family in the world; it is not even the largest. Unfortunately, we do not know as much about some of the other families for a variety of reasons, a lack of written records from long ago, for one. *Ethnologue: Languages of the world*, an annual reference work that provides information about the world's languages, lists 116 language families worldwide; what follows is a brief discussion of the major ones in terms of number of speakers and number of languages, based on data from *Ethnologue: Languages of the world*.

The largest family group, in terms of number of languages, is the **Niger-Congo** family, which includes 1,500 languages, one-fifth of the world's total number. In all, over 700 million people speak these languages, which are spread over much of Africa. In terms of the numbers of native speakers, the largest languages in the Niger-Congo family are Wolof, Ewe, Yoruba, Igbo, Swahili, and Zulu. The **Austronesian** family, with 1,300 languages, is the second largest in terms of number of languages and is spoken in a widespread geographic area from Madagascar to Hawaii and in New Zealand, the Philippines, and the Malay peninsula. There are approximately 390 million speakers of these languages, among which are Hawaiian, Maori in New Zealand, Tagalog in the Philippines, Malagasy in Madagascar, and Malay in Malaysia.

In terms of number of native speakers, Indo-European is the largest, with the **Sino-Tibetan** language family second. This latter family consists of most of the languages spoken in China (Mandarin, Cantonese, Hunan, and others), as well as Tibetan and Burmese, in all about 400 languages. Together, approximately 4.6 billion people speak a language in one of these two language families.

Hebrew, Arabic, Amharic, Hausa, and Somali are all part of the **Afroasiatic** family, which comprises 300 languages, both contemporary and ancient. Ancient Egyptian was an Afroasiatic language, as were Babylonian and Aramaic, all languages spoken long ago. Today there are around 450 million speakers of Afroasiatic languages, mostly in northern Africa and the Middle East.

The situation in the Americas is complex and not fully understood yet. Some linguists estimate there are 15 language families: Eskimo-Aleut, Algonquin, Athabaskan, and Iroquoian in North America and Oto-Manguean, Arawakan, Tupian, Quecha, Mayan, and Totnaca in Central and South America. No evidence for a larger family that includes them all has yet been found.

The family tree model is useful in illustrating how languages are related, but it does not explain everything. One problem is where to put the many creoles around the world. As we saw in Chapter 12, creoles are languages that developed out of contact between two languages. English-based creoles, for example, are not really descendants of Old English the way Modern English is, so where do they fit in this model? And where do sign languages fit in? There's no clear answer to those questions.

A VERY BRIEF HISTORY OF ENGLISH

As noted earlier, English is a Germanic language, but it is quite different from its cousins German, Swedish, Norwegian, Danish, and Dutch. So how did it become English? Linguists divide its history into three major periods: **Old English** (449–1100 CE), **Middle English** (1100–1500), and **Modern English** (1500—present), the first two stages being marked by major invasions into the British Isles.

The languages originally spoken in the British Isles were Celtic languages, members of an Indo-European language family distinct from Germanic. These original inhabitants spoke Cornish, Manx, Gaelic, and Welsh and continued to do so after the Romans invaded and then left in 79 CE. Except for a few place names, the language of these first Roman invaders left little mark on the languages spoken in the area. Many of these Celtic languages nearly disappeared, however, when the next invasion came.

Old English

In 449, several Germanic-speaking groups invaded Britain, this time coming to stay: the Angles, Saxons, and Jutes, who arrived from what is now Holland, Germany, and Denmark. In several waves over many years, these invaders settled in England, pushing the original inhabitants back to Wales and Scotland. Many terms for the land and people of Great Britain reflect both Celtic and Germanic origins: *Britain* comes from a Celtic word, while *England* evolved out of *Angle-land*, the land of the Angles. Aside from a few place names and other words, what became Old English borrowed very little from the indigenous Celtic languages.

Because the Angles, Saxons, and Jutes spoke related languages, they could understand one another, and although they often fought among themselves, they also traded and intermarried. Eventually, a common language emerged, what we call Old English, which like any language consisted of several regional varieties.

Old English changed over the centuries because of natural language change and further invasions. Norsemen, also called Vikings, began invading in the 8th to 10th centuries, eventually settling in the northeastern part of England. Again, intermarriage and trade brought the two groups into contact. The language spoken by the invaders, Old Norse, was also a Germanic language and similar to the English spoken by the Anglo-Saxons. Because they had enough elements in common, the two languages began to merge. We can see the borrowings from Old Norse in the English pronoun system (*they, them*, and *their* come from Old Norse); in place names such as *Greenwich* and *Darby*; and in words that begin with [sk] such as *skill*, *sky, skin*. Since the consonant cluster [sk] did not exist in Old English, we know these words came from Old Norse. Today, for example, we have two separate words, *shirt* and *skirt*, both of which derive from the same Proto-Germanic word for short garment. The former is of Anglo-Saxon origin, the latter Old Norse.

If you wanted to learn to speak Old English today, you'd need to study it like a foreign language; it is that different from Modern English. For one thing, it was highly inflected. As we noted in Chapter 3, Modern English has only eight inflectional morphemes. Old English had hundreds. It marked nouns for case, gender, and number, so that the word for *ship* was *scip* if it was the subject or direct object in a sentence, but *scipes* if it was possessive, and *scipe* if it was the indirect object. And there was an entirely different set of endings if it was plural: *scipu, scipa*, or *scipum*, each meaning *ships*. Adjectives and verbs were similarly inflected.

Many of these inflectional morphemes began to disappear over time; exactly why is not clear. It may be partially due to the fact that Norse and Old English speakers lived side by side. Although the two languages shared many Germanic roots, their inflectional endings differed, so for ease of communication, people may have just left those endings off. In any case, many inflections began dropping out of English at this time, resulting in a more simplified morphology that became even simpler after the next great invasion to affect the English language: the Norman Conquest in 1066.

Middle English

The year 1066 marked a turning point for both Old English and the people who spoke it. In that year, the Normans, a French-speaking group from Normandy, conquered England, with the Duke of Normandy, William, becoming King of England and distributing land to his French-speaking nobles. French now became the language of the court, the legal system, and the nobility. In fact, for a century after the Norman Conquest, the kings of England did not even speak the English language, though the common people, who had little contact with courtly life, continued to do so.

Within 200 years, however, the kings and their nobles lost most of their lands in Normandy, a loss that eventually led to a break with their ties to France. By the end of the 14th century, English had again become the language of the land, spoken by nobles and commoners alike. It was, however, a different English than that spoken before the Normans arrived, one that was in many ways simplified but that now contained many new words.

Those new words are one of the most striking differences between Old English and Middle English. Around 10,000 words are thought to have entered the language during this time, mostly words relating to the court, administration and law, the military, education, religion, fashion, and food. The simplification of morphology that began during the later Old English period continued, with more loss of inflection. One result of this loss was a more fixed word order. If inflections indicate which word in a sentence is the subject and which the object, word order can vary greatly, as it could in Old English. Without those inflections, word order becomes important. In Middle English, then, the subject–verb–object word order we are familiar with becomes more common. In Middle English and through early Modern English, we also see an increase in both the number and functions of prepositions, which now indicate the kinds of semantic relationships among words that previously had been indicated through inflection.

English phonology changed as well. Several initial consonant clusters dropped the initial sound. So /hr/ in *hrof* became just /r/ in *roof*; /hl/ in *hlaf* became /l/ in *loaf*; and /kn/ in *cnif* became /n/ in *knife*. One other important change was the gradual loss of the final schwa [ə] in many words, a loss that continued into Modern English.

Great Vowel Shift

The biggest change in phonology occurred in the late Middle English and early Modern English periods. Between 1400 and 1600, English vowels gradually underwent the **Great Vowel Shift**. This shift applied only to long vowels, those vowels held longer in pronunciation. In Middle English, there were seven of them: [iː], [eː], [ɛː], [uː], [oː], [ɔː], and [aː]. (Remember [ː] indicates that the vowel is long.) As a result of the Great Vowel Shift, each of these vowels changed its place of articulation to a place higher in the mouth and thus came to be pronounced differently. (You might want to review the chart of Modern English vowel

TABLE 13.3 Great Vowel Shift

	Middle English	Modern English
stone	[stɔ:n]	[ston]
sweet	[swe:t]	[swit]
name	[na:mə]	[nem]
food	[fo:d]	[fud]
house	[hu:s]	[haws]
geese	[ge:s]	[gis]
mice	[mi:s]	[mays]

sounds in Chapter 4.) So [e:] became [i], [ɛ:] became [e], [o:] became [u], and so on. And what happened to [i:] and [u:], which could go no higher because they were already high vowels? They became the diphthongs [ay] and [aw], respectively. Table 13.3 shows some of this shift.

The Great Vowel Shift is a striking example of how phonological change is systematic, not random or individual. This shift applied to long vowels but not short vowels, and it applied across the board to all long vowels. It did not, however, occur in all dialects of English. Those spoken in Scotland, for example, still tend to maintain the earlier pronunciation of these vowels.

How do you spell that again?

English is well known for having inconsistent if not chaotic spelling. Part of the reason for this seeming chaos is the Great Vowel Shift. Through this shift, the pronunciation of thousands of words changed, but their spelling did not. Printing, which tends to standardize spelling, began in England before the shift occurred, and the spelling reflected the pre-shift pronunciation. Before the shift, for example, *goose* was spelled with two *oo*s to reflect the long [o:] sound used there. When the long [o:] became a [u], the spelling stayed the same, but the pronunciation changed. The shift also accounts for the strange differing pronunciations of related words. Words like *crime/criminal* or *serene/serenity*, which used to be pronounced with the same vowel sound, no longer are because the vowel in the first word was long and thus went through the shift, while that in the second was short and did not.

Some other changes during Middle English also contributed to our inconsistent spelling. Words spelled with *-ough*, such as *though*, used to be pronounced with a velar fricative. That sound dropped out of the language during this period, but the spelling stayed. And as mentioned previously, consonants in initial consonant clusters and final schwa sounds also disappeared, leaving us, for example, spelling *knife* but saying [nayf]. No wonder we have spelling bees.

Modern English

With the Great Vowel Shift and other changes, we begin to see a language that more closely resembles the Modern English we speak today. Early Modern English is the English of Shakespeare, different from ours in many ways but still recognizable and intelligible. There is an amazing expansion in the vocabulary during this early period, especially from about 1500–1800. English continued to borrow words from Latin and Ancient Greek but also began borrowing from languages across the globe as the British explored and colonized many parts of the world. New words entered the language from languages as different as Malay, Hindi, Algonquin, and Arabic, as we saw in Chapter 3.

Inflectional endings continued their disappearing act, leaving us with only those eight we discussed in Chapter 3. The verb endings we sometimes see in Shakespeare, -*est* and -*eth*, dropped out over this period. The distinction between *thou* and *you* disappeared as well. Before this time, *thou* was generally used for one person and *you* for more than one. Though speakers of many regional varieties continued to use it, by the mid-17th century *thou* had pretty much disappeared, leaving only *you* in Standard English and leaving English speakers no easy way to distinguish singular and plural, for *you* came to mean both. With that loss, new forms cropped up. The *y'all* in southern varieties of the United States is perhaps the most well-known, but we also find *youse* [yuz] in New York City and some parts of Ireland and increasingly *you guys* in many areas. Each of these is considered informal, perhaps even wrong, but because they fill a need, they continue to be used.

Continued change and global spread

What we call Modern English has, of course, continued to change. One of the most important changes is its global spread. With British colonization of parts of Africa, Asia, and the Americas from the 17th through the 20th centuries and the spread of American culture in the 20th and 21st centuries, English has gone around the world, changing in not only form but function as well. As a result, we now have a situation where there are multiple Englishes spoken not just in Britain and the United States, but in such disparate places as Nigeria, Singapore, Tanzania, and Papua New Guinea, among many others. It is estimated that one to two billion people worldwide speak English, though of course they do not all speak the same English.

How do we make sense of these multiple **World Englishes**? Perhaps the most influential scheme of categorization, that developed by Kachru (1986), posits three circles, differentiated by when and how English was brought to an area and the functions it now serves.

The **inner circle** refers to speakers of English in Great Britain, Ireland, the United States, Canada, Australia, and New Zealand. All except Great Britain and Ireland are the result of settler colonization in the 17th to 19th centuries, when people from Great Britain and Ireland came to new areas and settled, displacing most of the original inhabitants and their languages. In these countries, English became the native language of most of the population and the primary language of the country.

The **outer circle** refers to areas that were colonized by the British but did not have the same influx of settlers that the inner circle did. In these countries, English is not the native language or home language of most of the population. Instead, it is a widely spoken second language used in the government, law, education, and national commerce. Or it may be one of the official languages of a country, as happened in many previously colonized countries in Africa and South Asia: Kenya, Nigeria, Uganda, Ghana, India, and Pakistan, among others. The majority of people retain their own community languages and may use English as a lingua franca among different language groups.

The **expanding circle** refers to those areas where English has little or no historical or governmental role, but it is still learned and used by many, in such countries as China, Nepal, South Korea, Russia, and Egypt. People learn it as a foreign language in school, often for a specific purpose such as tourism or international communication. This last function points to the evolution of English into a **global lingua franca**, a language used by speakers of many languages when interacting with speakers of other languages.

This categorization is complicated by the changing situation on the ground. In an outer circle country such as Singapore, English is increasingly being learned as a native language and used as a home language, especially among the educated, thus confounding the definitions of inner and outer circles.

Another confounding factor is the increasing number of what are called **New Englishes**, new varieties of English and English-based creoles emerging in what was considered the outer or expanding circles. Most are Postcolonial Englishes, new forms of English that have evolved in areas that had been colonized by the British. Over time, as English came to be used by more of those living in these areas, the new varieties that emerged began to differ more and more from the language of Britain, often having been influenced by the indigenous languages spoken there. The new varieties that have emerged will continue to change, following their own paths as the social and cultural circumstances in which they are used change as well. The English spoken in Nigeria, for example, has its own rules for pronunciation and its own vocabulary, some of which are shared with British English or American English but by no means all.

English is currently used as an official language or a de facto official language in approximately 75 countries (Crystal, 2007). The question of ownership looms large in discussion of these World Englishes. Is English the language of those peoples who have historically used it, those in what is called the inner circle (Great Britain, Canada, the United States, Australia, New Zealand, etc.), or is it equally the language of those speakers of new varieties who have adopted it and begun to remake it for their own purposes? Although there are more speakers in the latter category than in the former, some claim these New Englishes are not really English. Such claims ignore the reality of language change and spread. Each of those varieties has the right to be called English, if the speakers desire it, and deserves as much respect as the varieties spoken in Boston, Sydney, Toronto, or London.

English is also used as a lingua franca in many activities worldwide; air traffic control, for example, takes place entirely in English. Computer technology is similarly discussed mostly in English. Some estimate that 80% of the world's scientific journals are written in English. I can attest to the latter; when I lived in Poland in the 1990s, I helped edit the *Polish Journal of Soil Science*, written entirely in English, even though it was written and read by Polish speakers, many of whom did not speak English well.

ORIGINS OF AMERICAN SIGN LANGUAGE

Our discussion of language origins and families so far has focused solely on spoken languages. What about the origins of the many sign languages used around the world? *Ethnologue: Languages of the world* lists 130, though the exact number is not known. Among them are Chinese, Tibetan, South African, Indo-Pakistani, Czech, Tanzanian, and Russian Sign Languages. They are natural languages just as spoken languages are, but they are not necessarily related to the spoken languages used in the same area. For example, although Spanish is the dominant language in both Mexico and Spain, the sign languages used in those two countries are unrelated. Sign languages do not develop out of a spoken language but rather as independent languages among groups who need them. Unfortunately, we don't know much about the origins of most sign languages and their possible family relationships.

We do, however, know a great deal about the origins of at least two of them: Nicaraguan Sign Language and American Sign Language (ASL). In the 1970s and 1980s, Nicaraguan Sign Language emerged naturally when deaf children in Nicaragua, who had been isolated from one another, were brought together for the first time in a school created especially for them. This sign language emerged not in the classroom, where teachers tried to teach them Spanish, but in the school yard and other areas where the children needed to communicate. Out of this need, they soon developed a sign language of their own, Nicaraguan Sign Language.

American Sign Language, used in the United States and English-speaking parts of Canada, came about through a different route. It is, interestingly, not related to British Sign Language; in fact, the two languages are mutually unintelligible. It is instead related to French Sign Language, which developed, as often happens, in close connection with a school for deaf children, in this case one founded by Abbe de L'Eppe in Paris in 1755. After opening his school, L'Eppe soon noticed that the children were already using a sign system to communicate with one another. These signs, with some further development by L'Eppe, became French Sign Language. Something similar happened in 1817 when Thomas Gallaudet and Laurent Clerc founded a school for the deaf in Hartford, Connecticut. American Sign Language developed out of both French Sign Language, which Gallaudet and Clerc brought to the school, and signs that the students had already been using, including Martha's Vineyard Sign Language, mentioned in Chapter 12. ASL, which went on to become the dominant sign language in the United States, still shares much of its vocabulary with French Sign Language.

LANGUAGE LOSS AND ENDANGERMENT

The amount of diversity in the world's languages, not to mention varieties of those languages, is staggering. That diversity is also, unfortunately, diminishing every day as more and more languages are disappearing. In Chapter 12 we discussed language shift in the United States, where most immigrant communities shift to speaking only English within two or three generations. That shift means the community language is lost. The language they spoke, however, is usually still spoken elsewhere in the world. My father's immigrant Italian community, for example, became monolingual English within that time span, but the Italian language itself was not in danger of becoming extinct because it is still spoken in Italy and elsewhere.

What happens, though, when all the speakers of a language shift completely to another language? Then you get **language loss** or **language death**, a phenomenon that is happening increasingly worldwide. A language dies when all of its speakers either shift to another language or else die off, so that there are no more people in the world who can speak, sign, or understand it. Many people think Latin is a dead language, but Latin is not really dead. It has just evolved into several different languages, so it is alive and being used by millions of French, Italian, Spanish, and Portuguese speakers.

Languages become **endangered**, on their way to disappearing, when one generation of speakers no longer uses their language with their children or when languages, especially those spoken by a small number of people, come to be used in fewer and fewer areas of life. There are various estimates of the number of endangered languages. According to *Ethnologue: Languages of the world*, over 3,000 languages are currently endangered: that's 41% of the world's languages. Some predict that by the end of the 21st century, 90% will be lost (Krauss, 1992); others put the figure a bit lower. Whatever the prediction, all agree the situation is dire. According to the Foundation for Endangered Languages, 52% of the world's languages are spoken by fewer than 10,000 people each, with another 28% spoken by fewer than 1,000 individuals. These languages are in danger of dying out within the foreseeable future.

This loss affects different parts of the world differently. The vast majority of languages, around 96%, are spoken by small numbers of people, only 4% of the world's population. That means that only a small fraction of the world's 7,000 languages, around 4%, are spoken by 96% of the world's population. Those few widely spoken languages (Chinese, Hindi, English, Spanish, and Arabic, for example) are not in danger of becoming extinct, but the remaining languages are. The communities that speak these endangered languages tend to be small indigenous or minority communities, and it is those communities that carry most of the world's linguistic diversity. The two areas where language loss is happening at the greatest rates today are North America and Australia, with the loss of half or more of their indigenous languages just between 1970 and 2005 (Maffi, 2011).

Sign languages can also become endangered if users shift to a more dominant sign language. That seems to be happening with Hawaiian Sign Language as more and more users shift to American Sign Language. Catalan, Icelandic, and Spanish Sign Languages are also currently endangered (*Ethnologue: Languages of the world*).

Why should we care?

Many linguists have likened the loss of linguistic diversity to the loss of biodiversity, the loss of species and ecosystems happening now. Both losses are irretrievable; once a language or a species is gone, it's gone forever. Is that really such a problem? To my mind, yes.

Knowledge loss

What is lost when the world loses a language? For one thing, knowledge. Each language encodes cultural knowledge: values, beliefs, worldviews, and information about the natural world and how to live sustainably with it. For most indigenous languages, which make up 80%–85% of the world's languages (Maffi, 2011), this knowledge is encoded not in books or written material, but orally: in songs, myths, rituals, stories, poetry, art, and ceremonies of all sorts. One type of knowledge of special concern is what is called traditional ecological knowledge, knowledge these groups have about their natural environment, knowledge that may turn out to be key to solving the world's environmental problems. If the community that loses its language is the only one that speaks it, that knowledge is lost forever. And since most endangered languages are unwritten, if they are lost, we will never know what has been lost.

Social justice

Even if such important knowledge did not exist, language loss is a social justice issue. As Crawford (1995) points out, "language death does not happen in privileged communities. It happens to the dispossessed and the disempowered, people who most need their cultural resources to survive" (p. 35). Language loss does not happen in isolation; it occurs as part of a general pattern of loss of culture, with loss of language making it more difficult for a community to tackle social problems such as poverty or substance abuse. For communities, language plays a key role in creating and maintaining social cohesion, especially when that cohesion is threatened by outside pressures. We saw in Chapter 12 that teaching children in their home languages in school leads to lower rates of school failure. Maffi (2011) notes that in British Columbia, Canada, youth in First Nations communities that continue to speak their native language have much lower rates of suicide than in those communities where the native language is dying out.

Linguistic human rights

Every community has the right to use and transmit its language without hindrance from others, what are known as **linguistic human rights**. Although not always recognized by nation states, these rights are a fundamental part of human rights, those rights possessed by every person, regardless of status. The United Nations recognizes "the right for individuals and communities to maintain their own social, cultural and linguistic identities, without any discrimination or pressure for assimilation" (Maffi, 2011, p. 7) Threats to a community's language are threats to those identities. The right to continue to use one's language as a way to preserve one's culture is one aspect of linguistic human rights. Yet as we will see, indigenous groups worldwide experience enormous pressure to assimilate economically, culturally, and linguistically to the dominant culture.

So should it matter to those of us who are not speakers of an endangered language? Yes. One of the defining characteristics of our common humanity is language in all its variety. It is part of the diversity of life on Earth, and any diminishment of that diversity diminishes humanity as a whole. As Maffi (2011) puts it, "If linguistic diversity is part and parcel of the diversity of life in nature and culture, then any loss in linguistic diversity is a loss in the vitality and resilience of the whole web of life" (p. 9).

Biocultural diversity

Just as there is an amazing diversity in the forms that life can take on Earth, there is an amazing diversity in worldviews, values, beliefs, knowledge, and art that languages encode. Biocultural, linguistic, and cultural diversity are all key to the survival of the human race. In biology, the strongest ecosystems are those which are the most diverse; the same holds true for language ecosystems, which preserve and sustain linguistic diversity for the future benefit of all humankind. And just as every species, no matter how seemingly insignificant to us as humans, can tell us something about life itself, every language, spoken or signed, prestigious or not, spoken by millions or not, can tell us something essential about life that we did not know before.

Some people argue it's no big deal to lose a language. They see languages as more or less interchangeable. In this view, each language may have different terms to label parts of our world, but those labels are only superficial differences. Whether we call something *a flower* or *une fleur* (French) or *he puawai* (Maori), it is still a flower. Others dispute this view, noting that language serves as a filter through which we learn about and see the world around us, so that we notice some parts of that world and not others and experience parts of that world differently in different languages. It is not that languages determine our perception of the world, but they offer different filters, what Mühlhäusler (2001) calls "provisional interpretations." Because the world is so complex, we need the perspectives and provisional interpretations provided by different languages to understand it. Thus, loss of any one language means a loss in human understanding of the world.

Causes of language loss

The causes of language loss are local and global, multiple and varied: natural, economic, social, and political. Local natural disasters can lead to the decimation of populations: floods, earthquakes, famines, or droughts can be especially devastating to linguistic communities with small populations. Most language loss is not the result of natural causes, however; it is caused by other humans, whether directly or indirectly. Although languages have always died, the rate of loss has increased dramatically in the last 500 years. Colonization of much of the world by European nations led to a mass extinction of languages, often by decimating the indigenous populations through disease or military conquest. In Brazil, fewer than 200 of the approximately 1,000 languages spoken when Europeans first arrived are still vital today (Crystal, 2010). Contemporary cultural domination by major languages such as English, Chinese, French, or Hindi also contributes. Some have even called English a "killer language" because of its pernicious effect on linguistic diversity.

Economic pressure can lead to language loss as many areas of the world join the global market economy. Indigenous peoples and languages of the Amazon rain forest can serve as an illustrative example. Ever greater swaths of the rain forest are being cut down by those who seek to exploit it for economic gain. In some cases, indigenous peoples have been violently expelled from their ancestral lands to facilitate exploitation of the forest. As a result, they can no longer support themselves as they have in the past and are forced either to work as laborers or move to nearby cities. To survive, they must learn the dominant language, in this case Portuguese. Such changes make it hard for them to maintain their cultural identity and language.

As people around the world increasingly migrate to cities from rural areas, urbanization is contributing to language loss. In cities, speaking the local dominant language, or a more global one like English, is often necessary for getting a job. Cities are also areas where groups speaking many different languages live and work together, necessitating a lingua franca. As people are forced to learn a new language to get by, they lose touch with their first language, often leading to its loss.

Education, surprisingly, is one of the main causes of endangerment. As noted in Chapter 12, around the world, education increasingly takes place in only a few major world languages. Brenzinger (1998) notes that in Africa nearly all education past elementary schooling takes places in a language other than the student's native language, a situation that encourages the idea that indigenous native languages are not suitable to modern life. Education also creates pressure to assimilate into the dominant culture, which usually means pressure to assimilate to the dominant language. I once taught a student from Nigeria who, until she took my course on endangered languages, had never thought it worrisome that she spoke only English, not the local language of her community, which was being spoken by fewer and fewer people her age. Speaking English was an important part of her identity, an identity that, unfortunately, included shame about her community's language, another contributor to language loss.

English in Nigeria, as in many parts of the world, is an important means to advancement and success; the same goes for Spanish or Portuguese in Latin America, Swahili or English in East Africa, French or English in parts of West Africa. These dominant languages are often used in public discourse, in the media, on the internet, in government and in courts, as well as in education. Invariably, these languages come to be seen as necessary for the modern global economy and culture. And too often indigenous languages become stigmatized as primitive, not capable of carrying the knowledge necessary for economic or cultural advancement, and useful only for home life or religious ceremonies. Partly because of this and because the dominant language can lead to better jobs, parents may not pass on their own language to their children, instead encouraging them to learn the dominant language—a certain path to language extinction.

Stemming the loss

Language revitalization is a term that covers efforts to revive languages that are dead and to maintain those that are endangered. Increasingly, indigenous and local communities around the world have begun to do both. These communities are working to pass on their languages to the next generation and to gain recognition of their cultural and linguistic rights from national governments. Programs and initiatives to do so are varied, as are the contexts in which they occur. The following are some of the actions being taken.

Raising awareness

Many local communities and global organizations are working to raise awareness of the problem. New organizations have been created whose goal is not only to record information about endangered languages, but also to bring the issue of their pending loss to public attention. They encourage governments to create language policies that respect multilingualism, and they support local communities in their efforts. Local communities, the ones most affected, are the ones that must decide what should be done, but regional or national government support is also often necessary. Such support can be monetary or as part of a language policy that, for example, might allow elders, often the only ones who still speak a language fluently, to become certified as teachers without the requisite credentials.

Connecting linguistic, cultural, and biological diversity

Many advocates for linguistic diversity recognize that for most indigenous peoples, land, culture, and language are not separate entities, but an integrated whole that forms and nourishes their identity as a distinct people. Too often, language loss goes hand in hand with the loss of a community's culture and land. It is thus devastating on several fronts at once. These advocates aim to raise awareness of this connection so as to alleviate all three types of losses.

Education

Whether through formal schooling or informal learning, education can play a key role in revitalizing any language. If educational policy mandates schooling in the dominant language only, local languages will suffer. If, instead, policy mandates using the local language as an equal partner in the classroom, it increases the chances of that language remaining vital. Local control of education can also increase those chances. In the 1980s, the Maori in New Zealand created **language nests**, *kohanga reo* in Maori, to encourage the transmission of their language to the next generation. In these nests, preschool children learned the Maori language from elders in the community. Soon primary schools were created that did the same thing. Now there are secondary schools and universities that focus on Maori culture and teach in Maori.

In North America, the Mohawk have borrowed the concept of language nests, using it to help revitalize their language. In Hawaii as a result of efforts by native Hawaiians, the Hawaiian language is being increasingly taught in schools so that more children become fluent in it. The University of Hawaii at Hilo uses Hawaiian as the medium of instruction for their college of Hawaiian language, which also works to revive Hawaiian culture. Many universities in the United States and elsewhere have established language academies to help indigenous leaders prepare the materials needed to teach their languages.

Community activism

Several indigenous groups have used various strategies in their efforts to revitalize their cultures and languages. In New Zealand, the Maori have had some success in getting recognition from the dominant society of their rights, including language rights. Today, Maori is an official language in New Zealand, along with New Zealand Sign Language and English. In Paraguay, Guarani, the indigenous language spoken by over 90% of the population, gained official status in 1992 and is now widely accepted as an emblem of national identity (Crystal, 2010). It is one of the few indigenous languages that is being learned by a large number of non-indigenous people. In Wales, community efforts have led to an increase in the number of speakers of Welsh for the first time in 100 years, with 19% of the population now speaking it (*Ethnologue: Languages of the world*). Welsh became officially equal to English as result of the Welsh Language Act of 1993. Welsh-medium primary schools now exist, and perhaps most importantly, the majority of Welsh-speaking parents are now raising their children to speak Welsh (Morgan, 2001).

Documentation

The need to document endangered languages is urgent. Many linguists have, in recent decades, taken on this task, trying to document as many endangered languages as possible before they are lost forever. Such documenting can at least preserve some aspects of a language and perhaps serve as a basis for revitalization in the future. For example, when descendants of speakers of Kaurna, an Australian Aboriginal language, became interested in reviving it, documentation existed that allowed them to start the revitalization process, even though no one had spoken Kaurna for almost a hundred years (Wurm, 1998).

Much work has been done to stem the loss of languages, but the outlook globally remains dire. Crystal (2010) estimates that as of 2000, there were 51 languages with just one speaker left. The last speaker of Manx on the Isle of Man died in 1974, the last speaker of Kasabe in Cameroon in 1995, the last speaker of Ubykh in the Caucasus in 1992, all taking their languages with them.

CHAPTER SUMMARY

- Human language probably originated with the rise of modern humans around 150,000–200,00 years ago and spread globally when humans began leaving Africa around 60,000 years ago.
- Language families are related languages that have descended from a common linguistic ancestor. Indo-European and Sino-Tibetan are the largest of these families in terms of number of speakers.
- A proto-language is a language reconstructed by linguists by comparing regular sound correspondences in daughter languages. It is hypothesized to be the parent of all languages in a particular language family.
- Proto-Indo-European is the parent of all Indo-European languages. The original speakers of Proto-Indo-European are thought to have lived around 5,000 years ago and then spread throughout Europe to the Middle East and to India. The language they took with them changed and developed into several subfamilies.
- The history of English is generally divided into three major stages: Old English, Middle English, and Modern English. Each differs from its preceding stage in pronunciation, morphology, syntax, and vocabulary.
- As English has spread, many new varieties have developed, with their own pronunciations, morphology, syntax, and vocabulary. These varieties are collectively known as World Englishes. New Englishes are emerging in many postcolonial areas.
- A large number of the languages used today are in danger of dying. This loss will have dire consequences not only for those whose language becomes extinct, but for all of us.
- Efforts to stem this loss are continuing, with local communities working to revive or maintain their languages and cultures. Some have been successful, but the situation remains dire.

KEY TERMS

continuity/discontinuity theories of language origin
proto-language
language family
genetic relationships
Indo-European language family
Proto-Indo-European
cognates
regular sound correspondence
Proto-Germanic
language isolate
Niger-Congo language family
Austronesian language family
Sino-Tibetan language family

Afroasiatic language family
Old English
Middle English
Modern English
great vowel shift
World Englishes
global lingua franca
New Englishes
language loss/language endangerment
endangered language
linguistic human rights
biocultural diversity
language revitalization
language nest

EXPLORATIONS

Exploration 1: Exploring linguistic diversity

Langscape Magazine, an online publication, offers stories about linguistic and biocultural diversity. Go online to www.terralingua.org; choose an article of interest, read and summarize it to share with your small group. Together identify what you have learned about the world's languages and their connection to biodiversity.

Exploration 2: Language origin stories

Most cultures have stories about the origins of language and languages. The Tower of Babel from the Bible is one well-known one. Do you know of any others? If not, see if you can track down one from a culture other than your own. Share it in groups.

Exploration 3: World Englishes

There are many varieties of English besides the well-known ones of the United States, the British Isles, Australia, Canada, New Zealand, and South Africa. Research one of these other varieties (Nigerian English, Singapore English, or one of your choosing) or one of the many creoles based on English (Tok Pisin, Jamaican Creole, Barbadian Creole, or one of your choosing; there are estimated to be 25 of them). What can you find out about its history and current status? Share your findings in small groups.

Exploration 4: One endangered language

A good online source for discovering more about languages and language families is *Ethnologue: Languages of the world* at www.ethnologue.com. Using *Ethnologue* or another online source such as www.sil.org/about/endangered-languages, investigate one endangered language. There is a map of endangered languages at www.sil.org/worldwide. How many speakers are there now? What is the prognosis for its survival? How has it become endangered? Share your findings in small groups.

Exploration 5: Exploring language families

Using *Ethnologue,* www.ethnologue.com/family-index.asp, or other sources, investigate a language other than English, preferably a non-Indo-European one. What language family is it part of? What languages is it related to? How many people speak it? Where? Report to your group on what you have found out about its history.

Exploration 5: English as a lingua franca

Many social media sites allow us to communicate with people in other countries; do you ever do so? If yes, what language do you use when communicating with people whose first language is not English? What does that tell you about the spread of English worldwide?

FURTHER READING

Crowley, T., & Bowern, C. (2010). *An introduction to historical linguistics.* Oxford University Press.

Harrison, K. (2010). *The last speakers.* National Geographic.

Jenkins, J. (2013). *Global Englishes: A resource book for students* (3rd ed.). Routledge.

Nettle, D., & Romaine, S. (2000). *Vanishing voices: The extinction of the world's languages.* Oxford University Press.

The Linguists—Kanopy. http://linguistlist.org/topic/ebonics/. A fascinating video about two linguists documenting endangered languages.

Van Gelderen, E. (2006). *A history of the English language.* John Benjamins. A good introduction to the history of English.

Watkins, C. (1981). Indo-European and the Indo-Europeans. In *The American Heritage dictionary of the English language* (pp. 1496–1502). Houghton Mifflin.

REFERENCES

Brenzinger, M. (1998). Various ways of dying and different kinds of death: scholarly approaches to language endangerment on the African continent. In K. Matsumura (Ed.), *Studies in endangered languages (Papers from the International Symposium on Endangered Languages, Tokyo, 18–20 November 1995,* pp. 85–100). Hituzi Syobo.

Crawford, J. (1995). Endangered Native American Languages: What is to be done and why? *The Bilingual Research Journal, 19*(1), 17–38.

Crystal, D. (2007). *English as a global language.* Cambridge University Press.

Crystal, D. (2010). *Language death.* Cambridge University Press.

Dunbar, R. (1997). *Grooming, gossip, and the evolution of language.* Harvard University Press.

Ethnologue: Languages of the world. www.ethnologue.com/. Retrieved May 2, 2020.

Kachru, B. (1986). *The alchemy of English.* Oxford University Press.

Krauss, M. (1992). The world's languages in crisis. *Language, 68,* 4–10.

Maffi, L. (2011). Linguistic diversity: What's the fuss all about? *Terralingua; Langscape,* (II/8), 3–12.

Morgan, G. (2001). Welsh: A European case of language maintenance. In L. Hinton & K. Hale (Eds.), *The green book of language revitalization in practice* (pp. 107–113). Academic Press.

Mühlhäusler, P. (2001). Babel revisited. In A. Fill & P. Mühlhäusler (Eds.), *The ecolinguistics reader* (pp. 159–164). Continuum.

Wurm, S. (1998). Methods of language maintenance and revival, with selected cases of language endangerment in the world. In K. Matsumura (Ed.), *Studies in endangered languages (Papers from the International Symposium on Endangered Languages, Tokyo, 18–20 November 1995,* pp. 191–211). Hituzi Syobo.

CHAPTER 14

Ecolinguistics

Language and the environment

....

> **First glance**
>
> What is ecolinguistics?
> Language and its natural environment
> Metaphors for the natural world
> Eco-critical linguistics
> - Anthropocentrism: Human centrality, human exceptionalism
> - Greenwashing, euphemisms, erasure: How we make it all sound okay.

INTRODUCTION

We can start with a question that may seem a long way from the phonemes and phrase structure rules we examined earlier: *"Do linguistic patterns, literally, affect the survival and well-being of the human species as well as other species on Earth?"* (Steffensen & Fill, 2014, p. 9). Though it may seem unrelated on the surface, it is a question that linguists, especially ecolinguists, have begun to ask in the last few decades. The field of **ecolinguistics**, a new branch of linguistics, examines how language is related to the environments in which it exists and how our language use is connected to how we act in the natural world, especially actions that contribute to the destruction of the environment.

The environments that language exists in are many. Language exists in our minds, and it is this cognitive environment that we examined in Chapters 3 through 7 when we discussed the knowledge we call on whenever we use language. Language exists in a social environment,

DOI: 10.4324/9780429269059-14

and it is this environment we examined in Chapters 8 through 12 when we discussed how we use language in everyday interactions, how we use it to signal and create our social identities, and how its use varies across those social identities. Language exists in a symbolic environment, the context in which languages and varieties interact; we examined this environment in Chapters 12 and 13 when we discussed multilingualism, language birth and death, and language loss, all key concerns for ecolinguistics.

In this chapter we focus on an environment not usually addressed in mainstream linguistics: the natural environment of language, what ecolinguists call its human ecology. It is this environment that ecolinguists are especially concerned with. Rather than a self-contained system, language for ecolinguists is ecologically embedded, always part of a larger ecosystem that includes all of the environments mentioned earlier. After all, after we learn to use language, we still exist in the physical world.

Mühlhäusler (2003) defines ecolinguistics as the study of how "humans communicate in, with and about the environment" (p. 35). Stibbe (2015) defines it as the field of linguistics that explores "patterns of language that influence how people both think about, and treat, the world," including other humans and the planet of which we are a part (p. 1). He adds that ecolinguistics examines how language influences the relationships of humans with each other, with other organisms, and with the ecosystems that all life depends on.

LANGUAGE AND ITS NATURAL ENVIRONMENT

Any examination of language and its relation to its natural environment is complicated by the fact that, as Sapir pointed out over 100 years ago, the very concepts of nature and landscape are socially constructed. Maffi (2001) enlarges on this idea when she notes,

> Landscapes are anthropogenic [created by humans] not only in the sense that they are physically modified by human intervention, but also because they are symbolically brought into the sphere of human communication by language: by the words, expressions, stories, legends, songs, and verbal interactions that encode and convey human relationships with the environment and inscribe the history of those relationships onto the land.
>
> (p. 12)

Metaphors for the natural world

One important way landscape and nature are brought into the sphere of human communication is through metaphors. As noted in Chapter 3, metaphors are tools "for experiencing and perceiving the world," ways of ordering and reordering human knowledge (Steffensen & Fill, 2014, p. 2). Metaphors of nature are of special concern, for they reflect how we see nature and influence how we act in it. A common metaphor in English is that nature is a singular entity; we use the pronoun *it* for nature, not *they*, even though nature is not singular; it is "a multiplicity of things and living processes" (Williams, 1980, p. 69). This singular nature is also metaphorically talked about as something to be controlled, even conquered. We see this when we use terms like *pest control*, *forest management*, and *genetic engineering*, among others. Animals and land are spoken of as things to be controlled too: animals are domesticated or hunted; land is cultivated; trees are harvested; coal is mined. Feminists point to the many metaphors of nature that are gendered: *Mother Nature* or *Mother Earth*, for example. And many metaphorical expressions about the land are similarly gendered: *virgin territory, penetrating the wilderness*. Such metaphors cast both nature and women as properly under the control of men. Areas of nature that we cannot control are metaphorically discussed as somehow acting on their own: nature takes revenge (*you can't fool mother nature*), and it destroys buildings (*natural disasters*). These conventionalized metaphors can structure the way we think and act. If we see nature as something that exists for us to control, then we can do what we want to it.

ECO-CRITICAL LINGUISTICS

Eco-critical linguistics, like the critical discourse analysis (CDA) we discussed in Chapter 9, examines discourse all around us for hidden messages. To review, CDA analyzes discourse for ideologies, beliefs, and values embedded in it. Generally, CDA focuses on how discourse reproduces power relations and inequalities among social groups. Eco-critical linguistics enlarges that focus in two ways. First, it sees its work as speaking for those who literally cannot speak for themselves: non-human animals, plants, other organisms, and future generations of humans and other living beings. Second, it examines the influence of our language use on the ways we see and interact with the environment; it asks how our discourse represents as normal and acceptable, even necessary, actions that may destroy life on our planet. Like CDA, eco-critical linguistics seeks to reveal those hidden messages that may influence us to act in certain ways, especially the ways we act in the natural world. In critical eco-linguistic theory, the way we as humans treat the natural world is influenced by our view of the world, and our view of the world is at least partially constructed through discourse.

Halliday (2001) argues that just as languages can contain the ideologies of sexism or racism or classism, they can also contain ideologies that construct the world in ways that are detrimental to life on Earth. As an example, he points out the many ways that growth is represented as a positive thing throughout many discourses, what he calls **growthism**. Corollaries to this growthism (*many is better than few, more is better than less, large is better than small, up is better than down*) are represented as general principles of life. This is especially evident in the discourse of economics, in which growth is always presented as a good thing. Collocations reinforce this perspective with phrases like *profits fell sharply* (never *gently*) or *markets are shrinking*. That last example is an interesting one. I tried to find a synonym for *shrinking* that does not have a negative connotation; I couldn't find one. That's how prevalent growthism is in our language. Halliday's point is that the ideology of growthism is built into our language, and that ideology can be dangerous because the implicit message, repeated over and over in multiple phrases, is that it is always good for economies and markets to grow, no matter the consequences for society or the environment.

Similarly, in multiple ways, *progress* is presented as a good. Progress means we move forward (forward is good, backward bad). New industries or technological innovations are mapped onto this idea. They are represented as inherently good, even if their effect is to move us backward in terms of nature. These types of innovations are also represented as inevitable, just as progress itself is presented as inevitable: *you can't stop progress* is a common response to complaints about new gadgets or technologies that do damage to the social or natural ecology. And because these innovations are represented as progress, efforts to protect nature from being despoiled through their use are represented as blocking and fighting progress.

Technological progress is inevitable is an example of what Stibbe (2015) calls **stories-we-live-by**, mental models of the world that exist across a culture at large rather than in just one individual's mind. These are not stories in the traditional sense of a narrative, but rather discourses that convey particular worldviews. They are produced and reproduced in everyday discourse, though not necessarily overtly, and are often so invisibly embedded that they are not noticed as stories at all; instead, they are seen as just the way things are. Ecolinguists are interested in those stories and how they construct our view of nature and our place in it. They seek to analyze common and not-so-common discourses to reveal their hidden stories and to challenge those that lead to and justify actions destructive of the ecosystems that all life depends on.

Anthropocentrism

Anthropocentrism, a key story-we-live-by, includes the stories of human centrality and human exceptionalism. The story of **human centrality** places humans at the center of the world and represents the natural world in terms of its usefulness to humans, turning the land and the creatures that live on it into natural resources for our use. The story of **human exceptionalism** represents humans as radically different from other living things and as separate from the rest of nature. Both stories are woven into everyday discourse.

We encounter these stories when we call humans *stewards of the earth*, a notion common in many religions, and one that implies that humans are the designated caretakers of nature, rather than a part of it. We also encounter them in the English lexical system, which encodes a distinction between humans and other life forms, even animals closely related to us. Thus, our pronoun system distinguishes between a human being (and perhaps also one of our pets), who is *he* or *she*, and any other living creature, who is an *it*. As Kimmerer (2013) notes, in English a tree is not a *who* but a *what*, an object to be used rather than a fellow living organism. In many North American indigenous languages, that's not so: in Potawatomimowin, an Anishinaabe language, a tree is "a non-human forest person" (p. 144). Kimmerer goes on to note that "just about everything we use is the result of another's life, but that simple reality is rarely acknowledged" in our discourse (p. 148). In fact, it is sometimes hard to even express that idea in English. How do we talk about trees, lakes, or rivers having rights?

Our verb system similarly sets humans apart from other parts of nature: we use verbs such as *think, believe, know,* or *plan* almost exclusively for humans. Non-human animate beings, animals, and plants, for example, and all inanimate entities do not have agency in our discourse; they do not think or plan. We rarely talk of trees or forests as doing something, but as Halliday (2001) points out, they cleanse the atmosphere, stop flooding, and stabilize the soil, all important actions for life on Earth.

Our way of talking about the environment is deeply anthropocentric. The term *environmental degradation*, for example, implies degradation of environmental conditions that humans find useful but not of those conditions that bacteria or mosquitoes do. The terms we use for the land and the plants that live on it—*barren, productive, virgin, rich, wasteland*—describe the earth as useful or not only to us: w*eeds* are plants we do not want; *natural resource*s are those parts of the world that we can use for our purposes. Although in much of our discourse nature is represented as a resource to be used to provide for our sustenance (*the bounty of nature*) and other needs (*nature as healer*), as Odum (quoted in Mühlhäusler, 2003, p. 38) points out, nature is "not just a supply depot;" it is "the home . . . in which we must live."

The story of human exceptionality places humans as separate from the rest of nature, unlike other creatures on Earth. When we say things like *both humans and animals*, we are representing humans as not animals, though of course we are. Stibbe (2015) points out that in much of philosophy as well as linguistics, what makes us human is found in what makes us different from other animals rather than in what we share with them. Language is often presented as the quintessential phenomenon of human exceptionality, as when linguists claim that language is unique to humans and that in understanding it, we are understanding what makes us humans. In most linguistics theory, humans are the only species with language—by definition. Until recently, little scholarship addressed the aspects of human language that are shared by non-human animal communication systems. Some ecolinguists argue that rather than seeing human language as unrelated to animal communication, we should investigate the continuity between the two, as in the syntax of bird songs, for example.

Ecolinguistics is interested not just in discourse about the environment but in any discourses that might influence how we treat nature. Some discourses commonly examined include those of advertising, ecotourism, the animal product industry, and global agribusiness. Advertising regularly makes use of nature discourse and images to make products appear less damaging to the environment, a process known as **greenwashing**. Products are described as *sustainable*, *natural*, and *environmentally sound*, even when they are not. The use of *all natural* to describe foods that are made from genetically modified grain or are full of artificial flavors is one example. My personal favorite is a slogan for an Australian insecticide cited by Mühlhäusler (2003): *kills all insects—safe for the environment* (p. 137). Obviously, insects do not count as part of the environment.

Advertising for ecotourism similarly greenwashes its effects. Ecotourism is touted as ecologically sound, with pictures of pristine beaches and claims of non-intrusive encounters with nature, a sustainable way to see the world. That may be true, but such advertising also conceals its *consumerist essence*. From an eco-critical linguistics perspective, that consumerist essence is important to reveal, since overconsumption, whether at home or in one's travels, is a key contributor to the dangers our planet faces.

Stibbe (2015) critiques the discourse of the animal product industry, the industry which raises and slaughters animals for their flesh, what we call *meat*. His analysis shows how this discourse represents animals as objects, machines, and resources. The entire slaughter process is presented as benign through various techniques: **euphemisms** such as *housing* for animal cages or *carcasses* for animal bodies, for example, or false comparisons such as likening breeding sows to machinery, which, of course, cannot feel pain. Slaughter itself euphemistically becomes *meat production*.

Another technique common in this discourse is erasure. **Erasure** represents an area of life (people, experiences, identities, animals, nature, all sorts of things) as unimportant or unworthy of mention or consideration. In the discourse of the animal product industry, for example, keeping animals in cages is called necessary to protect them from predators, but the most lethal predators, the people who slaughter them, are erased. In some environmental advocacy discourse, human agency is similarly erased. To say high levels of carbon dioxide contribute to climate change is true, but it represents carbon levels as causes when they are instead the result of human actions. What is erased are the institutions, corporations, and people who produce those high levels of carbon dioxide.

Vandana Shiva, an Indian physicist and environmental activist, succinctly critiques the discourse of global agribusiness: "When patents are granted for seeds and plants, as in the case of basmati, theft is defined as creation and saving and sharing seed is defined as theft of intellectual property" (quoted in Alexander, 2009, p. 118).

It's not that any of these discourses directly determine how we see the world or force us to act in a certain way. Their common everyday use, however, may create a world view that encourages us to think and act in ways that exploit the natural world for our own purposes and, in the process, help destroy it. The discourse of human exceptionalism and centrality may well contribute not only to our growing destruction of non-human lifeforms, but also to the belief, shared by many, that such destruction is justified if it benefits humans.

Although some linguists disagree about the appropriateness of doing so, for many eco-linguists their work includes more than critiquing discourse that contributes to ecological destruction. It includes raising consciousness about that discourse. Eco-critical linguists, according to Stibbe (2015), work to "reveal the hidden stories that exist behind and between the lines" with the specific aim of questioning those stories to determine if they "encourage people to destroy or protect the ecosystems that life depends on" (p. 5). They help us realize that we have never been separate from nature nor have we controlled the non-human parts of it, but that we have always been inextricably bound up with those parts and with all of nature. As part of that effort, ecolinguists also seek to bring attention to discourses, such as nature poetry, that inspire us to care for the natural world and encourage us to allow all beings, not just humans, to survive and thrive.

CHAPTER SUMMARY

- Ecolinguistics examines the relationship of language to its symbolic and natural environments, especially how language encodes human relationships to the natural environment.
- Metaphors, especially metaphors about nature, offer insights into this relationship.
- Eco-critical linguistics examines the underlying ideologies present in discourse to identify those that are potentially detrimental to the ecosystems on which life depends.
- Discourses analyzed by ecologists includes those of advertising, agribusiness, ecotourism, and the animal product industries.
- Raising awareness of the potentially destructive effects of certain discourses and of the potentially beneficial effects of other discourses, such as nature poetry, is an important part of the work of ecolinguistics.

KEY TERMS

ecolinguistics

cognitive, sociocultural, symbolic, and
natural environments of language

metaphors (see also Chapter 3)

eco-critical linguistics

critical discourse analysis (see also Chapter 9)

growthism

stories-we-live-by

anthropocentrism

human centrality

human exceptionality

greenwashing

erasure

euphemism

EXPLORATIONS

Exploration 1

The International Ecolinguistics Journal includes scholarly articles and creative works. It is accessible at https://www.ecolinguistics-association.org/Journal. Choose an article or creative work of interest to you.

Writing prompt: If you've chosen a scholarly article, summarize it in a few paragraphs. Then add your response to the main claims of the article. If you've chosen a creative work, write a paragraph or two about your reactions to that work.

Discussion prompt: If you've chosen a scholarly article, summarize it for your small group, being sure to include your response. If you've chosen a creative work, describe it (or read it aloud if a poem) to your small group, again being sure to include your reactions. As a group, discuss any commonalities or themes you identify across the articles or works.

Exploration 2

The Stories We Live By is a free online course in ecolinguistics by Arran Stibbe at the University of Gloucester. The unit on identity and men's health magazines is especially interesting. Access the course at https://www.storiesweliveby.org.uk/. You will need to register, but there is no cost. Go to "Part 6: Identities" and click on the handouts and video to hear Stibbe's analysis of these magazines.

Choose a lifestyle magazine of interest to you and do a similar analysis. Be sure to examine the advertisements, the cover, and the stories within. How does this magazine encourage you to be dissatisfied with yourself? What products are presented as a way of becoming a better self? What discourse is used to encourage consumption, even overconsumption, of these products? How does this discourse connect to the degradation of the environment?

Exploration 3

Check out a website for ecotourist attractions or tours. What do you notice?

Exploration 4

There are many TED Talks about our place in nature vis-à-vis other organisms. I've included a few of them. Check them out, then share responses in your small groups.

Kelsey Leonard, *Why lakes and rivers should have the same rights as humans* https://www.youtube.com/watch?v=opdCfb8cCFw

How trees talk to each other | Suzanne Simard https://www.youtube.com/watch?v=Un2yBgIAxYs

What animals are thinking and feeling, and why it should matter | Carl Safina https://www.youtube.com/watch?v=-wkdH_wluhw

FURTHER READING

Fill, A., & Mühlhäusler, P. (Eds.). (2001). *The ecolinguistics reader.* Continuum.

Kimmerer, R. (2013). *Braiding sweetgrass: Indigenous wisdom, scientific knowledge, and the teachings of plants.* Milkweed Editions.

Stibbe, A. (2015). *Ecolinguistics: Language, ecology, and the stories we live by.* Routledge.

REFERENCES

Alexander, R. (2009). *Framing discourse on the environment: A critical discourse approach.* Routledge.

Halliday, M. (2001). New ways of meaning: The challenge to applied linguistics. In A. Fill & P. Mühlhäusler (Eds.), *The ecolinguistic reader: Language, ecology, and environment* (pp. 175–202). Continuum.

Kimmerer, R. (2013). *Braiding sweetgrass: Indigenous wisdom, scientific knowledge, and the teachings of plants.* Milkweed Editions.

Maffi, L. (2001). Introduction. In L. Maffi (Ed.), *On biocultural diversity: Linking language, knowledge, and the environment* (pp. 1–50). Smithsonian Institution Press.

Mühlhäusler, P. (2003). *Language of environment, environment of language: A course in ecolinguistics.* Battlebridge.

Steffensen, S., & Fill, A. (2014). Ecolinguistics: The state of the art and future horizons. *Language Sciences*, 41(6), 6–25.

Stibbe, A. (2015). *Ecolinguistics: Language, ecology, and the stories we live by.* Routledge.

Williams, R. (1980). *Problems in materialism and culture.* Verso Editions & NLB.

Index

Printed in the United States
by Baker & Taylor Publisher Services